Framing Shakespeare on Film

Framing Shakespeare on Film

Kathy M. Howlett

OHIO UNIVERSITY PRESS

ATHENS

PR
3093
. H69
2000

Ohio University Press, Athens, Ohio 45701
© 2000 by Kathy M. Howlett
Printed in the United States of America
All rights reserved

Ohio University Press books are printed on acid-free paper ♾™

03 02 01 00   5 4 3 2 1

Library of Congress Cataloging-in-Publication Data

Howlett, Kathy M.
Framing Shakespeare on film / Kathy M. Howlett.
        p.   cm.
Includes filmography (p.).
Includes bibliographical references (p.) and index.
ISBN 0-8214-1247-7 (cloth : alk. paper)
1. Shakespeare, William, 1564-1616—Film and video adaptations.
2. English drama—Film and video adaptations. I. Title.
PR3093.H69 1999
791.43'6—dc21   98-50057

"Remember thee?"

In loving memory of my mother

Marie Toth Howlett

Contents

Illustrations

Chapter Three

Chapter Four

Chapter Five

Chapter Six

Chapter Seven

Credits

Some of the frame enlargements and production stills used in the text are in the public domain, while others were obtained from a variety of sources.

Introduction: Kenneth Branagh's *A Midwinter's Tale* courtesy of Castle Rock Entertainment. Photo credit: David Appleby.

Chapter One: Franco Zeffirelli's *Hamlet* courtesy of Warner Brothers.

Chapter Two: Orson Welles's *Othello* courtesy of Castle Hill Productions, Inc.; Vittore Carpaccio's "Sant'Agostino nello studio" courtesy of Scuola di San Giorgio degli Schiavoni, Venice, Italy; Vittore Carpaccio's "Storie di Sant'Orsola" courtesy of Gallerie dell'Accademia, Venice, Italy; preliminary drawing of Carpaccio's "The Vision of St. Augustine" courtesy of The British Museum, London, England.

Chapter Three: Kenneth Branagh's *Henry V* from the collection of the Museum of Modern Art Stills Archive, New York.

Chapter Four: Akira Kurosawa's *Ran* from the collection of the Museum of Modern Art Stills Archive, New York.

Chapter Five: Richard Loncraine's *Richard III* courtesy of MGM/United Artists and Bayley Paré.

Chapter Six: Orson Welles's *Chimes at Midnight* videotape copyright permission from Arthur Cantor Film Collection, New York; Gus Van Sant's *My Own Private Idaho* courtesy of New Line Cinema.

Chapter Seven: Kenneth Branagh's *A Midwinter's Tale* courtesy of Castle Rock Entertainment. Photo credit: David Appleby.

Acknowledgments

The essays in this book were originally presented as conference papers at meetings of the Shakespeare Association of America. They found a more than tolerant audience among friends, colleagues, and Shakespeare scholars over a period of several years, from which emerged this book.

I owe an enormous debt to friends and colleagues at Northeastern University who supported me throughout the writing of this book. In particular, my co-director of the Program in Cinema Studies at Northeastern University, Inez Hedges, whose work on framing theory influenced my approach to Shakespeare on film; my colleague Gerald Herman, whose knowledge of film and German history inspired my chapter on *Richard III;* Francis Blessington, whose intellectual tenacity forced me to grapple with unresolved problems in the manuscript; Joseph Westlund, dear friend and Shakespeare scholar, whose probing questions and demand for clarity helped reshape my critical thinking on important psychoanalytic issues; and Marina Leslie, whose work on early modern utopias led me to write about cinematic ones. There are others, too, who helped shape my ideas as I worked them out in the classroom, not least of whom are the faculty from other disciplines with whom I team-taught Shakespeare on film — Inez Hedges, Gerald Herman, Nancy Kindelin, Sam Bishop, Billy DeAngelis, and Del Lewis — as well as the many undergraduate and graduate students who brought their insights to my classes on Shakespeare, Shakespeare on Film, and Film and Text.

Without the generous support of research grants from Northeastern University, in the form of a Junior Research Grant and a Research and

Scholarship Development Fund Grant, I would not have been able to begin the crucial work on this book. A Northeastern University Faculty Development Fund Grant also allowed me to attend the World Shakespeare Conference in Tokyo, Japan, in 1991 where, in a seminar on Shakespeare on film, I first met some of the brilliant scholars who would influence my thinking on this topic: Anthony Davies, Kenneth Rothwell, Peter Donaldson, Jack Jorgens, and Samuel Crowl. That acquaintance was sustained through the years as I presented parts of my chapters in the annual meetings of the Shakespeare Association of America, and came to appreciate the insights that these scholars, as well as others, brought to the field of Shakespeare on film.

In particular, I gratefully acknowledge three individuals, whose work on Shakespeare on film influenced my own: Samuel Crowl, Peter Donaldson, and Herb Coursen. I am especially grateful for the generous support and guidance of Samuel Crowl, who from first to last has encouraged me in this project, and for Peter Donaldson's kind consideration in reviewing my manuscript and in supporting my work as a part of a conference on Shakespeare/Film/Hypertext at M.I.T. I also am grateful to Herb Coursen, whose tough-minded questions and comments on my manuscript ultimately made this a better book.

There are others who contributed to the writing of this book over the years, in particular, Virginia Vaughan, who kindly invited me to share my work on *Othello* at the Center for Literary and Cultural Studies at Harvard University and shared her own work on *Othello*. And to others, for whose input, in various ways, I am grateful: Michael Mullin, Linda Boose, Barbara Hodgdon, Robert Willson, Jr., Stephen Buhler, Lisa Starks, Courtney Lehmann, and Barbara Freedman. David Sanders, my editor, was remarkably patient as I revised the manuscript and then sorted through the copyright permissions and tracked down citations. My husband, David DePree, supported me through the writing of this book from its first inception, shouldering family burdens so that I could find time to write. My dearest friend Claudia Thomas was an enthusiastic supporter and listener, and Peter Kairoff graciously aided in my correspondence with Italian museums. Kevin Paul and the students in the Media Lab at Northeastern University helped me acquire the images I needed. And although he did not live to see me begin this project, I owe a debt of gratitude to John Hazel Smith, scholar, mentor, and friend, who demonstrated the transformative power of Shakespeare's drama every day in the classroom.

As I reach back in memory to those who inspired me to begin this book, I realize that my original debt is to the person who introduced me to Shakespeare on film, when, so many years ago, playing with my friends, I was called home to watch a movie. And although I only reluctantly left my games to sit down before the large black and white television in our living room, I never forgot that first mesmerizing encounter with Shakespeare and the soft lyricism of Olivier's Hamlet, the ghost, and the mystery of Elsinore. My deepest gratitude I owe to my mother, who first showed me those rare visions. I dedicate this book to her memory—so little to give to someone who gave me so much.

My appreciation to *Literature/Film Quarterly* for permission to reprint the essay that originally appeared in the fall 1996 issue under the title "'Are You Trying to Make Me Commit Suicide?': Gender, Identity, and Spatial Arrangements in Kurosawa's *Ran.*" A version of "Playing on the Rim of the Frame: Kenneth Branagh's *A Midwinter's Tale*" appears in a forthcoming issue of *The Upstart Crow: A Shakespeare Journal.*

Framing Shakespeare on Film

Rare Visions

In the hands of twentieth-century film directors, Shakespeare's plays seem transformed beyond recognition from the theater Shakespeare created for his audience and time. In Gus Van Sant's *My Own Private Idaho* (1991) Falstaff is one of Portland's homeless, in Franco Zeffirelli's *Hamlet* (1990) the prince assumes the heroic destiny of a Western film hero, and in Akira Kurosawa's *Ran* (1985) King Lear is a great lord of a Japanese feudal empire. The transformations seem, like those of Bottom's dream, to be past explanation. To some critics they appear to be as much a violation of Shakespeare's drama as the mechanicals' performance is of the tragedy of Pyramus and Thisbe. This book is an effort to expound those rare visions that have captured the imaginations of American film audiences by demonstrating that Shakespeare is still centrally in these films, despite their deviation from the text or radical reformulation of character and situation. The successful Shakespeare film can transform Shakespeare's text while remaining rooted in Shakespearean conceptions.

Modern audiences are adept at responding to cultural and gendered encodings, but do not always comprehend how the director employs cinematic elements in telling Shakespeare's story. Similarly, the Shakespeare scholar is often skeptical of films that seem to deviate too widely from their familiar theatrical incarnations. Critics emphasize the differences, and lose sight of the fact that, no matter how far some films deviate from the material and literal facts of the plot and action and even language, these films can still be truthful representations of Shakespeare's plays. The very dilemma is the point.

Film adaptations of Shakespeare's plays necessarily partake in the critical and ideological discourse by which a culture understands Shakespeare's drama. As Graham Holderness points out, when Laurence Olivier created his *Henry V,* critical reception of Shakespeare's play underscored the heroic dimension of the king, whereas the critical consensus of the text had altered by the time Kenneth Branagh came to produce his film version of the same play.[1] For every generation, for every culture, and for every director, what constitutes an "authentic" version of Shakespeare's drama is subject to a discernible context of personal, sexual, social, and cultural signifiers. When these film adaptations are successful, the visual signifiers communicate the complexity of the plays: they open up a multiplicity of interpretations that strike at the heart of the drama and lay open ideological issues that time, theatrical practice, and critics have ignored. As Virginia Vaughan observes, productions of Shakespeare's plays are "not simply a product of a cultural milieu but also a maker of cultural meanings."[2] Cinematic adaptations of Shakespeare's plays reveal that textual meaning is not diminished by contemporary film's contextualizing visions but is confirmed and created anew.

This book does not measure the success of a film adaptation of Shakespeare's work by its faithfulness to elements of plot or to its theatrical incarnations. Kurosawa's *Ran* and *Throne of Blood* are good examples of how successful adaptations may retain only vestigial elements of Shakespeare's drama and yet prove to be excellent Shakespeare films. Discussions of a production's fidelity to the Shakespearean text, useful as they are, tend to address what is absent in the film rather than what is present.[3] While Shakespeare may seem quite lost in Idaho or in feudal Japan, my point is that he is in fact there, though sometimes not in terms of superficial plot or even the poetry.

At times the cinematic liberties a director takes may seem, on the surface of things, to be capricious visual indulgences, mere bids to capture a contemporary audience. But if the viewer probes a little more deeply into the cinematic context, in these departures from the original text will be discovered something that is nevertheless authentically Shakespeare, something that rings profoundly true about the way the imaginative director approaches Shakespeare's texts. The films often imbibe their visual influences from sources unknown or undreamt of by Shakespeare, yet *because* of those influences they produce a cinematic vision of Shakespeare's story that captures its most essential elements. Just because "The eye of man hath not heard, the ear of man hath not seen" (*MND* IV.i.209–10) these rare visions of Shakespeare's drama before, does not mean that these cinematic transformations have no substance or form as Shakespeare films. My point is that, as utter and complete as these cinematic transformations may seem, the essential concepts remain as one finds them in Shakespeare's text. Like Theseus, who finds a truth beneath the rough surface of the mechanicals' play, one discovers in even the most vulgar and modernized of these cinematic adaptations "as much as from the rattling tongue / Of saucy and audacious eloquence" (*MND* V.i.102–3) that is Shakespeare's drama.[4]

The techniques employed by directors of Shakespeare films are inspired by Shakespeare's plays, their world and ideas, and those concepts are identifiable within the cinematic frame. Even as I point out the various influences external to the text that produce the cinematic visions of the plays, including other Shakespeare films, I reconnect the viewer's experience of the cinematic frame to Shakespeare's text and world. When I speak of "influence" I mean two intertwined aspects of cinematic framing, the one made representable by the creative imagination of the other. I am interested in a director's aesthetic awareness, not as a painstakingly constructed theory of art or as a psychoanalytic inquiry into the mind of the artist, but as a guide to understanding how a director frames questions of identification and definition in the Shakespeare film. Influence shapes the director's creative imagination and provides clues to how the mind transforms the proverbial bush into a bear, or how the director turns Shakespeare's theater into cinematic spectacle.

Of necessity, my approach is intertextual, since I straddle two separate areas of discourse, Shakespeare and film. By pursuing the relationship between textual and film criticism, I demonstrate that Shakespeare's plays contain within them cultural, ideological, rhetorical, and psychological elements that have cinematic implications. This approach does not preclude or diminish the significance of the text. On the contrary, this book refines and advances a textually self-conscious discussion of the framing of

Shakespeare's plays as a negotiation between the creative influences in the director's art and the Shakespearean text. However, instead of dismantling the distinctions between film and text, I ask when the distinction matters—how and when the difference reshapes the audience's understanding of character or theme. I do not concentrate on the content as much as the context or how the variables of framing create the cinematic spectacle that reshapes the concepts within the text. The frame is important not just as the place where the story is told or how the story is told. In a significant way it *is* the story. Framing is the key to a film's aesthetic, since it is the first step in comprehending Shakespeare on film.

When I refer to "framing" in the following chapters, I mean something somewhat different than cinematic framing, although the techniques of cinematic framing necessarily contribute to what the viewer perceives as the Shakespearean "frame." Let me first address the issue of cinematic framing, and how it contributes to what the viewer perceives as Shakespeare on film. When I speak of cinematic framing I do not simply refer to the rectangular screen that permits the audience a view of the action but to how the arrangement of objects within the cinematic frame interprets the Shakespearean story according to a dynamic of space existing between the camera and the objects it surveys. Since the cinematic frame is the audience's "*synoptic center* of the film's experience of the world it sees," as Vivian Sobchack explains, it "literally provides the *premises* for perception as expressed experience."[5] The cinematic frame reinvents what the viewer sees and experiences through a variety of techniques: the fluidity of camera positioning, the frequency of the change of shot, the arrangement and linking of the screen images, and cuts between shots. Variable framing, the process of camera movements and cutting, establishes the viewer's understanding of the gestalt of objects within the cinematic frame and their relevance to the unfolding narrative.

Perhaps the reason Shakespeare's drama has translated successfully to the medium of film and proven to be popular with contemporary film audiences is the great emphasis Shakespeare's drama gives to spectacle itself. Voltaire praised Shakespeare's plays for their fearless exhibitionism and capacity to "address themselves to the eyes." Centuries later Jan Kott concurred that "all Shakespeare's plays are great spectacles . . . a theatre for the eyes" that is "very similar to the beginnings of film."[6] Today critics ponder the powerful reception of Shakespeare's drama across cultures and time, and conclude that "it is this *address to the eyes* which is remarkable, a fearless scopophilia that brings everything onto the stage, not only carnage and ghosts but thought itself, as it emerges out of the private depths."[7] In fact, this conjoining of spectacle and thought, or, more specifically, the deployment of visual imagery to bring out thought, is one of the ways that constructivists discuss the viewer's experience of watching film. In this regard, the film viewer, like the audience in Shakespeare's theater, does not passively imbibe the spectacle before him. Instead, according to David Bordwell, the cinematic screen actively engages the viewer's perceptual capacities, prior knowledge and experience, and the material and structure of the film itself, in an experience that is "more a mental system than an optical one."[8] One could conclude, therefore, that the spectacle of Shakespeare on film, rather than diminishing the viewer's active engagement with the drama, reinforces and even intensifies it. Primarily, this intensification is achieved through the capabilities of variable framing. Variable framing translates the scopophilia of the stage from a vaulting space of often indistinct action seen at a distance to the intimate space of the cinematic frame, affording the viewer of a Shakespeare film an intelligibility of relationship and clarity of vision that theatrical representation lacks. As Noël Carroll observes, the techniques of variable framing enhance the viewer's engagement with the cinematic spectacle in ways that the original dramatic representation is incapable of, reorganizing and constructing cinematic images "with an economy, legibility, and coherence" that "gratifies the mind's quest for order" and thereby intensifies the viewer's engagement with the screen.[9] Shakespeare films, therefore, are driven by what Carroll calls an "*erotetic* model of narrative," in that questions and answers "are saliently posed and answered in important ways by means of variable framing."[10] As I will demonstrate, the question and answer model of cinematic experience is intimately tied to the problem-solving activity that is Shakespeare on film.

A substantial scholarship now addresses cinematic adaptation and its relationship to contemporary criticism of Shakespeare's plays and to the directors and cultures that produce the films. Samuel Crowl and Barbara

Hodgdon show how film performances function as criticism of the text. Graham Holderness argues that the director's awareness of textual criticism infuses a film's interpretation of the play. Peter Donaldson locates the meaning of a film adaptation as an aspect of the director's subjective and personal experience, and John Collick reads cinematic adaptations of Shakespeare's texts as cultural productions.[11] Anthony Davies attends to the interpretative differences between theatrical and cinematic space, and Lorne Buchman investigates spatio-temporal structures in cinematic adaptations of Shakespeare's plays.[12]

However, Holderness detects in scholarship on Shakespeare films a pervasive "canonical" approach in its selective focus upon a circle of "great" films and directors. Holderness charges that critics of Shakespeare films tend to ignore or dismiss those films that do not meet an auteur theory of film production or that deviate from naturalistic representations of Shakespeare's drama. The result has been a body of scholarship that fails to explore "alternative possibilities which might chal-lenge the basis of structural totality."[13] According to Holderness, even the best of these studies demonstrates a "hierarchical and élitist" form of "cultural politics," supported by a "Great Tradition of 'Shakespeare-on-film' which sustains outmoded nineteenth and early twentieth-century models of narrative, character, action, imagery, and form."[14] Ironically, the same films that are so suspect to Shakespeare on film scholars reflect the concerns of much contemporary literary criticism, from Marxism to textual bibliography, in rendering a vision of the Shakespearean text that is "unstable, self-contradictory, fissured, labile, permeated by a radical indecideability."[15]

Although Holderness's critique of the state of current Shakespeare on film scholarship belies much of its basis in performance theory and cultural studies, he accurately assesses a general resistance to films that fracture and fragment the Shakespearean text. In this regard, I share Holderness's sentiments that the scope of Shakespeare on film scholarship must be enlarged to encompass new cinematic visions, and that even the most radical transformations can be successful in capturing the "elusive, shifting complexity of the Shakespeare text."[16] Indeed, Holderness illuminates the issue with which this book is centrally concerned — that of the relationship between a Shakespeare film and Shakespeare's drama, or what we perceive in the cinematic frame to be the essential "Shakespeare."

What constitutes the drama we have come to know as "Shakespeare"? The notion that there exists an original performing manuscript by which one can assess a production's fidelity to the original Shakespeare is, as Stephen Orgel bluntly asserts, "a figment." Orgel maintains that the task of "getting back to the original Shakespeare" is an impossible one, for the idea of a complete or absolute text is inconsistent with Renaissance theatrical practice.[17] Yet contemporary film critics often continue to judge Shakespeare films by an impossible and absolute standard—as being "Shakespeare" or "like the original Shakespeare." The problem of assessing what constitutes a Shakespeare film, then, appears even more daunting when we consider the basic instability of the Shakespearean text itself. So how are we to assess what constitutes a Shakespeare film?

We cannot determine what is a Shakespeare film according to our perceptions of narrative structures in Shakespeare's plays, since Shakespeare recycled everything, and the ideas he used were often obvious to his contemporaries. However, Shakespeare's incorporation of past forms in his drama and the proliferation of Shakespeare films that consciously invoke earlier Shakespeare films and performances suggest to cultural critics like Leo Braudy that Shakespeare films exist as an identifiable genre. According to Braudy, Shakespeare films share with other genre films a self-consciousness and preoccupation with the past. The "past" of a Shakespeare film, like that of other genre films, is not based "on the reality of a society or the reality of the past, but on the individual's perception of those superhuman orders and what they mean."[18] In other words, Shakespeare films explore a horizon of expectations about a past that constitutes an essential "Shakespeare."

Inez Hedges observes that in genre films audience expectations include not only knowledge of particular literary, dramatic, and cinematic conventions but also knowledge of the world. Audiences might therefore evaluate Shakespeare's work against expectations "established either by evaluating signals in the work itself or by knowledge of the society at the time."[19] Similarly, Charles Altieri argues that canonized works tend to project ideals with which an audience identifies as "shared values in a past culture that influence the present."[20] Those ideals may serve as artistic models that provide "a repertory of inventions and a challenge to our capacity to further develop a genre or style" or as "alternatives" that "the past provides in order to shape possible selves in the present."[21] But Susan Bennett emphasizes that the object of our idealizing tendencies may have little or no relationship to the realities of past—or present—values and forms. Bennett argues that the "past" that is "Shakespeare" comprises imagined and mythical qualities, which act as a corrective to a less than ideal present. To "Shakespeare" we ascribe the meaning of our collective nostalgia for an idealized past "overdetermined by the social institutions for whom it has some use and [with which] the reader's relationship with that text is necessarily mediated."[22] Even as we ascribe our ideals to "Shakespeare," we recognize that those ideals never match reality. The current vogue in Shakespeare films therefore raises questions about how directors and audiences understand the genre of Shakespeare films and the past it invokes—as an "enshrinement" of the past or a "rummaging in the garbage heap of broken images"?[23] Filmmakers seem to be self-consciously examining this question, a recent example being Kevin Costner's *The Postman* (Warner Brothers, 1997). Set in 2013 in the apocalyptic wasteland of the former United States, the film features a drifter called "Shakespeare" who wanders the Pacific Northwest reciting fragments of Shakespeare's plays and inspiring a post-apocalyptic generation with the forgotten ideals of a past culture.

In surveying the proliferation of sequels and genre films in the last decade of the twentieth century, Leo Braudy speculates that genre films speak to the audience's desire for repetition and formula. Braudy asserts that repetition "helps perform the same function as a funeral service does for mourners: turning discomfort, fear, and anxiety into matters of ritual, elegance, and even routine," for "those who seek to forget the past are swallowed up by it."[24] As filmmakers and viewers collectively embrace Shakespeare at the end of the twentieth century, Shakespeare films allow anxieties about the future to be translated into the recognized forms and rituals of an idealized past. That is not to say that film audiences want to see Shakespeare's plays in their historical settings; on the contrary, they willingly liberate Shakespeare's drama from a historically determined set of conventions. However, even as audiences embrace variation and are surprised or even shocked by the transformations on screen, they simultaneously long for the repetitions that mark the genre Shakespeare on film.

The recent popularity of Shakespeare films does not testify to a change in audiences' viewing habits, or that audiences are more sophisticated or literary in their tastes. In fact, the capacity for audience involvement seems unrelated to how Shakespeare scholars or film critics assess a film's value. As sociologist Erving Goffman observes, audiences have a great capacity "to adjust and calibrate in order to get on with getting involved," whether or not the production they view is good or bad.[25] And audiences still assess films in box-office terms, even Shakespeare films. The recent commercial success of Baz Luhrmann's *Romeo and Juliet* (1996), for example, illustrates how Shakespeare films can exploit generic and recognitional abilities in viewers, so that the untrained spectator is able to master visual conventions with little or no reference to linguistic ones ("the original Shakespeare").

Tellingly, Bertolt Brecht comments that Shakespeare's "plays may have been made like films are now."[26] Transparently basing his work upon existing plays, Shakespeare discovered dramatic possibilities and alternative readings in the plays' montage of fragments. The plays were works in process, yielding new possibilities with each enactment. For Brecht, Shakespeare's "theatre was a source of discovery that was just like life," in which the dramatist discovered fresh ideas each day in a "spirit of experiment" that Brecht calls Shakespeare's "global transformations."[27] According to Brecht, an essential Shakespeare does not exist in the plots, characters, and themes transparently culled from existing plays. Instead, Brecht detects in Shakespeare's work an "essence" that comprises fragments perpetually in process, shaped and reshaped through time and imagination.

For "Shakespeare" to exist outside assumptions of plot, character, language, theatrical conventions, or even quality of performance suggests that "Shakespeare" may not be a concept in itself but, rather, a way concepts are organized by convention. Marvin Minsky's frame theory, which analyzes frames as aesthetic models of communication, helps clarify how Shakespearean concepts are framed in cinematic terms. Minsky asserts that in a frame "'concepts' are interrelated in different ways when in different contexts, and no single hierarchical ordering is generally satisfactory for all goals."[28] In other words, the conceptual frames by which an audience imaginatively experiences Shakespeare's ideas are the key to their endurance, but *how* they are organized within the cinematic frame is subject to variation. Nevertheless, despite the variation, we understand these ideas and films to be "Shakespeare."

The gap between our expectations of Shakespeare's drama and what we view on the cinematic screen exposes the limits of the ideal we hold as "Shakespeare." However, the fact that our ideals can never be matched by reality is the very source of their attractiveness and power. In his theory of aesthetic communication, Minsky describes the frame in ways that are significant for understanding the process by which we experience Shakespeare on film:

> We can think of a frame as describing an "ideal." If an ideal does not match reality because it is "basically" wrong, it must be replaced. But it is in the nature of ideals that they are really elegant simplifications; their attractiveness derives from their simplicity, but their real power depends upon additional knowledge about interactions between them! Accordingly we need not abandon an ideal because of a failure to substantiate it, provided one can explain the discrepancy in terms of such an interaction.[29]

Similarly, because a Shakespeare film does not match the ideals that scholars establish as "Shakespeare" does not mean that Shakespearean concepts are not there. It is in the interaction between the real and ideal — the gap between the concepts we believe to be Shakespeare and their incarnations in the cinematic frame — that we discover an immanence of meanings.

The Shakespeare "frame" can be understood as both a concept of genre and the organization of experience. As Inez Hedges points out, genre frames are the highest level of organizing artistic works: "In frame theory, the reading or perception of a work is viewed as an inductive process in which the reader/perceiver tries to 'match' perceived conceptual structures with conceptual frames stored in memory. In the matching process he or she employs a 'search' technique, calling up one frame after another until a match is made."[30] Or, as Marvin Minsky asserts, "In seeing a room, or understanding a story, one assembles a network of frames and subframes. Everything noticed or guessed, rightly or wrongly, is represented in this network."[31] One might therefore infer that Shakespeare films are a problem-solving activity.[32] Viewers participate in an inductive process of matching a story within a network of frames and subframes within the global frame that is "Shakespeare." Similarly, when watching a Shakespeare film, the viewer's perception is both immediate and revisionist, in that the viewer continually tests what he understands against a growing amount of visual data.

Marvin Minsky offers a simple example of how an audience determines meaning within a frame that is useful to this discussion. According to Minsky, "A *frame* is a data-structure for representing a stereotyped situation, like being in a certain kind of living room, or going to a child's birthday party."[33] Minsky employs the example of a birthday party to demonstrate that through a proliferation of objects—or variables within the frame—we recognize the "frame" of a birthday party. We see a cake, presents, and balloons, and thereby deduce from their inclusion within the frame that we are viewing a birthday party. The phenomenological power of the theory hinges on the inclusion of expectations of what we would see at a birthday party, presumptions based on convention and life experiences. In that same frame of expectations, elements may be omitted. However, we continue to recognize the scene as a birthday party. For example, if the candles are missing from the cake, we still know that what we view within the frame is a birthday party. Similarly, "a frame may contain a great many details whose supposition is not specifically warranted by the situation."[34] If we see an American flag or a school bus, these objects do not cause us to revise our understanding that what we view within the frame is a birthday party. Minsky's analysis of frames suggests a flexible approach to how we ascertain what constitutes a Shakespeare film. Instead of demanding a rigid hierarchy and format, viewers integrate two kinds of knowledge—"gross, global frames of reference as well as smaller, local structures."[35] In other words, Shakespeare on film gives to Shakespeare's "global" drama a local habitation and a *frame*.

Sociologist Goffman's analysis of framing emphasizes the viewer's capacity for accepting variation within a frame. A frame, according to Goffman, "does not so much introduce restrictions on what can be meaningful as it does open up variability." Goffman observes that "persons seem to have a very fundamental capacity to accept changes in organizational premises which, once made, render a whole strip of activity different from what it is modeled on and yet somehow meaningful, in the sense that these systematic differences can be corrected for and kept from disorganizing perception, while at the same time involvement in the story line is maintained."[36] Variations within the frame do not disrupt the meaning for the viewer, as long as the viewer remains capable of involvement in the story. Shakespeare on film, like any other film narrative, is an inferential, cognitive activity that requires the viewer "frame and fix perceptual hypotheses by reckoning in probabilities weighted to the situation and to prior knowledge."[37] The viewer of a Shakespeare film will test visual information against a particular framework for understanding—such as the play itself or its theatrical representation—and may even anticipate information or create linkages where none exist. However, the perceptual abilities of the viewer, such as his or her level of sophistication, can directly affect framing in that levels of understanding transform how a viewer receives the information in the frame.

Shakespeare films raise the question of artistic self-consciousness. As a genre they define their originality against a history of previous performances and films, and therefore are contained within an even larger frame of aesthetic perspective. Goffman claims that this is a central concept in frame analysis, which he calls "keying," or the process of transcription. Keying is an "open transformation of something modeled after something else (or after a transformation of something else)."[38] Staged events may also be "rekeyings," as when Falstaff rehearses Hal's interviews with his father-king in *Henry IV, Part I*.[39] As Goffman makes clear in this example, the audience only understands the scene between Hal and Falstaff as long as it understands the meaning of the frame that is being invoked—the father-son interview: "a key can translate only what is already meaningful in terms of a primary framework," for "it is the keying of that framework that is the material that is transposed."[40] For example, the self-consciousness of a film like Gus Van Sant's *My Own Private Idaho* arises from its representation as art-within-art, in that the film simultaneously directs the viewer back toward Welles's *Chimes at Midnight* and Shakespeare's *Henriad* as a means of self-validating the frame text, or "rekeying." In this respect, *My Own Private Idaho* illustrates reflexivity in consciously conjuring the presence of two artistic works — one textual, the other filmic — that mutually relativize one another. Within the context of the film's literary and cinematic antecedents, Van Sant also introduces the context of our contemporary world against which we test the truth of the concepts within the frame, demonstrating how textual meaning is not only discovered but remade by casting Shakespeare's drama in meaningful juxtaposition with cinematic antecedents and with contemporary issues and problems.

Zeffirelli's *Hamlet* exhibits discursive practices within a single frame, in that within the frame there are other recognizable influences, although related through a subtle process of dissemination. In Zeffirelli's construction of what Hedges calls the "'topic' frame" of the film, the viewer finds that not all elements in the frame can be "accommodated by the hypothesized frame." The result is that the viewer will "try, inductively, to find a pre-existing frame in which they will fit, or, deductively, to produce a new frame."[41] In other words, when Shakespeare films exist outside existing models, the viewer must create a new "frame" or strategy for understanding the new arrangement of conceptions recognizable as "Shakespeare." Because Zeffirelli's *Hamlet* introduces a new frame encoded with the familiar patterns of the film Western, the film involves the viewer in what Hedges calls a "frame-*making*" cognitive activity, which relies upon strategies of understanding that the perceiver has learned through experience.[42] In altering the patterns through which we view Shakespeare, Zeffirelli challenges viewers to new insights or frames of knowledge. These are strategies of contextualization, or ways of dealing with new information, in which "cognitive strategies which are of a general nature . . . are activated in the construction of new frames."[43]

The aesthetics of frame theory form the basis of my approach to Shakespeare on film. The films that I discuss offer particularly clear examples of how the concerns of frame analysis are implicated in our comprehension of the images in the cinematic frame we understand as "Shakespeare." Each of the films I examine demonstrates how the viewer's expectations for understanding the genre that is Shakespeare on film—as intextual conceptual frames that include Shakespeare's drama, the world, and our ideals—is manipulated by the directors' use of cinematic framing. As I argue in the following chapters, our cinematic experience of "Shakespeare" may involve frame-making or frame-breaking, framing ambivalence, or parodic reframing.

I begin with two films, Zeffirelli's *Hamlet* and Welles's *Othello*, that are centrally concerned with the question of framing conventions, even as they introduce variation in the organizational principles of Shakespeare's story. As I have suggested, Zeffirelli's transformation of the Shakespearean text is subtle in that it partakes of distinctly cinematic techniques and conventions to which American audiences favorably respond. Paradoxically, by introducing conventions outside the frame of audience expectations of the genre of Shakespeare on film, Zeffirelli recovers essential aspects of Shakespeare's play. Orson Welles's *Othello* also draws on genre conventions outside those associated with Shakespeare's drama or Shakespeare on film. Welles explores the limits of film narrative in tracing the textual echoes of desire through the painterly conventions of Renaissance Venetian narrative art. He challenges traditional concepts of objecthood and observer by signaling to his viewers the collapse of conventional cause-and-effect action, reconstituting cinematically the effect achieved in Vittore Carpaccio's paintings. The film investigates the tortured passions of Othello through the interplay of sadistic and masochistic impulses ("cine-repetitions"), a technique derived from Welles's personal rehearsal of voyeuristic pleasures and influenced by the paintings of Carpaccio.[44]

In Kenneth Branagh's *Henry V* we experience confrontational cinematic techniques: "crossing the line," a method of employing reaction shots to convey the visual effect of the fragmentation and invasion of space. Branagh's film demonstrates how cinematic techniques can wage an interpretative struggle (historical, political, and ideological) in the construction of the hero's identity and contribute to what Erving Goffman calls "ambiguity of frame," or those moments when the viewer may suspect Henry's role or motivation in the film. Yet, as Goffman emphasizes, viewers "actively project their frames of reference into the world immediately around them," and, because events on screen "ordinarily confirm these projections, causing the assumptions to disappear into the smooth flow of activity," the narrative remains undisturbed by ambiguity of frame.[45]

Framing also has political implications for the representation of the female subject, as we see in Akira Kurosawa's *Ran,* a recontextualization of Shakespeare's *King Lear* within the Jidai Geki genre, which glorifies the ancient samurai and his masculine code. *Ran* reveals how gender conflict and confusion can "break" the frame that defines masculine identity.[46] This is a term derived from Inez Hedges's work on cinematic framing, in which she employs the term more generally to suggest the violation of the intertextual conventions from which frames are constructed. Frame-breaking occurs when the expectations of the audience are not met or are challenged, when the frame pushes against the limits of its genre or against the limits of sense.

Richard Loncraine's *Richard III* recontextualizes Shakespeare's medieval tyrant within a modern fascist England, thereby allowing the audience to examine late twentieth-century culture's mythologizing process as a retroactive reconstruction of history. The film illustrates that the viewer is most vulnerable in understanding the frame that is the past, and dramatizes that the only corrective to delusion and error in framing is for the audience to reexamine the issue of transformation itself.[47]

In *Richard III* the viewer also experiences what Goffman calls "self-referencing *reflexive* frame breaks," in which the viewer's "engrossment is not merely an indicator of how well things are going, but by definition is also the main issue: the performer is charged with inducing it, and the audience expects to enjoy it."[48] When Richard directly and intimately addresses his audience, and comments upon himself as performer, it results in a reflexive frame break — a mixing of levels of being. It is entirely consistent with the methods of framing in Shakespeare's play that Loncraine's film should violate his audience's experience of the frame through methods Richard employs with others, such as breaching boundaries in face-to-face interactions. However, at the end of the film we experience not simply the unreality of Richard's end but also a disruptive face-to-face interaction with Richmond. This interpenetration of frames is a "frame-directed remark" that Goffman calls the "manufacture of negative experience" in which "an audience can be jarred from protective psychological distance by threats to frame."[49] At the end of the film one discovers the consequences of the vulnerabilities of framing, when the audience realizes that it too has been a victim of deception and delusion. And when Richard bursts into demonic laughter at the end of the film and plunges to his fiery end, the scene marks the limits that his current role can hold him, in that the mythic character he has played is larger than the frame's context.

Shakespeare films may also parody framing mechanisms used in other films to interrogate theme and character, as it does in Gus Van Sant's *My Own Private Idaho*. Van Sant's film looks back to Falstaff's tavern world and the filmic stylization that Welles accords that world in *Chimes at Midnight*. By parodying the world that Welles creates, Van Sant illuminates social truths imbedded within the Shakespearean text and explores their relevance in twentieth-century America. As Robert Stam observes, "Parody, far from being a marginal sub-genre within the history of literature or film, can be seen as an ever-present tendency which renders explicit the intrinsic processes of textuality."[50] *My Own Private Idaho* parodies outgrown artistic conventions—the "past" that is Shakespeare on film—to dissociate himself from it, and underscores the historical inappropriateness of Welles's vision by rehistoricizing the artistic process.

Branagh's *A Midwinter's Tale* (1995) draws the viewer's attention to the fact that the frame itself represents a paradox of inside and outside, in that the status of the frame is relational, much as are the Shakespearean concepts that the viewer perceives within the frame. The paradox of framing is primarily a problem of borders, for what refers to the outside border—the frame—also refers to the inside, and thereby raises the question "Where is the film frame's frame?" Branagh addresses this query by creating a context through which the viewer experiences the *play* frame's frame, which alerts the viewer to the existence of frames outside the boundaries of the theatrical frame, or what Goffman calls the "rim" of the frame.[51] The film simultaneously calls attention to *itself* as rehearsal, in that the audience is continually aware of the *film* frame's frame through its self-conscious disparagement of the market pressures of Hollywood, its

FIGURE O.I. The film frame's frame: Kenneth Branagh directs Michael Maloney as Joe Harper as Hamlet in *A Midwinter's Tale*. (Courtesy of Castle Rock Entertainment. Photo credit: David Appleby)

parody of Laurence Olivier's *Hamlet* (1948) as the standard to which all *Hamlet*s are held, and its showcasing of many of the same actors who comically rehearse *Hamlet* for roles in Branagh's film *Hamlet* (1996).

However, it is important to note that the grouping of elements of Shakespeare's *Hamlet* within this new configuration called "rehearsal" does not annihilate meaning in the inner frame that we understand as Shakespeare's play. Instead, the film folds the outside (the rehearsal) back into the inside (Shakespeare's *Hamlet*), and forces the viewer to recognize that those elements usually considered outside the frame of Shakespeare on film—the actors' experiences and values, theater and film history, genre conventions, culture, social contexts—are essential elements in comprehending Shakespeare. This process of internalization gives the viewer the sense of watching as through the workings of a richly annotated manuscript, in which Branagh's film is only a partial citation in a complex network of historical and cultural elements that comprise "Shakespeare." Branagh's film reveals a significant point about Shakespeare films, in that the plays themselves are always larger than that which holds them, for what is "outside" the text is always folded back into the "inside" of the drama itself.

As the "canonical" or idealized Shakespeare play inside the rehearsal frame of Branagh's *A Midwinter's Tale, Hamlet* assists in the viewer's effort to organize the film's visual material, but only to a point. Much of the comedy in *A Midwinter's Tale* is derived from the way the film upsets common assumptions about *Hamlet* and invalidates common inferences and hypotheses about Shakespeare's drama and its theatrical and film history. In fact, Branagh sometimes invokes expectations by bidding the viewer to anticipate and extrapolate, and then presents solutions that defeat the audience's expectations. The film illustrates that the viewer's engagement with cinematic spectacle is a search for meaning, in which the viewer searches out the details that fit Shakespeare's *Hamlet* and even tries to make the elements apparently external to the *Hamlet* story "fit" the conventions of the *Hamlet* paradigm. In this respect Branagh's *A Midwinter's Tale* is a comic investigation of how the frames of representation that comprise our experience of the world, our ideals we call "Shakespeare," and our expectations of the intertextual genre called Shakespeare on film unite in creating our experience of the cinematic frame in which we discover "Shakespeare."

Not surprisingly, the title of Branagh's film recalls Shakespeare's *A Midsummer Night's Dream* and its rehearsal of a tragedy transformed into comedy by the mechanicals. Like the film audience's response to the rehearsal of *Hamlet* in *A Midwinter's Tale,* the character who views the mechanicals' rehearsal of Pyramus and Thisbe remarks that "when I saw rehearsed, I must confess, / Made mine eyes water; but more merry tears / The passion of loud laughter never shed" (*MND* V.i.68–70). The comedy of Branagh's film imitates strategies in Shakespeare's *A Midsummer Night's Dream,* in that Shakespeare's comedy demands that the viewer retain simultaneously various levels of imaginative experience (the worlds of Theseus and Hippolita, the fairies, mechanicals, and lovers), only to confuse the viewer's understanding of their priority or exclusivity. Branagh's intention seems similar, in that his film challenges hierarchical ordering of the audience's under-standing of the concepts that comprise Shakespeare's drama. In reorganiz-ing, resisting, and even erasing textual meaning, Branagh points to various aspects of cinematic and theatrical spectacle that cannot be accounted for by the text alone. Conversely, in the process of searching for textual mean-ing, the film also demonstrates that the play is "a matter of a translation that effaces as it reaches toward an original." As Barbara Freedman observes, "A play is, after all, a projected performance of an original that can never be retrieved or realized as such."[52] As a projection of some impossible ideal, rehearsal allows even the rudest of these mechanicals to discover something wondrous in the transformative power of moonlight and the visions it bod-ies forth. So too we find that in the transformative light of the cinema we glimpse those shapes the poet's pen created from airy nothing, those rare visions that, as strange as some contemporary cinematic projections may seem, grow to something of great constancy.

However, the concept of imagination or "dream" in film spectator-ship does not suggest that the viewer becomes, like Bottom, absorbed in the world of the fiction itself or duped into believing that the events on the cinematic screen are real.[53] As Murray Smith cautions, the concept of imagination explored in cinematic fiction is "neither simply an arena of subjection, nor of escapism, nor of fantasy, nor of aesthetic (in the sense of asocial) attention," but instead "denotes our capacity to frame mental representations of absent objects (real but non-present objects) or unreal (fictional) objects."[54] The viewer who watches a Shakespeare film never represses his awareness of cinematic conventions. Nor does the viewer hold any mistaken belief about the reality of what he sees on the cine-matic screen. Shakespeare films are mimetically powerful because they are capable of moving us, like Shakespeare's drama, by the activation of our imagination, and prompt us to reflect upon what we see in ways that are epistemologically and phenomenologically distinctive from that of normal awareness. For even Bottom, in his crude way, reflects upon his "rare vision."

Chapter One

The Frame's the Thing

Franco Zeffirelli's *Hamlet*

Franco Zeffirelli's *Hamlet* (1990) illus-
trates discursive practices within a single frame. For while the audience
attends to what might be called the "topic frame" of the film—Shakespeare's
Hamlet—the film also exhibits other recognizable influences that introduce variation in the organizational principles of Shakespeare's play. By
introducing a new frame encoded with familiar patterns from a popular
American film genre, the Western, Zeffirelli involves the viewer in a
frame-making cognitive activity that challenges the viewer to new
insights about the nature of Hamlet's conflict. However, many film and
Shakespeare critics do not find these changes meaningful. Although they
aptly detect popular film influences in Zeffirelli's *Hamlet* that realign
audience expectations and therefore make this film substantially different
from previous film and stage incarnations of Shakespeare's play, they overlook the film's dominant visual motif, one with deep roots in popular
American film. Iconographic elements work in conjunction with
specific cinematic strategies in constructing a film narrative encoded
with the social and cultural signifiers of the American film Western.

When Zeffirelli's *Hamlet* was first released, reviewers characterized the
film as a popularized version of Shakespeare's play.[1] Indeed, Zeffirelli's
Hamlet has sustained a level of popular success that Olivier's *Hamlet* or even
the more recent four-hour "epic" *Hamlet* directed by Kenneth Branagh
has failed to achieve.[2] Yet it is the film's supposed pandering to the popular
that has made it questionable in the eyes of film and Shakespeare critics,
who object to elements in Zeffirelli's production perceived to be external

to the literary *Hamlet* and derived from popular film culture. For example, although Neil Taylor finds Zeffirelli to be "by far the most radical reshaper of the text," and points to the influences of popular film when he wryly comments that this film follows the film "conventions of Beverly Hills cops," as Hamlet "rides out of town into the open countryside in order to commune with nature," yet Taylor fails to see how those changes are meaningful.[3] Even as astute a critic as Barbara Hodgdon concludes that Zeffirelli's "*Hamlet* is merely a classical arabesque between *Lethal Weapon 2* and *Lethal Weapon 3.*"[4] Casting Mel Gibson in the role of Prince Hamlet contributes to what Hodgdon perceives as the film's popularization of Shakespeare's story, in that Gibson's Hamlet is an extension of the film roles for which he has become famous, a Hollywood screen presence that exudes the "appealingly legitimate masculinity" of an action hero.[5]

These critics generally believe that, in popularizing *Hamlet* within the conventions of American film, Zeffirelli departs from expectations of the play, notably ones rooted in theatrical tradition. What they do not see is that this director taps into aspects of Shakespeare's *Hamlet* that resonate within the context of American mythology and film. Turning away from theatrical models to cinematic ones, Zeffirelli concentrates on those aspects of the revenge drama that are shared by the film Western, as conflicts over morality, justice, family authority, and the value of violence as it relates to the construction of masculinity.

Zeffirelli engages his audience in Hamlet's revenge tragedy through associations with the American gunslinger and myths of the American West, a marriage of genres that captures essential elements within the Quarto 1 version of Shakespeare's *Hamlet*. Critics have noted that Zeffirelli's filmscript closely parallels the Quarto 1 (Q1) text of the play, which is a more swiftly moving version of *Hamlet,* with characterizations that are "less complex and ambiguous than in Q2/F1."[6] Zeffirelli strips the film of political complexities and implications, deleting the character of Fortinbras and playing down the political impact of Claudius's assumption of power, while creating a preponderance of private scenes, changes that accord with the Q1 manuscript. Zeffirelli's decision to diminish political and social entanglements also accommodates the frame of the film Western, in which the interactions of society are personal and archetypal, and not political.

Barbara Hodgdon speculates that Zeffirelli's use of the QI *Hamlet* "opens up a space for a text that is not quite Shakespeare and not quite *Hamlet,* a space where the traffic between literary and popular reading formations flows in more than one direction."[7] Although Hodgdon is skeptical that Zeffirelli's film remains "Shakespeare" because of its introduction of organizational principles that interrelate the play's concepts in a different hierarchical ordering and context, the fundamental power of the Western is that it allows Zeffirelli to experiment with alternative interpretations of Shakespeare's play. Specifically, the cinematic space encoded as Western opens up an ideological landscape that frees *Hamlet* from the interpretative constraints that have defined previous film adaptations of the play by allowing the audience to view simultaneously the "traffic" between two mediating frames. As Leo Braudy observes, "The acceptance of the frame of western conventions allows a freedom to experiment in crossing boundaries that might be impossible" in other genres.[8] In fact, Zeffirelli's film engages Shakespeare's *Hamlet* as a problem of borders, not only in its application of discursive framing practices, but illustrated narratively through a concentration upon liminal scenes and cinematically through the collapse of spatio-temporal boundaries.

By exploiting viewers' recognitional abilities of a Western "past," Zeffirelli reshapes *Hamlet* within the contours of past mythologies that continue to be a vital mythology of our American present. The mythic status of the cowboy has ancient roots in the character of the drifter, extending as far back as Homeric epic, but as an American invention the Western myth emerged in the late nineteenth century as a nostalgic invocation of a pastoral world and as a dream of escape from the narrowing confines of middle-class existence, family ties, and the pressures of an industrialized society. Contemporary film versions of the myth reinforce the allure of the frontier as posed precipitously on the edge of encroaching psychological and modernizing pressures. Although the form may vary somewhat in twentieth-century film, the myth remains essentially intact as an investigation of the terrain of gender identification, in which the construction of masculinity resides not in what a man does but in how he does it.[9] Even in these bare outlines one detects the central concerns of Shakespeare's play. As a mode that renders in particular shape the contradictions that assail Hamlet, the Western genre investigates the ideal of masculinity as founded upon fundamental oppositions between idealism and savagery, sensitivity and violence, unresolvable tensions played out on the divide between worlds encoded as masculine and feminine.

Zeffirelli is not the first director of Shakespeare films to use a Western motif, as anyone who has watched Kurosawa's films or the battle sequences in Olivier's *Henry V* knows.[10] Perhaps these directors intuit the connection between Shakespeare's drama and the film Western, for, as Leo Braudy observes, the "methods of the western" are "reminiscent of the way Shakespeare infuses old stories with new characters to express the tension between past and present. All pay homage to past works even while they vary their elements and comment on their meaning."[11] It is in keeping with Shakespeare's own methods, and those of the Western, that Zeffirelli underscores his similarities with past films of *Hamlet* while emphasizing his creative differences, repudiating past formulations of Hamlet's character while casting Shakespeare's protagonist in a familiar set of plot conventions. This, in essence, is the relevance of the Western frame for a twentieth-century *Hamlet,* in that it visually articulates the dilemma presented by Shakespeare's drama as "the past's continuing grip on the present, which reshapes the past to present needs."[12]

Zeffirelli admits his irritation with critics who "want art to be as 'difficult' as possible, an elitest [*sic*] kind of thing."[13] Instead, the director reaches out to his viewers with a myth recognizable as images of the American West, and creates a cinematic space that is both expressive of the hero's continuity with the viewer and accessible to the non-Shakespearean. Although Barbara Hodgdon complains that "Zeffirelli's *Hamlet* never quite intersects with late twentieth-century history," this film's great strength is that it does provide the viewer with a familiar context by which to recognize contemporary conventions and morality as retold within the context of an invented Western "past."[14] The mythic symbolism of the American West transcends historical contingencies, even those of medieval Elsinore. The reality of the landscape need not be historically accurate as a representation of the American West, but in its sensuous concreteness it must be capable of conveying the highly charged passions of human conflicts and experiences the viewer associates with the Western genre.

Outside the castle walls of Elsinore Zeffirelli's camera captures an open and alluring visual space that evokes the dramatic opaqueness of the American Western within the natural realism of the Northern European kingdom of Elsinore, and employs the psychology of this popular cinematic image so that the audience may identify with its hero. Ironically, the film fuses the constituent elements and structures of the Western genre without the viewer's awareness of how its familiar patterning reshapes Hamlet's story, for it is one of the commonplaces of cinematic representation that the viewer often fails to perceive what is familiar. Instead, the viewer takes the familiar patterns of the Western for granted, and accepts the way in which problematic or confusing aspects of Hamlet's character and conflict are recontextualized by the explanatory quality of the Western film narration.

In fact, Zeffirelli does what Shakespeare may have done before him, in shaping *Hamlet* as a response to other circulating versions of the play and in accordance with shifting tastes in theater. As Hodgdon notes, Shakespeare's "'new' *Hamlet* [was] more suited to changing dramatic tastes," and was contemporaneous with shifts in acting style toward a "'life-like' action" and away from "the exaggerated affectations associated with strutting players."[15] Zeffirelli's film eliminates the emblematic gestures of theatrical convention and Expressionistic stage-sets associated with Olivier's *Hamlet,* and emphasizes natural action in a natural world.

Critical appraisals of Zeffirelli's *Hamlet* make much of Laurence Olivier's earlier *Hamlet* as source and inspiration.[16] Zeffirelli freely admits that Olivier was "my hero since I was a boy," and in adult life his personal friend and collaborator on film and theater productions.[17] Zeffirelli, however, declares his difference from Olivier's theatrical and somewhat feminized performance of the role by remaking *Hamlet* with an actor whose cinematic persona represents the contemporary audience's masculine ideal.[18] Hodgdon observes that critics tend to emphasize "Hamlet's intellectual dilemma, his subjectivity and interiority" at the cost of his physical representation.[19] Consequently, casting Mel Gibson in the role of Hamlet challenges conceptions of character and conflict favored by literary critics who perceive the play primarily in terms of its "*intellectual* pleasures." However, Zeffirelli's film requires an actor who can sustain two "frames" simultaneously, who could carry the narrative that is Shakespeare's play and yet not disrupt the careful patterning of the Western. It is not that Gibson's presence deflects the play's "intellectual pleasures," as Hodgdon implies, but that Zeffirelli has conceived Hamlet's story as conforming to the sensuous contours of the film Western, a genre that requires the prominent display of the male body.

Robert Warshow declares of the Western film hero's physical representation, "No matter what he has done, he looks right."[20] Lee Clark Mitchell similarly observes, "In no other genre is such an emphasis laid upon youthful male good looks," or "for clear eyes, strong chins, handsome faces, and virile bodies over which the camera can linger to disclose what it is that supposedly contributes to self-restraint."[21] Here, too, Hodgdon intuits the result of commingling Shakespeare and the conventions of the film Western, for she declares Gibson "seems just right" as an ideal of cultural masculinity in Zeffirelli's *Hamlet*.[22] Zeffirelli acknowledges that Mel Gibson's star status was "vital" to the production.[23] Gibson's screen persona carries a measure of the invulnerability that marks the Western hero, as demonstrated in a screen career that began in George Miller's *Mad Max* (1979), a film that exhibits the "fragments and fetishes" of the film Western translated into "alien forms and distant contexts."[24] The choice of Gibson is in keeping with the conventions of the Hollywood Western for, like John Wayne or Gary Cooper, Gibson's presence is larger than the part he plays, less impersonation than personation. The actor, therefore, retains his "identity" on screen even as representational signs capture the actor within the framed action of the drama. However, the result of casting Gibson in the role is that audiences judge his performance — and Zeffirelli's film — by the other films he has made, instead of by Shakespeare or by other Zeffirelli films. It is no accident that Zeffirelli's film is popularly known as "Mel Gibson's *Hamlet*."

Yet even a Hollywood screen idol of Mel Gibson's stature and obvious box-office appeal does not dominate the focus of Zeffirelli's camera. As Neil Taylor points out, "Mel Gibson appears in a smaller proportion of shots than any of the other Hamlets" — only 45 percent.[25] The camera concentrates on the sheer spectacle of landscape that surrounds Hamlet as much as on the man himself, and illustrates the cinematic strategies of the film Western, where to "be a man" meant to be one with the terrain. In the film Western the interconnections between landscape description and character portrayal are closely aligned. As Mitchell observes, the genre's concentration on male physiques "feeds a broader cultural longing for renewal, one that occurs in a special landscape (the American West) because that landscape is associated with personal transformation."[26] In part, the Western elements explain the sometimes contradictory responses that critics have to Gibson's screen presence.[27] In Hollywood films in general and in the Western in particular, the figure of the active male requires the three-dimensional space of the landscape upon which to project his internalized representation of his imaginary existence. To recall Laura Mulvey's oft-cited essay on the pleasures of the gaze, the idealized masculinity of the male movie star is "a figure in a landscape," a figure whose glamorous characteristics are "not those of the erotic object of the gaze, but those of the more perfect, more complete, more powerful ideal ego."[28] As in the film Western, in Zeffirelli's *Hamlet* the spectator finds his or her attention split between the spectacle and the narrative in which Hamlet plays the central role, in that the spectator's vision is continually guided to the spectacle of the landscape in which the Hamlet is situated even as the viewer identifies with Gibson's imagined omnipotence.

How we understand Hamlet's character is largely determined by how we interpret the world that surrounds him, a world that is often read as a projection by the character rather than as an objective reality. Olivier's *Hamlet* is a stunning example of the way in which an audience interprets the film's expressionistic sets and camera's wandering gaze as projections of Hamlet's introspective assessments and disturbed mental state. Hamlet's world functions like Shakespeare's rhetorical devices in providing "a scenic pointer to ambiguous regions in human character that cannot be explained in terms of motive."[29] In fact, Bert O. States observes that analogous techniques are at work in Shakespeare's *Hamlet* and in the art of the film director, for "Shakespearean 'cinematography' makes use of the same device [as employed by film directors] for advancing character ambiguity by framing the character against the rhetorical sky of the play's world."[30] In both text and film "we are invited to read character and world as two terms of a metaphor."[31] Zeffirelli's approach is purely cinematic, in that his film captures the sensuous surfaces of reality as a means to establishing Hamlet's subjective self. The film establishes mood by the way the protagonist is situated in a landscape that reflects the vastness, incongruity, and melancholy that we associate with him. Firm distinctions between actor and landscape collapse in the dialectical interplay between the human constructions of family and court that constrain him and his yearning for a transcendent reality as represented in Hamlet's relationship to the natural world.

Zeffirelli's film crystallizes Hamlet's conflicts through cinematic elements that make visible what otherwise would have remained inaccessible. This film's originality lies in the prosaic nature of its symbolization, which brings abstraction to profane concreteness. Zeffirelli rejects highly stylized stage action, in which language must carry meaning, and reverses the proportions and orders of importance, so that action itself remains, in the strictest sense, naturalistic. Yet by focusing upon the level of realistic action and the sensual reality of Hamlet's world, the film suggests something that lies beyond the senses, and reflects the conditions of existence as both immanent and objective material and transcendent and subjective consciousness.

According to Mel Gibson, Zeffirelli's cinematic techniques distinguish him from other directors with whom he has worked: "Zeffirelli— his thing is the look of a frame that's really interesting. He has to have certain things happening at a certain timing in the frame."[32] Gibson's comments suggest that movement itself carries meaning, in that it frees objects from their stationary restrictions and arranges them in dynamic relationships. It is a technique Lorne Buchman has observed in other Shakespeare films, one that achieves "a vertical meaning of the text" by traveling and exposing "the level of dramatic action operating underneath, to give form to an aspect of the performance text that is 'below.'"[33] The spatio-temporal dynamic allows the director to express Hamlet's transitional inner states (the dramatic action that lies "below") by coordinating the "look" of the cinematic frame with the rhythms of the objects as they move within space, in conjunction with the movement of the camera itself. In the arrangement of objects ("the look of the frame") as they move in space (a "certain timing"), Zeffirelli also accommodates the strategies of the film Western to the topic frame of Shakespeare's play.

The Western film is a genre that exploits contradictions between stasis and movement in the image of the hero himself. As Lee Clark Mitchell observes, astride his horse the cowboy remains "motionless on display even while transversing the landscape, registering supreme self-control in the nonetheless energetic process of crossing (and recrossing) our field of vision, fixed in the center of the frame."[34] In the rhythms of the "unfractured, undistorted, fully coherent male body" as it travels across the landscape, the viewer takes the measure of the man and discovers, in the process, a rich and multilayered meaning of composed movements made of a multitude of equally rich and varied elements that embody a more abstract "order."[35] In the tension between the flowing and the fixed movement of camera and the objects that it surveys there also emerges a spatial context through which mythical thinking visualizes sacred experience. As Yvette Biró points out, "Every realistic movement in the history of the film has proved to be very sensitive to the ephemeral and throbbing nature of the flow of everyday events," since filmmakers have observed that "metaphoric power is created not only by the simple juxtaposition of diverse images, or by the encounter of unusual spectacles, but also by strongly articulated changes of rhythm."[36] Consequently, although physical reality remains unquestionably present on the screen in the conventions of the film Western, abstraction is not impossible, just hidden, and discernable through the time-space freedom of the objects within the cinematic frame.

"This goodly frame, the earth"

The landscapes in film Westerns are as distinctive as their heroes. Whereas John Ford carefully constructs the film landscape with distinctive natural formations towering in the distance, the later Italian Westerns of Sergio Leone evoke an alien and undistinguished landscape. Zeffirelli presents his hero against an open terrain reminiscent of mythic conflicts in a heroic style. The film's scenes that operate within Western conventions and expectations follow Hamlet's violent rejection of Ophelia and his "To be or not to be" scene in the royal crypt, scenes that confine Hamlet to Elsinore. The Western motif dominates in Acts II and III, when Hamlet is increasingly estranged from social relationships and looks toward the natural world, beginning with the scene in which he reclines on a hillside outside the walls of Elsinore as Rosencrantz and Guildenstern approach. In this scene Hamlet is a figure in repose, in relaxed association with nature. The eventlessly concrete realization of his reclining figure against the sounds and sights of the landscape contribute to the viewer's sense of the sensuous reality of time as it weighs heavily on Hamlet. The very barrenness of the spectacle, in conjunction with the sounds of lapping waves and the screeching of gulls against the broad expanse of sea and sky, provides temporal width to the scene, in that purely coincidental and independent elements within the common action-space of the cinematic composition also draw the viewer's attention.

This shot calls upon the viewer's ability to calibrate for cues that work in dramatic juxtaposition to the natural realism of the Danish coast. The ocean and sky merging in a hazy blue in the far background and the sounds of gulls overhead reside in conjunction with Western elements in the frame. Hamlet may bask in the northern sunlight of a Danish coast, but the scene incorporates a familiar pastoral motif of horses grazing in the foreground. By introducing within the topic frame of Shakespeare's *Hamlet* familiar patterns from popular American mythology of the hero's relationship to the physical world, the film conveys an impression of Hamlet's moral clarity as reflected in the clarity of his masculine form against the barren landscape. The viewer modifies the mental constructs he understands as *Hamlet* by using his knowledge of Western filmmaking conventions to construct a new mental representation of Hamlet's story time and space. Paradoxically, the more original Zeffirelli is in his conception of Hamlet's story, the more conventional the Western elements appear, so that audiences intuit and respond to the organization of elements accommodated by Shakespeare's play (figure 1.1).

Yet the familiar motifs of the Western film—of an expansive sky and land and the free movement of men on horses—can also lull the viewer into believing that Hamlet is as open as the world that frames him. Because the landscapes are filmed in a realistic mode, the viewer has certain expectations of what the landscape should mean, how the plot should

FIGURE 1.1. The "Western" terrain outside the walls of Elsinore in Zeffirelli's *Hamlet*. (Courtesy of Warner Brothers)

FIGURE 1.2. The "saloon" structure in Zeffirelli's *Hamlet*. (Courtesy of Warner Brothers)

work, and how the hero should act. But even the Western genre may play against its conventions to search for truths not exhausted by the realistic surface that the camera surveys, and, as a consequence, Gibson's Hamlet is not without moral ambiguity. He retains the darker shadings of the avenger and killer when he warns Laertes: "Yet have I in me something dangerous, / Which let thy wisdom fear" (V.i.263–64).

True to the narrative patterning of the Western film, when Hamlet and his companions leave the pasture's open spaces, they ride their galloping horses to a lonely, rustic structure looking every bit like exuberant cowboys galloping into a desolate Mexican outpost.[37] Peasant women walk past the horsemen, and one dead tree interrupts the openness of the composition in an iconic representation familiar in scenes from the American West. The men tether their horses, sit around a campfire cooking their food, and partake of a barbecue reminiscent of numerous film Westerns. The rustic structure that shelters the men during their repast also serves as a stage for Hamlet to act out his conflicts (figure 1.2). The staging metaphor is central to textual criticism of Hamlet and the play itself. Although the staging is realized within the context of the Western motif, it simultaneously gains prominence as part of the film's articulation of Hamlet's conflict. In Zeffirelli's film, the Western guise is one of the modes, and surprisingly contemporary at that, which "a man might play."

The building, like the saloon enclosure of the classic Western film, has an open floor that suggests a stage and proscenium setting, and provides an opportunity for the hero to insult and threaten spectators and actors alike.[38] Indeed, a violent outburst disrupts this lyrical interlude in Zeffirelli's film when calculated insult turns violent, and Hamlet kicks one of Claudius's spies off his stool. As Lee Clark Mitchell observes, "the Western can be reduced to oppositions between those who stand and those who fall down," and the "prone are always revealed in the end to be non-men."[39] Hamlet's assertion of masculine difference in this scene assumes the forms of the Western film, in physically distinguishing the upright man from Claudius's creature who sprawls on the ground. Hamlet defends his sense of honor and purity of self-image against those who would compromise those values, for his passionate anger and reactive violence is clearly a private response to men who will not be "even and direct" with him.

Released from the claustrophobic setting of Elsinore and surrounded by the open terrain of the landscape, Hamlet still searches for meaning within the social relationships that have defined his existence. He has not yet committed to a larger perspective of action, for he is still ruled by his personal sense of honor, and the landscape reinforces the viewer's awareness of his psychology and struggle. The most revelatory moments in Zeffirelli's film are expressed as the tensions between the confinements of social relationship and the open potential of sea and sky, much as the Western film expresses a dialectic between commitment to the community and the open potential of the range. Beyond the walls of Elsinore and the natural landscape into which Hamlet has been pursued by Claudius' spies lies the nothingness of sea and sky. Zeffirelli frequently frames Gibson's Hamlet in close-up or medium shot against the blue expanse of sea and sky, presenting a persistent visualization of the hero's impulse toward an abstract purity of identification, whereas Rosencrantz and Guildenstern pose before a thorny and entangled vegetation that suggests entrapment by history, personal motives, or the social roles they play.

In this scene Hamlet reflects on "What a piece of work is a man" (II.ii.304–5). When Hamlet begins his speech with a confession to Rosencrantz and Guildenstern that "this goodly frame, the earth, seems to me a sterile promontory" (lines 299–300), he turns away from the building and men to walk down a slope in a low-angle camera shot in which his head and upper body appear against a vast expanse of the sky. He appears to remain constant within the focus of the camera, giving the viewer the impression, as David Impastato observes, that "Hamlet walks but generates virtually no sense of forward progress."[40] Zeffirelli achieves this effect by synchronizing the pace of his dolly to the actor's pace, and filming Gibson in constant image-size with a frontal medium shot so that the hero appears fixed in space.

David Impastato astutely observes that Zeffirelli's use of medium shots conveys a sense of Hamlet's evolving relation to destiny, "not in terms of what he physically faces in the shot" but "rather in terms of what lies behind him."[41] As Hamlet begins his descent down the hill and toward the camera, the uppermost barren branches of a tree remain behind his head, reminding us of the entangled vegetation that frames

Rosencrantz and Guildenstern in an earlier shot and suggesting that he remains within the social world of masculine violence. And because Hamlet's image appears to remain constant within the cinematic screen, the viewer perceives that the hero is static. The viewer's spatial consciousness senses that Hamlet is fixed in space, making the point that images are often more powerful than the concepts they imply.

The manner in which Zeffirelli manipulates the moving dolly and the moving person carries significant metaphysical and textual implications. Because the camera maintains Gibson's image at exactly the same size and distance, the visual effect is of a man floating in one place. That Hamlet appears free-moving, striding forward yet seeming to go nowhere, is presented subliminally in a thematic interpretation of his psychological state by intensely visual means. In this scene Zeffirelli imbues Hamlet with a powerful and timeless iconography of a man who could count himself "a king of infinite space," capable of achieving freedom and selfhood within a vast and expansive terrain, but that he has "bad dreams" (II.ii.256–57), held back by a world of masculine violence and social obligations.

That Hamlet is at this point reciting "What a piece of work is a man" augments the viewer's understanding of his questioning and of his quandary. As Hamlet begins his speech he strolls forward with an expansive sky behind him, so that the space within the viewer's visual field establishes a context that subordinates Hamlet's character to the wide open spaces. When he turns away from his companions, they disappear into non-diegetic space, so that Hamlet appears to turn away from the world that has entangled him. His position in the cinematic frame raises the dilemma that is key to the whole film and play: Hamlet feels he is static when in fact he is caught up in the relentless process of time and the world. The fixed order or spatiality of Zeffirelli's composition achieves a psychic representation that arises from its temporal sequencing so that consciousness appears in spatial metaphors.

This pensive moment abruptly ends, however, when Hamlet spies the traveling troupe of actors beneath the tattered roof of their covered wagon. These actors are at the other end of the spectrum from Olivier's classically trained, all-male troupe; restraint is not among their acting skills. In fact, the troupe resembles the traveling actors of Zeffirelli's youth,

which he sometimes saw in the Tuscan countryside, where "traveling troupes of performers . . . would come and perform" and tell their stories with "blows and gestures." Zeffirelli claims to have "always believed more in their fantasies than in anything else," and uses a similar sort of raucous entertainment in the Mousetrap scene to reveal the truth hidden behind the fiction of Claudius's good intentions.[42] In *Hamlet* the hero's eager adoption of the actors' motley garb and the troupe's general associations with aspects of the carnivalesque (laughter, irreverence, the grotesque, and the urge to turn the world upside down) invert our expectations of Hamlet's interactions with the actors as the "alienated, fragmentary and guilty adoption of a popular voice," and a symptom of "troubled intellectualism."[43] These actors suggest the liberties of the popular voice, and their introduction advances the popular motifs of the American West that Zeffirelli employs in the previous scene.[44] In fact, the actors include among their number a middle-aged woman, an elderly woman, a child, and a dog, visually linking them to narratives of migrations west and the hero's role in escorting the weary wagon train to the walled safety of a nearby fort.

Although Hamlet trumpets the actors' arrival as he leads them to the castle gate, once more within the castle environs he is solitary and entrapped, hemmed in by the stone walls and the narrow corridors through which he walks. Hamlet feels the tortures of his confinement, and his body expresses the pain of mental and physical constriction. At this moment Hamlet's gaze wanders outside the bars of the window to the actors disembarking from their covered wagon. In an anguished yet subdued moment singularly unlike Olivier's dramatic run to the spotlight and stage, Hamlet concludes "the play's the thing." This is a key moment in Zeffirelli's representation of Hamlet's dilemma, just as it is in Olivier's film, in which the camera oscillates between an image of Hamlet's tortured form within Elsinore and the spatial freedom he glimpses outside the bars of his prison.

Although pulled by enclosure, Gibson's Hamlet ultimately leaves behind the social world of masculine violence and its enclosed system of plot and behavior to explore an alternative space that expresses the possibilities of freedom and creative aspects of the self. Despite the confinement that weighs upon him and the social obligations that continually pull him back into the masculine world of violence, he is drawn back to the open space of the natural environment that passes through and beyond the film's frame. This is not the tempest-tossed sea and darkening sky upon which Olivier's Hamlet projects his inner perturbations as he contemplates "to be or not to be," but an alluring and expansive sea and sky that beckon to the man who seeks a truth beyond the narrow limits of his world and the individual self. As Gibson's Hamlet stands upon the castle ramparts or gazes out the window, he continually surveys the visual expanses of his world. Van Watson observes of Zeffirelli's film that "in frame after frame, in close-up after close-up, in soliloquy after soliloquy, Hamlet looks at everything and nothing."[45] Hamlet's incessant gaze outward is part of Zeffirelli's overall filming strategy, which segments images by "frequent changes of image," so that the average shot lasts less than six seconds.[46] For Hamlet, meaning is discovered in the space beyond the architectural boundaries of the castle and the objects and persons contained within it. His truth lies everywhere and nowhere, projected onto the spatial openness upon which he gazes, and not within a constellation of objects, as in Olivier's *Hamlet*. Zeffirelli's film presents a hero who, while responding to the pull of masculine encodings of identity, surveys the aesthetic boundaries of its representation.

"Good my lord, put your discourse into some frame"

According to the Western conventions that Zeffirelli employs, spatial openness holds out the possibility of escape from the masculine world of violence and the promise of personal transformation. In fact, Zeffirelli's autobiography records his personal engagement with the transformative power of the Western myth. Zeffirelli acknowledges that "foreign idealization" of myths "never quite matched up to the illusion," but he concedes that "sometimes you need a national myth and without one you can end up with nothing towards which to work. I know that theater people often have a very simplistic view of politics and tend to express very black and white patriotic sentiments but perhaps that is because we know the value of illusion, how it can help strengthen the weak and stimulate the weary. I think Shakespeare understood that very well."[47] Zeffirelli speaks from his own experience, for in the bleakest moments of his life he turned toward the myth of the American West to question and redirect prescriptions of identity.

Zeffirelli recalls how during the last days of World War II in Italy he came to Milan and saw the savagely desecrated bodies of Mussolini and his mistress laid out on two tables, a scene so gruesome that the sight, he claims, ended his innocence: "I felt my childhood ended in that room."[48] He decided to return to his father's home in Florence and recalls that the "Germans had abandoned a lot of horses when they withdrew, and one of the partisans had rounded them up. . . . We took six horses and headed for Bologna. . . . It was exhilarating, something out of the American Wild West."[49] Zeffirelli envisions his escape from the carnage in Milan in terms of the genre of the film Western, in which the rootless, wandering cowboy rides into the spatial openness of the Western landscape and discovers who he is. In fact, Westerns such as John Ford's *Stagecoach* consistently represent the social outcast, or the misfit in repressive "civilized" society, as finding his place in the open spaces of the West. Indeed, Zeffirelli claims that his "Western" experience changed him, in that he was inspired to retain the fabricated name "Zeffirelli" that marked him as a bastard child.

The spectre of bastardy also haunts Shakespeare's *Hamlet.* Laertes, at once sentimental and murderous, is led to his revenge and possible treason against his king because he fears the taint of bastard: "That drop of blood that's calm proclaims me bastard, / Cries cuckold to my father, / brands the harlot / Even here between the chaste unsmirchèd brow / Of my true mother" (IV.v.121–24). Laertes connects feminine betrayal with the denigration of the father's image, much as Hamlet does when he upbraids himself for failing to fly to his revenge while he "Must like a whore unpack my heart with words" (II.ii.586). Zeffirelli concretizes the attendant fears of feminine denigration and the son's liminality in the opening scene of the film. Hamlet's liminality as outsider among the intriguers and plotters of Elsinore sets in motion the camera's exploration of the space outside the parameters of paternal authority and definition, much as Zeffirelli's experience as bastard led him to seek a "cultural ideal" that "offered an alternative to the losses, grief, and confusion of his relation to his actual parents in childhood."[50] In *Hamlet* Zeffirelli transforms the protagonist's metaphysical dilemma into an active and literal engagement with the world, which also begins with a scene of death. The film reveals the painful singularity of Hamlet's personal loss of the father within its greater cultural signification in the opening scene. It begins, not as the play does, with the nervous sentry's recollection of a ghostly presence, but with the funeral of a king, a scene that also marks the hero's liminal state.

In Shakespeare's age mourning was a "liminal period" demonstrated by the "wearing of special garments" for an indeterminate period of time.[51] In fact, Hamlet's liminality is visually established in the opening scene by the brown mourning cloak he wears. The cloak distinguishes him from the other mourners and guests, but also provides a visible indicator that the wearer's "grief was different from and by implication unsharable by the other guests."[52] It was even thought that the garment altered the inner man who wore it, for it "put a man in mind of his own mortality, seeing it carrieth a remembrance of death with it."[53] Although a relatively minor detail, the same brown cloak reappears in the dumbshow worn by the actor who murders the king, visually connecting Hamlet and the actor who plays the murderous nephew Lucianus. The mourning cloak is the sort of detail that would interest Zeffirelli, who claims that he developed his "own style by paying attention to cultural truths," truths that emerged from historical research and close attention to detail.[54]

The opening scene also accords with the Western's rituals of burial as liminal markers of masculinity. As Mitchell points out, the Western genre is obsessed "with acknowledging death" as the "liminal marker in the construction of masculine identity."[55] The Western's obsession with proper burial enforces a link between landscape and death as a process of bodies being returned to the earth from which they emerged. In *Hamlet* the presence of the king's cold body, the expression of a few solemn words while mourners stand around, and the scattering of soil over the corpse, enforce the viewer's impression of the vulnerability of the masculine figure before forces beyond his control. As Mitchell notes, the Western "has always celebrated a certain necrological impulse, verging on the edges of death, invoking violence only to show how the restrained, fetish-laden body is not to be deprived of life but made to stand as a desirable emblem of masculinity, as a self-contained, animated (if finally inanimate) object."[56] By situating Hamlet physically within the walls of the tomb that holds his father, Zeffirelli alerts the viewer to the film's interpretative design, which literalizes the son's quandary as that of "crawling between heaven and earth." Without speaking a single word in the opening scene, Gibson's Hamlet exhibits the restraint Western films associate with the masculine figure as he stands on the edges of death, in which expanses of silence operate like the landscape in evoking depth of feeling in the son's bereavement and in exposing the hollowness of the uncle's verbal flourishes. This moment in the film provides the viewer with a reference for specific aspects of Hamlet's character that theatrical incarnations of the play generally do not or cannot emphasize, such as the disdain Hamlet clearly feels for unrestrained verbal excess, those "words, words, words" with which he mocks Polonius and mercilessly upbraids himself for unpacking his heart like a whore.

This fabricated scene also introduces the possibility of different kinds of disruptions in the viewer's understanding of Shakespeare's *Hamlet,* in that it requires the use of a model, or relevant framing cues. It provides a structure for the viewer by putting Hamlet's circumstances "into some frame" (III.ii.307-8). Zeffirelli fabricates a transformational frame for the viewer, a strip of activity keyed for *Hamlet* if the story were real, in which the Western provides a subtle patterning, albeit not clearly visible at all times, through which the audience incorporates both Hamlet's responses and the world to which Hamlet responds. Although the viewer may detect extratextual patternings, they do not distract from the story line because the viewer manages them in a disassociated way. Since the Western patterning bears no immediate reference to Shakespeare's story, it illustrates how the viewer's attention can be split in two, in that the viewer attends to both Hamlet's story and the pattern of the film Western.

"Our state to be disjoint and out of frame"

In the opening moments of the film Hamlet turns away from this triangulated gathering of mother, uncle, and son at the funeral of the dead father (a scene Linda Charnes calls "literally encrypted" oedipalism) to the outer world where the public mourners stand in mute attendance at the funeral of the king.[57] Merely perceiving is a more active penetration of events than might be assumed, since even the bystanders who attend the public memorial of a king actively project their frames of reference into the world immediately around them. It is their active engagement as public mourners in viewing the burial of their king that diminishes familial encodings of the play. The film viewer confirms the perspective of those in attendance by his own perceptions of the events unfolding before him (the ceremonial burial of a king) even as the transformational power of the scene's earlier assumptions disappears into the smooth flow of the ensuing film narrative. It is a moment of competing perceptions that recalls Claudius's assertion of monarchical stability when faced with Fortinbras's estimation of Denmark as "disjoint and out of frame" (I.ii.20). Fortinbras's perceptions are borne out by dramatic events, of course, but the comment has relevance for the way in which Zeffirelli cinematically conceives Hamlet's own precarious state.

In the opening moments of the film Hamlet removes himself from the exchange of furtive glances to cross the threshold of the tomb to move into the natural space of his audience in a fleetingly transgressive moment in the play's plot of filial and sexual identifications. It suggests the developmental transitions that the borders and liminal scenes narratively reproduce, threshold points that are stressed cinematically by various characters spying through cracks in doors, from windows and behind arras. In fact, the film's visual emphasis upon liminality and framing boundaries replicates strategies found in the film Western for addressing oedipal issues, as evidenced in the preponderance of border and liminal scenes in films such as *Shane* or *High Noon*.[58] The leitmotif of the threshold also appears in Zeffirelli's *Hamlet* as a concentration on windows and doors, and reinforces the viewer's perception that the journey to manhood is somewhere between motion and stasis, between the hero's movement across the threshold and his liminal positioning.

In coupling the aggressive cultural encodings of masculinity derived from the Western with Shakespeare's drama, Zeffirelli magnifies the salience of Hamlet's oedipal conflicts with the demands of the Western genre that masculine aggression be played out across the bodies of

women. However, the Western also aspires to a mythic resolution of cri-
ses, in that it addresses the "filial theme as a way of resolving Oedipal
issues" that the genre simultaneously manages to "compound or evade."[59]
This may explain why Laura Mulvey asserts that the Western protagonist
displays "a nostalgic celebration of phallic narcissistic omnipotence" that
is "difficult to integrate exactly into the Oedipal trajectory."[60] Like the
Western hero, Gibson's behavior does not conform to easy definitions of
oedipal desire but instead contributes to fantasy elements in Hamlet's
characterization, in that the film engages oedipal conflicts and then avoids
them. A striking and obvious instance of this occurs in the film's closet
scene and its representation of the intimacy between mother and son. The
critical confusion arises, in part, from the viewer's inability to prescribe an
adequate framework to the actions within the scene, in what looks to be
Hamlet's acting out of oedipal impulses.[61] However, Shakespeare's closet
scene is, as Lisa Jardine points out, "one of contradictory, inconsistent and
incompatible messages" to begin with.[62] Jardine suggests that the conflict
arises from an insufficiently clear demarcation between the domains of
public and private, given the public counsellor's presence in the intimate
space of the mother's closet and Hamlet's retreat from that space — "backwards, in disorder, dragging a dead body." The scene marks an erotic situation that Hamlet (and, by extension, the audience) cannot assimilate, in
that it signals competing and conflicting spatial thresholds.

The closet scene in Zeffirelli's *Hamlet* is an instance in which continuity for the audience as far as guidance as to the interactions between
characters requires the enactment of two systems of reference, one per-
taining to characters in the staged events of *Hamlet* and the other in accordance with the patterning of the film Western. In this scene the Western
context remains outside the focus of the main story line, but is nevertheless consequential in qualifying the scene's various components and
phases. Although the viewer may not attend to directional cues, evidential clues somewhat akin to stereotyping have a framing effect in dramatically restructuring the scene and alerting the viewer to a shift in
directional flow.

Zeffirelli's dramatic scripting of the relationship between mother and
son well before the viewer witnesses their encounter in the closet scene

allows for the manipulation of framing conventions that cut deeply into the viewer's organization of experience. Early in the film the viewer perceives the Queen scampering through the halls of Elsinore and galloping along the seacoast astride a white horse, her physicality and intellect giving actress Glenn Close's Gertrude the appearance of being the hero's equal. In this regard she displays a quasi-masculine independence and strength more in keeping with the Western film's barroom entertainer or prostitute than with most stage or film Gertrudes, and stands in stark contrast with Eileen Herlie's simpering and laconic Gertrude in Olivier's *Hamlet*. When Gibson's Hamlet speaks sharply to his mother, Close's Gertrude slaps her son across the face. Close's characterization of the Queen harbors a strength and intelligence that makes this Gertrude, as many critics suspect, a match for Gibson's Hamlet. To some extent, the sheer sensationalism of the closet scene in Zeffirelli's film almost seems a mere pretext for delivering what audiences crave—the coupling of the film's two glamorous co-stars. The emphatic and sexualized movements between mother and son on the bed are beset with interpretative problems that casting and direction only compound. Murray Biggs's description of Gertrude and Hamlet's encounter as "a full-blown, vulgarized, traditional screen romance between coevals," correctly gauges how general audiences respond to their pairing in this scene.[63] However, when interviewed Gibson admitted that a Freudian explanation of Gertrude's "more than motherly" behavior "bothers" him.[64] Gibson's remark, although vague, suggests that Gertrude's physicality simply cannot be explained in terms of Hamlet's uncontrollable psychological forces.

In fact, the film's introduction of Western elements reshapes the contours of Gertrude's performance as much as it does Hamlet's by assigning Gertrude a central position as the object of masculine desire. Strong women in the film Western have what Philip French calls "a strong whiff of erotic perversity."[65] In a genre that both investigates and celebrates excessive masculinity, any bid toward sexual equality savors of dangerous confidence and provokes erotic fascination. It should be no surprise that "the emergence of the Western coincides with the advent of America's second feminist movement, and that the genre's recurrent rise and fall coincides more generally with interest aroused by feminist issues, moments when men have invariably had difficulty knowing how manhood should be achieved."[66] Hamlet's misogyny finds coherent expression within a Western context, not as perverse and obsessive oedipal musings but as the hero's active assertion of masculine identity under fire. However, in that Western narratives explore mythic origins of identity formulated as territorial expansion, Close's Gertrude lies within the Western's mythic representations that complicate the parent-child relationship of the play. As Laura Mulvey explains, when the image of the mother becomes implicated in the conceptual framework of myth, she becomes the "site of imbrication between body and psyche and society," and "metonymically associated with the cultural marginalisations of the woman's sphere."[67]

In the play Gertrude and Hamlet's encounter in the closet scene is constructed as hybrid narrative material that suggests the intersection of spatial thresholds. Similarly, the realistic surface of Zeffirelli's film explores Hamlet's unconscious in terms of topology, as a spatial journey. The film uses spatial figures and images to evoke the relation between a surface consciousness and those thoughts hidden from consciousness, giving Gertrude a symbolic role in Hamlet's complicated and ambivalent desire to journey back to a point of preverbal symbolizations (birth/death). In other words, Gertrude's sexual openness and her figuration as mother conjoin in her representation as an aspect of the hero's internal yearnings, which transforms her from a creature mired in carnality to a visual manifestation of the unseen. Hamlet's longing for spatial openness registered in the natural landscapes of the film has its corollary in the film's representation of femininity, as the capacity to move across the cinematic frame's aesthetic space. The literal openness of the physical terrain toward which Hamlet turns his gaze has its metaphoric equivalent in images of feminine fluidity, and is consistent with the Western genre's representation of womanhood "as a breaching of borders, an erasure of limits, a bridging of otherwise incompatible possibilities."[68]

To make sense of the closet scene one must consider its compositional similarity to the moment of Gertrude's death in the concluding moments of the film. Images of female sexuality and death merge in Zeffirelli's film in a pattern that lends Gertrude's representation coherence and meaning. In these two crucial scenes Zeffirelli suggests Gertrude's symbolic relevance through a visual coherence between scenes, or repetition of a motif, or presentation of character, by making Gertrude's physicality, characterized as her motherhood and openness (the unmarked and invisible reproductive female body), the visual representation of the hero's journey. The emphatic pelvic thrusts of both scenes (one indicating the mother's troubling sexuality, the other her death throes), are composed the same way, with Close in close-up and medium shot, lying slightly at an angle, and Gibson's Hamlet to the right of her body and above her. The similarity between these moments highlights Gertrude's symbolic significance, in which femininity is a primordial space of being which is created by the mother alone. Gertrude's movements recall the hero's journey from conception to nothingness, from womb to tomb, for which the mother is the dominate symbol and image, as the womb from which Hamlet springs and the source of his mortal and fleshly limits. The visual repetition is more than an instance of visual punning on the mother's "dying." The similarity between these moments alerts the viewer to the connection the film makes between those twin movements from conscious selfhood to oblivion, from birth to death. In comparing the scenes in which these repetitions occur, the viewer discovers that the surface reality is no more than artifice, that the visible surface recorded by the camera constitutes only part of a complex dialectic through which man discovers truth. Although Zeffirelli's camera looks outward at the realistic surface of the world, it does not exhaust the meaning of what it surveys, but provides a visual cue for the viewer "to discover those orders the watcher creates by his act of seeing."[69]

Woman's symbolic place, both stylistically and ideologically, is crucial to Zeffirelli's *Hamlet,* which is organized around dual feminine representations that are degraded and idealized projections of the same mystification. In the film's aesthetic representation of Gertrude and Ophelia's difference emerges a pattern of coherence and relationship, in that femininity appears as the cause and destination of the whole of human mystery and its desires, upon which Hamlet projects the unrepresentable. Their conjoined symbolic values counterbalance Hamlet's impulses toward violence and revenge and the masculine codes that bind him, and accord with the film's visual representations of landscape in terms of spatial openness and fluidity, in which images of femininity evoke a space of aesthetic representation and conceptualization, as realized in their repetition and refrainlike recurrences. As Yvette Biró observes, in cinematic moments of repetition the viewer discovers "death's oppressive power" in the facts of the physical world, in that movement and stasis alert the viewer to "the continual modification of the situation [that] is the spectacle of loss."[70]

If women are symbolic representations of Hamlet's conflicting desires, in which Gertrude stands as a type familiar as the erotic woman, then Ophelia is her redemptive counterpart, bound by established rules and conventions. In this context Ophelia represents the world and its moral codes from which Hamlet is disaffected, the sacrificed daughter whose identity is fatally linked with that of her father. Ophelia also bears certain similarities with Hamlet, since she is also held hostage to the violence and interpretative control of the men around her, who accord her, as Francis Barker observes, "a passivity and marginality which is both poignant and repulsive."[71] As in Hamlet's case, Ophelia's marginality conjoins with her position as chief mourner of a father inadequately commemorated, in which her unshaped articulation recalls a divine truth that stands in vivid contrast to Claudius's smooth statesmanship: "Her speech is nothing, / Yet the unshapèd use of it doth move / The hearers to collection" (IV.v.7–9). Like Hamlet, she bears the burden of memory that is death: "There's rosemary, that's for remembrance—pray you, love, remember" (IV.v.179). In the funerals of early modern England rosemary served to conceal the smell of putrefaction, but in the film Ophelia's truthtelling reminds her listeners of the decomposition that is death. Ophelia scatters no flowers, but instead distributes bones, an urgent remembrance of putrefaction and dissolution, a memento mori that links her, having lost her wits, with Hamlet's caustic wit in the graveyard. The substitution of bones for flowers is an instance of Zeffirelli's emphasis upon a physical reality that works against the text. Zeffirelli's realistic cinema focuses upon both the small details as well as the grand, sweeping landscapes, and thereby risks the viewer's failing to scan the objective surface of the screen for deeper meaning. By deviating from the play text, even in the minor detail of the flowers, Zeffirelli forces the viewer to attend to the surface of things, to link Ophelia's pain with Hamlet's, and to ponder the fact of the flesh's dissolution that is hidden by the flowers. By emphasizing the physical facts of death, Zeffirelli directs Ophelia away from paternal and social prescriptions of identity to the point of their literal dissolution.

Ophelia's madness and death are striking examples of Zeffirelli's realistic style in using the outer surface that the camera scans to reveal an inner truth. The similarity between the spatio-temporal framing of Ophelia's madness and the earlier shot of Hamlet in his "What a piece of work is a man" speech provides the viewer with a clue to Ophelia's representation as a repetition of Hamlet's struggle against enclosure and as a foreshadowing of his end. In this scene Ophelia's madness has a spectacular and virtually operatic grandness, and her sexual aggressiveness toward the guard and assault on Gertrude suggest the potential violence of her truth. In her bare feet and coarse, wet smock, she resembles a Christian martyr ranting at a decadent and unseeing court. Only in her psychic disintegration does she confront the truth of her betrayal and social alienation, and register a righteous anger in her search for meaning and justice. She leaves the king and queen with the assurance that "My brother shall know of it"(IV.v.71), and haltingly bids farewell to the gentlemen and ladies who grieve her dissolution. In a low-angle medium shot Ophelia moves away from the people who enclose her and for one moment stands completely still, with the palace's stone column directly behind her, so that she has the appearance of being crowned with its circle of supporting beams. The castle itself seems to crown her as its martyr, but, in destroying her, it also liberates her.

The camera records Ophelia's death from a distance, its significance projected upon the landscape that envelops her form. The viewer witnesses her escape to the open landscape beyond the walls of Elsinore. The brilliant sunlight and verdant greenery beckon her, her step is light, and the entire scene seems to suggest that she moves eagerly toward the water below. The camera cuts to Gertrude's narration of Ophelia's death, before the shot fades to a long distance shot of Ophelia's tiny figure floating upon the water. The viewer barely determines that it is Ophelia in the water before the camera moves away from the body and Gertrude completes her recital of events. As the camera slowly moves forward and upward it seems to capture the movement of Ophelia's ascent toward the oblivion of blue sky and water, punctuated with Gertrude's utterance, "Drowned, drowned" (IV.vii.185). The fluidity of the camera's movements, as it drifts toward the sea and expansive nothingness that claim Ophelia, registers a strikingly different moment than what we see in Olivier's film, where Ophelia's death is a constricted composition in what Jorgens describes as a "Rossetti-like image" and Davies specifies as a replication of "the Millais painting." Davies observes that Olivier's visualization of Ophelia's death has the effect of reducing "Gertrude's poetic description of the scene to a restricted and stale image."[72] The meaning of her death becomes a mere sentimental cliché as Ophelia descends into a more tightly restricted space, the little grave in which both Laertes and Hamlet intrude. The sentimental construction of Ophelia's death in Olivier's film coincides with the restrictions the cinematic frame places upon its significance. Her death expresses helplessness before an invisible authority that controls her end.

In comparison, Zeffirelli imbues Ophelia's death with a redemptive spirituality and heroic significance. Her drowning, as a consequence, seems not the result of the weight of her grief, as in Olivier's film, but a natural momentum toward release. Although Zeffirelli's realistic mode records Ophelia's death as morally neutral and mute fact, the viewer's experience of the landscape determines its significance as the freedom to explore a self beyond the limits of churchyard memorials, church monuments, and physical decomposition. In the expansive nothingness of blue sea and sky, punctuated by Gertrude's cries of "Drowned, drowned," the camera directs the viewer toward a nonhuman explanation of meaning, as if Ophelia departs "to some section of the world the camera specifically does *not* define."[73] The differences between the way Olivier and Zeffirelli record the death of Ophelia reflect the directors' differing perspectives on Hamlet's struggle against closure and limits. As Leo Braudy observes, "The kind of God, the kind of control, that forms part of a film director's themes" is "almost inseparable from his aesthetic vision of the way to make films."[74]

The spatial and temporal presentation of Ophelia's death illustrates what happens when space slowly detaches itself from objects, or, more accurately, when objects detach themselves from space. The slow movement of the camera lifts Ophelia's isolated figure out of its time-space coordinates into a magical-mythical level of experience, as if she were "like a creature native and endued / Unto that element" (IV.vii.180–81). Although Ophelia retains her own reality within the space of the screen, her death signals another self and reality that drifts into an inexhaustible and inaccessible beyond, "out of frame." Not unexpectedly, the shot of Ophelia's movement toward the horizon and eventual disappearance is similar to patterns familiar in the film Western: "If the prisoner we see in the opening shots of *The Roundup* suddenly sets out in an open space toward the horizon, we feel that this freedom bodes ill for him. We are looking at this suspicious, undermined movement and wait tensely for something irrevocable, as the prisoner just keeps going toward the geometric center of the frame, where, we are convinced, something must happen. He cannot go farther."[75] Ophelia is like the prisoner who escapes into an unknown territory, her diminished figure skipping lightly toward the center of the cinematic frame where, as Gertrude tells us, something does happen. But in its immaterial transcendence, which the viewer glimpses in the camera's final movement toward a space beyond the horizon, we begin to understand the significance of "out of frame" activities, which are often wrongly interpreted or incorrectly perceived. For not only do Fortinbras's little-attended marches across the borders of Denmark sweep the way for the ambitious prince to ascend to power in the final scene of the play, but the camera's fluid movement to a space outside the film narrative gestures toward Hamlet's unconscious desires and his end. The hero's longing for death marks him as a man who, although "standing tall" before the forces encoded as feminine, discovers their potential within himself.

"That frame outlives a thousand tenants"

The duel scene in *Hamlet* is a stunning example of Zeffirelli's skill as a filmmaker, which aspires to the standard of external reality while gesturing at the invisible and eternal. Osric is transformed from a self-serving fop to a gatekeeper of the undiscovered country, and establishes the weight and seriousness of the proposed duel with Laertes behind Hamlet's gibes and gambols. Osric delivers Laertes' challenge with ominous significance, grimly welcomes Hamlet when he enters the great hall, and directs him to his place upon the staging platform. Gone are Hamlet's ridicule of Osric found in the play and Osric's effeminate posturing seen in Olivier's *Hamlet*. In Olivier's film Osric's presence at the duel provides the viewer with a visual cue for degrading Laertes' character and motives. Olivier associates the fop and Laertes at the crucial moment in which Laertes chooses to use the poisoned rapier, linking his behavior with Osric's so that the treachery of the former is understood as an undermining of masculine codes by feminine influences. Zeffirelli, however, strips Hamlet's speech of his indignant response to Osric's apishness and allows Osric to deliver the challenge of the duel with dignity and a mysterious knowingness. The duel and the baited sword remain within the context of masculine codes of conduct, and femininity, which adversely affects Laertes' character and choices in Olivier's representation, is recast as a primordial state of being toward which Hamlet unconsciously wends.

In the duel scene Zeffirelli explores the aesthetics of stock characters and situations within Western genre conventions. Altering Osric's character frees Zeffirelli to redirect some of the clownishness typically reserved for Hamlet's encounter with Osric onto Gibson's Hamlet during the duel scene itself. Hamlet now consciously and entertainingly plays the clown, turning the swordplay into a frolic, winking at his mother, and exasperating the already impatient Laertes. However, Hamlet's clowning bravado during the duel turns to righteous anger when Laertes wounds him. He drops his sword and renders Laertes swift justice with a punch on the jaw. At this particular moment Hamlet's outrage and unpremeditated, immediate response are in keeping with the conventions of the Western hero, in that his motives are clearly understood within the context of the genre's conventions and morality. In the Western, the duel scene and fistfight define the hero, not in terms of justice or revenge as much as of his concept of honor and integrity of the self. Similarly, Hamlet does not violate accepted forms of combat, despite the cost to Elsinore and himself. And just as the spatial organization of the Western film requires the inevitable final shootout in which at least one of the participants be reduced to prone inactivity, the concluding moments of Zeffirelli's film fulfills its sublimated pattern of the film Western in depicting the hero's death within a spatial organization that contains the prone forms of his beaten antagonists.

When the Clown in the graveyard explains that the solution to his riddle is "gallows maker, for that frame outlives a thousand tenants" (V.i.43-44), his quiddities have resonance for the final catastrophe of Shakespeare's play and its memorialized reenactment as film Western. For the "frame" of Hamlet's story "outlives" its own dramatic enactment within the patterning of the film Western, even as the play's final spectacle of slaughter points the way, as Michael Neill observes, to "a new kind of theatre of the self—one in which an improvisatory readiness in the art of self-presentation is everything."[76] It is a story that ultimately defies the logic of bloody retribution by disassociating the hero from the ethics of revenge and by focusing upon the hero's encounter with his own death as a drama of masculine self-restraint and stoical resignation. The hero's readiness to submit to an authority greater than himself—whether to "this fell sergeant, Death" (V.ii.338) or "a divinity that shapes our ends" (V.ii.10)—inscribes Hamlet's death within a theatrical aesthetic of self-presentation that is reenacted in the film Western's ritual of dying.

At the moment of his death Hamlet lies with Horatio at his side and slightly to his right, reversing the positions between Hamlet and his mother in the closet scene and his mother's death. As the "potent poison quite o'ercrows" his spirit (V.ii.355), Hamlet's dying movements are versions of Gertrude's own, the agonized throes of death faintly resembling the sexualized violence of the closet scene, visually commingling desire and death as that "consummation / Devoutly to be wished" (III.i.64-65). As Hamlet becomes still and Horatio utters the last words of the film, "Good night, sweet prince, / And flights of angels sing thee to thy rest" (V.ii.361-62), the camera begins its slow and fluid movement upward and away from Hamlet, as if, on cue, Hamlet's spirit begins its ascent with flights of angels. The upward movement of the mobile camera clearly recalls Olivier's film and his Hamlet's end, but, to borrow a line from Ophelia, he wears his rue with a difference. In Olivier's film Hamlet's upraised body on the castle ramparts suggests his reenclosure in a plot and pattern imposed from some unseen authority, his diminished figure engulfed by a darkness that implies his mortal limits. In contrast, Zeffirelli's camera records a movement away from the powerlessness of personal grief and stultifying codes of masculine vengeance to a space outside the bounds of what the camera records, a space impossible to narrate, before which the audience experiences the heroic significance of Hamlet's death. The solemn music urges the claim that Hamlet's death is a release, like Ophelia's own, to an infinite space beyond the confines of this earthly frame. The swelling sound of the horns provides the viewer with connection, comment, and wonder about what has been seen.

The composition on the screen presents Hamlet's death as a journey in terms of his evolving relationship with what lies behind him — the staging upon which he fought the fatal duel and the bodies and courtiers that encircle him. The spatio-temporal dynamic evoked by the camera reverses the experience of Hamlet's "What a piece of work is a man" speech, in which the body in motion appears static. Now the body that remains motionless conveys the impression of spiritual ascent by the movement of the camera, which booms upward, as if to suggest the hero's apotheosis as a movement upward toward the freedom of spatial openness. The contradictions in the viewer's experience of movement within the cinematic frame have a corollary in the silence that punctuates Hamlet's end. For although death compels Hamlet's silence, the Western elements contribute to the viewer's impression that his silence, like that of the Western hero, is a "sovereign condition" which is "arduously achieved" and "not simply and passively assumed."[77] Paradoxically, even as the viewer appreciates the silence that crowns the perfect state of the constructed masculine form, and the hero's sheer effort of will which sustains that image, the viewer's gaze is drawn back to the physical body itself, and its impression of a natural and unfabricated masculinity.

As the camera moves away from a close-up of the dying Hamlet's countenance to a long shot of the great hall and the bodies that surround the raised platform upon which Hamlet's body lies, the viewer achieves a greater perspective of these tragic events. However, in contrast to the end of Olivier's film, which is a brilliant achievement of audience involvement and complicity, the last scene of Zeffirelli's *Hamlet* illuminates a sublimity in Hamlet's character that denies the audience explanation. As H. R. Coursen complains, "I feel a strong sense of incompleteness at the end of this film."[78] Such an ending contrasts with how the audience has come to understand Hamlet's character, whose motives are encoded with the Western's recognizable convention and morality, so that viewers respond, as Barbara Hodgdon does, in thinking "that nothing bad could happen to a body so perfectly formed."[79] But, of course, the point of violence in the Western is to illustrate the tension that exists between the potential dissolution of the hero's physical body and his performance of self-restraint, in which masculinity is revealed as an unresolvable condition.

In the final shot the viewer experiences aspects of Hamlet's character that force the viewer to acknowledge that this hero has not been predictable or understandable — that his end is, after all, a mystery. As the camera booms upward, it also moves away from the enclosure of conventions of genre and plot, including that of the film Western. Although the plot is solved and the facts brought together, Hamlet's mystery remains. The upward and outward movement of the camera away from Hamlet's body opens up the space of the irresolvable. It searches for a truth that lies outside the bounds of the cinematic frame and travels beyond its aesthetic boundaries, drifting upward into a diffuse space without frontiers.

Chapter Two

The Voyeuristic Pleasures of Perversion

Orson Welles's *Othello*

As Barbara Everett observes, Shakespeare's *Othello* is a tragedy that "turns on 'looking on,' on voyeurism, on proof" provided by "a mere handkerchief."[1] Orson Welles's 1952 production of *Othello* is an adaptation that emphasizes this voyeuristic impulse within Shakespeare's play. Although the film sacrifices a great deal of Shakespeare's language, narrative is replaced by visual relationships that require the involvement of the spectator in creating a coherent whole from the fragmented and oscillating perspectives of the camera. Welles emphasizes the viewer's sense of fragmentation through the excessive use of point of view shots. The film is tightly edited so that scenes are broken up into shots from different perspectives, frequently offering the spectator a "narcissistic doubling" of shot and reverse shot exchanges so that the spectator oscillates between the object choice and identification. Yet, as Peter Donaldson comments, in Welles's film "reversals of point of view are seen in relation to a sequence in which connection is sought but not found."[2] The editing style continually suggests to the viewer that he has missed something, has failed to glimpse all the action, much as Shakespeare's play depicts Othello puzzling over events he too has missed. A broken sequence of camera shots continually disrupts the viewer's understanding of events, creating a "'deliberately jerky' rhythm," which introduces, as James Naremore observes, "a slightly illogical ellipsis between some of the cuts."[3] This "gap" or imagined space of action between a scene's cinematic framing and "the look" or point of view creates what Welles has called "the voyeuristic pleasure of pain."[4]

The Voyeuristic Pleasure of Pain

Some critics argue that Welles's stylistic intention emerged from the necessity of shooting his film over a period of four years, encumbered by debt and repeatedly making fundraising forays so that shooting could resume. Barbara Leaming reports that "the sporadic manner in which Orson filmed *Othello* is reflected in its fractured texture."[5] It is certainly arguable that the need to interrupt filming to raise money for his project—and to deal with his disintegrating marriage with Rita Hayworth—determined not only the "fractured texture" of *Othello* but also the film's decided emphasis upon "the voyeuristic pleasure of pain." The psychological tensions replete in Welles's personal and professional life appear to discover their correlative in his imaginative excesses in theater and film.

One particular incident provides an illuminating glimpse into the Welles of this period. During the four years that Welles spent to complete *Othello* he undertook a variety of projects to help finance his film, though the larger project was never from his mind. Barbara Leaming reports that Welles went to Paris to star in his adaptation of Marlowe's *Dr. Faustus* with Micheal MacLiammoir (his Iago in the unfinished *Othello*) as his Mephistophilis. During the casting of *Dr. Faustus* Welles met the young Eartha Kitt, whom he decided to cast as Helen, and dismissed Suzanne Cloutier (Desdemona in *Othello*), to whom he had originally given the part of Helen. The onstage dynamic between Welles's Faust and Kitt's Helen suggests how her passivity (her desire not to let the audience perceive the events onstage despite her obvious pain) made her an ideal counterpart to Welles's impulse to enact "the voyeuristic pleasure of pain":

Miss Kitt played a young student who, seeing a statue of Faust in a museum, falls in love with him. The action that unfolds is the daydream she has about the statue's coming alive. As the spotlight falls on Orson he begins suddenly to move.

"And he stretches his arm out," Miss Kitt recalls. "The girl gets up on the other side of the stage. As she [Kitt] gets to Orson he takes her in his arms and he says, 'Helen, make me immortal with a kiss.' He's talking to the *audience* [emphasis Kitt's], and as he says, 'Helen, make me immortal with a kiss,' he pulls me up to him, he kisses me, but he *bites me* [emphasis Kitt's] at the same time. I mean that he bites me to such an extent that it was very painful." Miss Kitt suspected it was the conspicuous presence in the front row of an older gentleman friend of hers from the States that triggered Orson's jealous outburst: "I asked him later and he said that he was jealous. He said he got excited."[6]

Watching the gentleman in the audience watching him, Welles defends himself against his unconscious voyeurism by using his exhibitionistic tendencies. His fantasy is stimulated in catching the gaze of the older gentleman but his actions reveal the sadistic impulse evident in voyeuristic pleasure at the expense of the objectification of the image of woman.

Welles's oral erotics transform the oral pleasure of kisses into the excitement of sadistic jealousy. Kitt did not struggle when Welles's teeth dug into her lip; although she was in pain, she did not want the audience to know what was happening. Besides, she added, "I couldn't get away from him because he was too strong."[7] Later, she discovered blood dripping from her mouth and spotting the white apron she had to put on for the next scene. As the show continued, and she sang before the audience, Kitt recalled that "my face was getting bigger and bigger and bigger."[8] At the final curtain, when approached by Kitt to explain his behavior, Welles "sort of pushed me [Kitt] aside and said, 'I got excited.'"[9] As Welles's Faustus is transformed from a passive stage-presence (the statue) to a desiring agent, he simultaneously transforms Kitt's Helen from a desiring agent to a passive female object and possession inscribed within the male's desire. His erotic pleasure is determined by looking at the other person as object, but that pleasure is challenged by the spectator within the audience. Pleasure (kissing) becomes jealousy and excitement (biting) and later guilt (pushing Kitt aside and averting his gaze) when Welles discovers his own unstable position in the viewing process.[10]

To look closely at Welles's production of *Dr. Faustus* is to see how much in mind he always had his larger project, how in the very formulation of his play he was working out the issues of his film *Othello*. With MacLiammoir as his Mephistophilis/Iago, Welles recreates the psychological tensions evident in his *Othello* within another dramatic vehicle, one created to finance and sustain his filmic masterpiece. By substituting Kitt for Cloutier, Welles infuses his adaptation of *Dr. Faustus* with the racial difference that informs *Othello*. As the black Helen that Faustus yearns to possess, that symbol of female beauty and adultery so powerful that men bent on possessing her would destroy an entire civilization, Kitt becomes in Welles's adaptation a vital and active participant, whose desire stimulates the statue of Faustus into being. In this scene it is the frozen statue of Faustus, the monumental alabaster to which Othello compares Desdemona now made "concrete," who is gazed upon and imagined as returning the gaze of erotic desire. In his *Dr. Faustus* Welles inverts the imagined dynamic between black man and white woman in *Othello* to one of an active black *woman* whose desiring gaze stimulates desire within white *male* object. In turn, Welles as Faustus attempts to control the imagined desire of his Helen by kissing and biting her. Ironically, he bites her because he imagines he cannot control her imagined desire and because he imagines himself jealous. In biting her he succeeds in rendering her passive because she refuses to break character (determined by the gaze of the audience). Her pain, in fact, determines her position as controlled object who desires and is desired. Her pain is inscribed as blood upon an apron, much as Desdemona's is inscribed as red strawberries upon a handkerchief. Yet the very emblem of their pain—the white cloth spotted with red—has "magic in the web of it," for it is the talisman that preserves the threatened male self.[11] The rich imaginative associations between Welles's theatrical production of *Dr. Faustus* and his film *Othello* illuminate the ways in which he sought to explore the voyeuristic pleasure of pain.

In his 1978 documentary *Filming Othello* Welles would later describe his Othello as a man whose narcissism leads him to the "perverse pleasures of jealousy." Welles has called Othello "a perfect male type" who "kills Desdemona adoring her." In fact, as Welles's Othello comes more and more to see Desdemona through Iago's web of lies, he also finds himself aroused by the voyeuristic pleasure of seeing through the woman's eyes, the eyes of his victim and her imagined erotic gaze. The method by which he murders Desdemona makes explicit his need to be absorbed by an imagined desire. In her death scene Welles visually recreates Desdemona's objectification within the cinematic frame through Othello's erotic contemplation of her. However, the camera unexpectedly reverses the relationship between her presence as an object of curiosity and control to reveal, through a sequence of shots using the subjective camera, the connection between voyeurism and sadism, when the erotic impulse becomes fixated into perversion.

In the film's representation of Desdemona's death, Suzanne Cloutier is cool and still as any alabaster monument while Welles's Othello quietly contemplates the features of her beautiful, sleeping face (figure 2.1). The camera reveals Desdemona within the gaze of Othello's repressed desire, in which Othello sees, and thereby controls, the erotic gaze and desires of his sleeping wife. The fact that Desdemona remains prone and passive as Welles's Othello prepares to suffocate her reinforces his illusion of control. As Welles's Othello presses the gauze tight over Cloutier's face, the camera records her brief struggle from Othello's point of view as he contemplates with strangely erotic and perverse satisfaction Desdemona's distorted and transparently veiled face. Because Othello kisses Desdemona's lips as he strangles her in a grim parody of sexual desire, Jorgens suggests that "Othello kills her [Desdemona] not out of a sense of justice but out of a blend of twisted desire (he kisses her as he strangles her) and hatred for her inhuman perfection."[12] However, the scene's intense focus upon the instrument by which Othello attempts to control his wife's desires — the very sheets that she supposedly has contaminated — reveals how Othello's sadistic need to control her (all too human) sexuality operates within the structures of Othello's own desires, alternating between an idealizing exaltation of love (the frozen, idealized image) and a ritualized torture of his human female victim.

FIGURE 2.1. Desdemona's death in Welles's *Othello*. (Courtesy of Castle Hill Productions, Inc.)

As he suffocates her, Desdemona's gaze is unremittingly focused upon Othello. But the subjective camera also reveals Desdemona's perspective as she perceives the grim resolve of the husband who kills her. The juxtaposition of the shot of Desdemona's veiled and distorted face — the object of Othello's erotic gaze — with the subjective camera shot of Desdemona's gaze upon the man who murders her underscores the relationship between masochistic and sadistic impulses explored by the gaze of the camera.

In *Filming Othello* Welles describes his Othello as "monumentally male and his story is monumentally a male tragedy." While the experience of the "male tragedy" as explored in Welles's film suggests the narcissistic direction of male desire that must be aroused through the eyes of the woman, as in the example of the method of Othello's murder of Desdemona, the film also explores a homoerotic subtext through the fetishistic aspect of the film apparatus. In other words, the film reduces images of a person's sexuality that might be perceived as a threat and thus fetishizes by the pleasure of seeing the body in pieces.[13] As Janet Bergstrom demonstrates in her analysis of Hitchcock's *Psycho,* the camera implicates the viewer in its voyeuristic and sadistic relationship to the image it fragments. In several interesting respects Welles's *Othello* also explores the relationship between voyeurism and male aggression in a scene not unlike Hitchcock's now-famous shower scene.[14] The spectacle of the naked body, glimpsed but briefly and in fragments by the male who gazes upon it, and the sequence of rapid shot/reverse shot exchanges between the murderer and his victim, are devices used by both Welles and Hitchcock. In Welles's film, the murderer Iago also stalks his naked victims in the steamy baths, although Welles locates this scene of voyeurism and aggression in the Turkish baths of Cyprus rather than in the Bates Motel. However, in Welles's film the fetishized object of the camera's gaze is not the female presence, which in *Othello* becomes increasingly "cold and denying" as Peter Donaldson observes, but instead focuses upon the naked male presence as spectacle.[15]

The personal history between MacLiammoir and Welles accounts, to some extent, for the way that Welles chose to shoot the murder of Roderigo in *Othello.* Welles had met Hilton Edwards (Brabantio in Welles's *Othello*) and Micheal MacLiammoir, the co-directors of the Dublin Gate Theatre, in his youth, and rapidly became a star in the theater in which he debuted as an actor. But, as Welles tells it, "From the first he [MacLiammoir] was insanely jealous of the handsome young newcomer in whom his lover Hilton Edwards seemed to have taken special interest."[16] When the young Welles experienced sudden success in their shows "Micheal worked on stirring up Hilton's jealousy about the young American's having stolen the show."[17] Leaming reports that after one evening of heavy drinking between Welles and MacLiammoir, MacLiammoir "abruptly and mysteriously turned to Orson and said 'Never trust us!'"[18] That same night MacLiammoir would define the Irish character to Welles as "malice." In fact, these tensions between Welles and MacLiammoir, his later Iago, continued into the filming of *Othello:* Welles complained that MacLiammoir "'was always *on*—ferociously *on* . . . not to show his jealousy about Hilton, you see. Because Hilton loved me—I think Hilton genuinely did—at the moments when he was not under Micheal's influence.'"[19] The casting of Hilton and

MacLiammoir in his *Othello* illuminates the way Welles shaped his film to reinforce the patterns of fascination that existed from the first in Welles's early acting career. The fantasy of desire and malicious jealousy projected upon Hilton and MacLiammoir allowed Welles to play out an illusion of voyeuristic separation.

Arriving in Mogador on the northern coast of Morocco to shoot the first scene—the killing of Roderigo in a Turkish bath—MacLiammoir "discovered among the local population a great many masculine forty-five- and fifty-year-old men to his liking."[20] According to Welles, MacLiammoir was always attracted to "vigorous nonhomosexual types . . . good family men . . . and, ideally, members of the police force."[21] The defining feature of MacLiammoir's homosexuality is that he "narcissistically loves the phallic attributes of other male bodies."[22] MacLiammoir's activities even reached the attention of the governor of Mogador, according to Welles, who "insisted on giving me every day the report of everybody's behavior in Mogador the night before."[23] "At first I pretended that I didn't want to see it. But when I told Micheal that I knew what he'd done the night before, and saw what delight it gave him, then I read it like a newspaper!"[24] Welles "pretends" that he does not wish to "see it," perhaps because, as Laura Mulvey suggests, "the male figure cannot bear the burden of sexual objectification" and "is reluctant to gaze upon his exhibitionist like."[25] But Welles discovers the pleasures of the voyeuristic narrative because MacLiammoir's exhibitionism is made ideally passive through the medium of the official governor's reports, the police surveillance that privileges Welles's voyeuristic pleasure. MacLiammoir's obvious pleasure as well enables Welles to read the potentially threatening homoerotic look "as if it were a newspaper," neutralizing the guilt associated with voyeuristic pleasure by assuring himself of his voyeuristic separation from the activities reported. Yet, curiously, Welles's fascination catches him in the moral ambiguity of looking, the police narrative entwining him within the homoerotic display of desire, although he persists again in the illusion of voyeuristic separation.

Welles sets the scene of Roderigo's murder and Cassio's mutilation and attempted murder in a steamy Turkish bath. Obviously, the change in setting from that of the play is significant, and Welles offers a rather amusing and now well-known explanation for such a change. He tells of arriving in Mogador, Morocco, where the crew was to shoot *Othello's* Cyprus scenes and of discovering that the Italian backers who were to supply the money for the costumes had gone bankrupt. While Welles scrambled to find new backers to pay for the needed costumes, he had a large crew and cast with nothing to do. So, as Welles explains, he hit upon the idea that the killing of Roderigo was a scene that could be filmed without costumes—with a cast of naked men in a Turkish bath. The actors wear only towels, except, interestingly enough, Iago. Iago wears the Carpaccio-style costume Welles had dictated for this costume-drama. Fully clothed, he glides furtively among the naked men in clouds of steam, gazing from darkened corners at his intended victims. The handkerchief of Shakespeare's text is transformed in Welles's filmic imagination into the towels that the naked men grasp around them. Whether towel or handkerchief, the characters cling to these fragments of cloth as if they too would magically preserve the wholeness of their manhood while under the gaze of the voyeuristic spectator. In the chaos of Cassio's attempted murder and Roderigo's attempted escape, the camera follows the naked bodies of the scattering men as they cling to these remnants of cloth amid the swirling steam of the bath and the call of alarm (figure 2.2). The scene suggests the role of castration fear in the formation of male spectatorial pleasure, and the handkerchief/towel's function as a sort of talisman against that fear.

The fragmented editing of this scene again creates those "gaps" between action and point of view shots that prevent a coherent narrative and leave the viewer gazing upon the fragments of male bodies glimpsed momentarily in the swirl of the dense stream of the bath. Roderigo's bungled murder of Cassio provides an example of the way Welles uses a slightly illogical ellipsis between the cuts in this film. As Cassio lies naked and sweating in the bath, the naked Roderigo, grasping the towel around his waist with one hand and a dagger in the other, creeps up to his prone form. In a large two-shot, the camera located in front of the prone Cassio reveals only his head and half-torso, with Roderigo's head and upper body appearing behind. We see Roderigo fumble and drop something (we suppose it to be the dagger when we hear the heavy thud of metal on the wooden planks), as he moves out of the cinematic frame to the right.

Figure 2.2 Call for alarm in the Turkish bath in *Othello*. (Courtesy of Castle Hill Productions, Inc.)

The camera instantly cuts to the object upon the floor as a man's hand and arm enter the frame (although it is confusing whose arm it is). As one hand grasps the object on the floor, now revealed as the knife, the audience glimpses beside the knife a blurred object—Roderigo's dog—that rapidly disappears from the frame (figures 2.3–2.5). However, at this moment the dog is glimpsed only briefly, intruding upon the action before the scene cuts to Roderigo's attempted escape and the struggle between Cassio and Roderigo before a door frame. The distance traversed by the actors from the struggle on the floor to the struggle before the doorway suggests a brief lapse in time between these shots and a moment in the struggle obscured from the spectator's view. The jump from a subjective shot (from either Cassio's or Roderigo's perspective) to a shot of both men before the doorway creates an illogical ellipsis or gap between action and point of view, and the jerky movement of the camera gives the spectator the sensation, much like that of the men struggling in the bath, of the motion of bodies and swirl of steam that permits only a fragmented perspective of the entire action.

FIGURE 2.3. Roderigo's dog in *Othello*

FIGURE 2.4. The dog's innocent gaze

Figure 2.5. The dog flees the bungled murder. (Courtesy of Castle Hill Productions, Inc.)

The Turkish bath scene in Welles's *Othello* frames the male body as spectacle, but this scene is also haunted with sexual ambivalence and the threat of castration or feminization. As the naked Roderigo cowers beneath the slats in the floorboards and calls Iago's name, we see Iago unsheath his silvery sword above him and thrust it through the slats at the trapped and vulnerable Roderigo. Much as Desdemona is killed by controlling her fetishized image, Roderigo's body lies contained by the slats of the floorboard and shafts of light that illuminate slivers of his naked form. Entrapped, enclosed, and subject to the controlling gaze of Iago, Roderigo's body is literally fragmented by the sword thrusts through the floorboards, in a scene that illuminates the relationship between voyeuristic pleasures and the sadistic impulse.

In *Filming Othello* Welles describes his understanding of Iago's character as the "malice of impotence." He envisioned Iago as a man suffering from impotence, although as Naremore emphasizes, "the malady is never specified in the actual performance, which retains many of Shakespeare's ambiguities, but it becomes a 'subtext' for Micheál MacLiammóir's behavior."[26] MacLiammoir himself believed "there must be no 'passion' in Iago," and wished to emphasize "the secret isolation of impotence under these soldier's muscles."[27] MacLiammoir's performance may reveal no "soldier's muscles," but much in his performance suggests a predatory savagery, particularly in this Turkish bath scene and in Roderigo's murder. As Davies points out, the impotence suggested by this scene lies more in the moral impotence of watching one's own self-destruction, in that the camera reveals the point of view of the victim's terror and immobility. Welles's camera records the blade's slashing through the slats of the dripboards of the Turkish bath while, as Davies points out, "the movement of the camera also makes it partly a subjective shot of the sword's movements," so that the audience achieves Iago's perspective as the sword enters between the slats and the body of Roderigo.[28]

Welles complicates this murder by the addition of a perspective other than that of the murderer and his victim. Roderigo's terrier, which Welles describes as a type of "lap dog used by dandies in all the Carpaccio paintings," innocently views the struggle to kill Cassio and Iago's sadistic murder of Roderigo.[29] Antony Davies argues that the small, fluffy dog that appears constantly with Roderigo is a revelatory detail regarding Roderigo's foppish characterization and impotence.[30] When Roderigo is murdered, argues Davies, the appearance of the dog as a witness to this murder is but another comment upon the character of Roderigo:

> The dog's commentary on the character of Roderigo reaches its climax in the prelude to the murder scene in the Turkish bath. Its uncertain but trusting trot along the boards in the bath-chamber prepares us for the neurotic and puerile distractions of its master as he sits drawing love-graffiti on the wall, then fails in his half-hearted attempt to kill Cassio; and finally cowers under the boards trying to solicit Iago's reassurance.[31]

Indeed, the small dog is a constant presence in the Turkish bath scene, its tiny presence alert, wide-eyed, and anxious, and frequently looking at something the viewer cannot see. The dog is beside the dagger as Roderigo attempts to kill Cassio, and hovers nearby while Iago stalks Cassio. Impotent to act, the dog's gaze haunts this scene in such a way as to be more than a mere comment on Roderigo's foppish character. Because the dog appears at strategic moments when the spectator has an incomplete view of the action, its presence allows the viewer to identify with its reactive gaze before the camera cuts to a close-up shot of Iago's satisfied stare. It is with some irony that the murdered Roderigo cries out from beneath the floorboards "O damn'd Iago, O inhuman dog," because in this scene Welles allows the viewer's humanity to be expressed through the perspective of an innocent dog.

Carpaccio's "Eyewitness Style"

The visual inspiration for Welles's *Othello* has been the subject of some critical speculation. Jack Jorgens has detected Eisenstein's cinematic influence, and Barbara Hodgdon concludes that Welles's "stylistics derive from silent film, more especially from Carl Dryer's 1928 *La Passion de Jeanne d'Arc.*"[32] Yet critics have tended to ignore Welles's own admission that the visual inspiration for his film was discovered in the art of the Venetian Quattrocentro painter Vittore Carpaccio. Both Welles and Micheal MacLiammoir repeatedly acknowledge the film's indebtedness to Carpaccio in costuming.[33] Yet a comparison between Welles's *Othello* and Carpaccio's paintings and sketches suggest that Welles was indebted to Carpaccio for more than the clothes his actors wore (figures 2.6–2.7). A cursory glance through Carpaccio's works gives one the sense that even Welles's casting decisions may have been influenced by them: Desdemona (Suzanne Cloutier) resembles the slender blonde saint of Carpaccio's *Life of St. Ursula;* the courtesan Bianca (Doris Dowling) bears an uncanny resemblance to a courtesan in one of Carpaccio's sketches; the film's Michael Cassio (Michael Lawrence) looks like Carpaccio's portrayal of a man in a red hat; and the small dog in Welles's *Othello* resembles the Maltese terrier used in a number of Carpaccio paintings, including the cycle *Miracles of the True Cross.* Not only is the terrier used in Welles's *Othello* strikingly similar in appearance to the small dogs frequently seen in Carpaccio's masterpieces, but it functions within the cinematic frame much as does the terrier within Carpaccio's paintings.[34]

A study of Carpaccio's paintings suggests Welles's intention in making the gaze of the terrier in *Othello* such a pervasive part of the murder of Roderigo. One revealing example, in Carpaccio's painting of *St. Augustine in His Study,* c. 1502, in Scuola di San Giorgio degli Schiavoni, Venice, depicts St. Augustine at his table in a large and detailed room (figure 2.8). Critics have noted the "theatrical properties" or multiplication of objects that surround St. Augustine, which "tend to distract attention from the vision of the saint."[35] However, "Carpaccio the stage designer," as art critic Norbert Huse calls him, fails in Huse's estimation to achieve in the finished painting what his sketches were able to do:

> The room becomes a place for the exhibition of what on close inspection is a highly artificial arrangement of costly and interesting objects. The lack of overall relationships that isolates the objects shown to the point of alienating them is, however, probably involuntary, for in preliminary sketches Carpaccio had not only attempted but succeeded in supplying such relationships in light and atmosphere. . . . They [the

FIGURE 2.6. Two men await the ship in Carpaccio's "Life of St. Ursula." (Courtesy of Gallerie dell'Accademia, Venice)

FIGURE 2.7. Iago and Roderigo await Othello's ship in Welles's *Othello.* (Courtesy of Castle Hill Productions, Inc.)

FIGURE 2.8. Carpaccio's "St. Augustine in His Study" (c. 1502). (Courtesy of Scuola di San Giorgio degli Schiavoni, Venice)

FIGURE 2.9. Sketch for "St. Augustine in His Study." (Courtesy of The British Museum, London)

objects] are there for the viewer, not their owner. He [St. Augustine] too was presented more convincingly in the drawing, which showed him pausing in concentrated work, than in the finished picture, which is supposed to show his vision but finds no proper object for his gaze."[36]

Huse concludes that the final effect of Carpaccio's painting—the "lack of overall relationships that isolates the objects to the point of alienating them"—was unintentional, Carpaccio's failure to turn a successful sketch into a successful painting.[37] Yet in the finished painting of *St. Augustine in His Study* one "object" in particular attracts our gaze ("there for the viewer, not their owner"). Our gaze falls upon a small, alert, and upright dog on the floor at a short distance from the figure of St. Augustine. The dog in the painting is also conceived quite differently in Carpaccio's preliminary sketches, as a prone and ferret-like creature, whose presence is undistinguished from the other objects in the room (figure 2.9). However, in the final painting the detail of the dog diverts our attention from the larger figure of the saint.

Teresio Pignatti describes the quiet observer in Carpaccio's painting as a "Maltese puppy in the middle of the floor, the only living being besides the saint himself in this almost aquatic silence. The little animal sits motionless, his fluffy coat almost incandescent in the dazzling light; he seems to be gazing up at the fine cloud of dust particles floating down the shaft of light as it pours in from the window."[38] In Carpaccio's painting the small dog gazes upon its master and what preoccupies the man. Its small, light figure contrasts with the weightier and darker figure of St. Augustine, the entire painting cast in low, horizontal, rectangular formats. The angle of the gaze of the dog and St. Augustine's gaze outside the large window are in the same upward direction. Although the object of the saint's contemplation lies outside the purview of the spectator, the perspective of the dog's upward gaze suggests that it sees both the saint and the object. The viewer's attention is caught by the dog whose gaze seems to capture all that the viewer cannot see, and whose small physical presence within the painting pulls our attention away from the larger figure of the saint himself (figure 2.10). The theatrical arrangement of the scene emphasizes the small dog's role as "sole supporting actor" in a moment of considerable consequence, for his presence, as Brown notes, "provides the real clue that we are viewing something more exceptional than simply a scholar going about his daily tasks by the light of a window."[39]

FIGURE 2.10. Dog in "St. Augustine in His Study." (Courtesy of Scuola di San Giorgio degli Schiavoni, Venice)

Turning back to the Turkish bath scene in Welles's *Othello*, one finds a number of similarities between the way Welles films Roderigo's dog and the way Carpaccio portrays the terrier in *St. Augustine in His Study*. The dog in Welles's film appears incandescent as it stands in the dazzling shafts of light that strike its furry coat and head in the shadows of the Turkish bath. It is the innocent observer, a corollary to the innocent gaze of Desdemona who observes her own murder. The dog's gaze is haunting in this sequence of shots, because it sees clearly what we cannot and signals to the viewer, as does Carpaccio's dog, that we might be glimpsing something exceptional. A series of shot and reverse-shot exchanges reveals Iago's arm holding the sword and slashing at the body of Cassio, and then Cassio's collapse in pain. The subjective camera allows us to experience the vulnerability of the male body and the violence done to it as the viewer watches Cassio's crouching form, not unlike its experience of Roderigo's slaughter as Iago's blade penetrates through the cracks in the floorboards. In the midst of this series of exchanges the camera focuses upon the lone figure of the little dog looking up at the violence we cannot see. Its gaze is intense and unblinking, the voyeuristic gaze of the spectator whose vision is unimpaired and constant, and whose innocent gaze is a marked contrast to the perverse pleasure of Iago's gaze and the horror of Cassio's and Roderigo's. Through the gaze of the dog we view the physical degradation of the male body and its literal dismemberment, and yet sustain the illusion of voyeuristic separation.

In the death of Roderigo we see increasing fragmentation of the victim's body, in which the illusion of Renaissance space is reduced to the metonymical representation of the sword, the slats, and the gaze of the dog.[40] In effect, the viewer is subjected to the sort of "lurid metonymy for murder" into which Othello's logic is locked in the play, which connects "blood," "sheets," and "blot" as the visible signs of his wife's pollution.[41] The viewer of Welles's *Othello* similarly discovers his understanding of events reduced to a few discernible images or objects, a fracturing of vision that recalls Carpaccio's "eyewitness style," in which selected objects within a scene capture our imagination but fail to illuminate their relationship to the protagonist or to the narrative as a whole. Deprived of explanatory purpose or cause-and-effect relationship within the painting, the viewer must make his own connections between the objects and the narrative, much as a broken sequence of camera shots and reversals of point of view in Welles's *Othello* require that the spectator seek his own connections. The correspondences between this scene in Welles's film and Carpaccio's *Vision of St. Augustine* suggest that Welles discovered within Carpaccio's painterly vision a strategy of representation for translating the scopophile tragedy of *Othello* to the cinematic screen.[42]

Carpaccio's paintings offer an alternative view of truth that tempts the spectator to conclude something that is beyond his power to see. It is a "truth" that Welles's imaginative genius readily grasped as central to the story of his *Othello*. Much as Carpaccio's paintings challenge traditional concepts of objecthood and observer, the narcissistic doubling of shot and reverse-shot exchanges that characterizes the filmic stylization of Welles's *Othello* relentlessly challenges the viewer's point of view and undermines his ability to see relationships between characters and objects. The fragmented editing style, characterized by a broken sequence of camera shots, leaves the spectator straining to glimpse the sequences not seen, the relationships not revealed, only surmised through the voyeuristic gaze of another. Our view lingers on the tiny figures of Carpaccio's terrier or Roderigo's dog because, like Othello, we fail to achieve a vision beyond a fragmented truth.

"'Tis a pageant / To keep us in false gaze"

Carpaccio's theatrical representation of the problematics of display and spectatorship recalls the struggle facing the Venetian Council in the first act of Shakespeare's *Othello,* in which the assembled statesmen are denied a secure position by which to judge the intentions of the Turkish fleet. Their attempts to grasp the "truth" behind the Turkish fleet's erratic movements reveal the dangers implicit in spectatorship; conflicting reports frustrate attempts to impose order or meaning, for "There is no composition in these news, / That gives them credit," and information suggesting the number and direction of the Turkish advance are "disproportion'd" (I.iii.1–3). Nevertheless, the Duke claims "it is possible enough to judgement," although events soon reveal that this is bad judgment. The movements of the fleet are mere theatrical display, "a pageant, / To keep us in false gaze" (I.iii.9, 18–19).[43] In this brief scene Shakespeare encapsulates the problematics of spectacle visually demonstrated in the large-scale narrative paintings of Carpaccio and replicated in the cinema of Orson Welles.

Carpaccio's works involve a visual strategy that presents a "pageant" that keeps the spectator in a "false gaze." In a series of paintings Carpaccio displays a confusion of competing events and objects, diverting the viewer's concentration from the central narrative while inviting him to make judgments based upon events and relationships that are obscure. The spectator fails to see any relationship or ordering by which to interpret the scene, no "composition" by which truth might be discovered through the objects and their relationships, only a "pageant" or theatrical spectacle, a "false gaze," by which men interpret and judge, sometimes tragically so.

Most significant of Carpaccio's large-scale narrative paintings is his *Life of St. Ursula,* the earliest surviving cycle of the eyewitness school. Carpaccio painted the eight narrative scenes based on the life of St. Ursula for the Scuola D. Sant' Orsola when he was only twenty-five years old, establishing his artistic reputation at about the same age that Welles established his. In a series of long, horizontal canvases Carpaccio unfolds the story of a beautiful and martyred St. Ursula in images that clearly suggest the reworked objective reality of cinematic images. The low, horizontal and rectangular formats of Carpaccio's paintings present a perspective to the spectator not unlike the breadth and dramatic sweep of the unfolding cinematic screen. Indeed, as Patricia Fortini Brown remarks, critics have often associated Carpaccio's *Life of St. Ursula* with the experience of viewing film: "As others have observed, the effect [of the composition] is one of unfolding: a sequence of gestures of a single movement as if recorded in a strip of movie frames."[44] Carpaccio's visual narrative of the tragic Saint Ursula, in a series constructed with conceptions of space and perspective analogous to that found on the cinematic screen, provided Welles with the ideal model for a cinematic version of Shakespeare's story of tragic love and death. A close examination of the introductory and closing sequences of Welles's *Othello* reveals the extent to which his film is derived from the sequence of images portrayed in Carpaccio's *Life of St. Ursula,* and, from one particular painting in this cycle, *The Martyrdom of the Pilgrims and Funeral of St. Ursula,* c. 1493 (figure 2.11).

In the late 1940s Vittorio Moschini established that the narrative sequence of Carpaccio's paintings on the walls of the Accademia Galleries originally followed a clockwise arrangement, which begins and ends with *The Martyrdom of the Pilgrims and Funeral of St. Ursula.*[45] This is the recon-

FIGURE 2.11. Carpaccio's "The Martyrdom of the Pilgrims and Funeral of St. Ursula" (c. 1493). (Courtesy of Gallerie dell'Accademia, Venice)

structed narrative sequence that Orson Welles would have seen in Venice in the 1950s as he prepared for the shooting of his *Othello.* Carpaccio's cycle depicts the most important stages in the life of the saint, including the arrival in Cologne that made Ursula a martyr as well as the martyrdom and burial. The arrangement of the paintings on the south, west, north, and east walls of the chapel suggests the circular structure of the narrative, beginning and ending with the funeral of the saint. So, too, the much-observed circular structure of Welles's *Othello* opens and closes with the funeral of Othello and Desdemona.[46] Although Shakespeare's play begins with villains hidden in darkness and concludes with a demand for truncated funeral rites, Welles chose, instead, to parade the spectacle of tragedy and death before his viewers. In fact, ceremonial entries and exits are integral to Carpaccio's and Welles's conceptions of the narrative of their martyred protagonists. Their narratives are conceived as a series of greetings and farewells, in which the funeral procession—the martyred woman's farewell to the worldly stage—is the event that invites the viewer to enter the scene of the narrative.

The Martyrdom of the Pilgrims and Funeral of St. Ursula depicts a solemn funeral procession, with the body of Saint Ursula carried by soldiers and mourners (figures 2.12–2.13). The painting displays the dead body of the young, blonde Ursula carried on a funeral bier before a fortress, above which banners wave as the distinctive profile of the holy men follow in the

Figure 2.12. "The Funeral of St. Ursula," detail. (Courtesy of Gallerie dell'Accademia, Venice)

procession. The fortress walls are cast in relief against the brilliant sky as banners on the fortress wave in the breeze. Carpaccio's theatrical imagination casts this particular scene almost upon a stage. His painting provides a full view of the landscape from a perspective well above the heads of the people and at some distance from the crowd, although the funeral procession that carries the body of Saint Ursula seems to be moving slowly from our view. In the opening sequence of Welles's film the camera captures a view similar to that revealed in the funeral of the saint, from an elevated perspective of a funeral procession that moves past the viewer. As in the Carpaccio painting of the funeral of Saint Ursula, Welles's *Othello* places the solemn processional and funeral immediately and significantly within the spectator's view (figures 2.14–2.15).

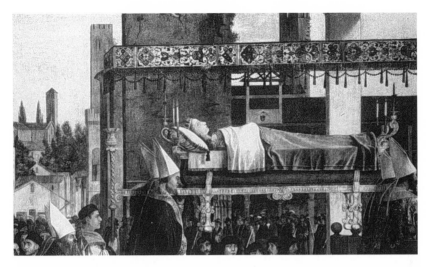

FIGURE 2.13. "The Funeral of St. Ursula," detail. (Courtesy of Gallerie dell'Accademia, Venice)

FIGURE 2.14. Desdemona's funeral procession in Welles's *Othello*. (Courtesy of Castle Hill Productions, Inc.)

FigURE 2.15. Desdemona's funeral procession. (Courtesy of Castle Hill Productions, Inc.)

Spectators are an essential part of the pageant in Carpaccio's paintings and in Welles's film. In fact, Welles's film imitates various poses and activities in which Carpaccio's *Life of St. Ursula* captures its spectators — climbing staircases, playing trumpets, or pressing against the crowd to glimpse the procession that passes before them. In the opening funeral sequence Welles, like Carpaccio, captures his spectators in mid-gesture as they watch the funeral processional, their gaze registering for the viewer the significance of the events that seem to be exiting the frame and passing from view. Carpaccio's painting details the small figures below who observe St. Ursula's funeral procession, whereas Welles's camera pans across the faces of the audience below, including men such as Cassio and Ludovico, who have been spectators to this tragedy. Their gaze, like that of the small dogs who observe the murder of Roderigo and the vision of St. Augustine, determines our own position in the viewing process, providing "mirrors of ourselves" and "reflecting back upon us our demeanor and attitudes as we pause before the panel" and as we gaze upon the cinematic screen.[47]

The opening funeral sequence in Welles's film owes its considerable dramatic effect to a precise articulation of temporal pace and spatial form. Ponderous and ritualized movement is conveyed through the rhythmic placement of solids and voids—of mourners, marchers, biers, and sky—and is reminiscent of Carpaccio's articulation of temporal pace and forms in the funeral procession in *The Martyrdom of the Pilgrims and Funeral of St. Ursula*. Carpaccio understood the dramatic effect achieved through the interplay of space and the placement of forms: "Unlike most of his contemporaries," Brown observes, "he knew what to leave out." Carpaccio conveys the ponderous movement of ritual through "an acute sense of interval, of gesture, of cadence, and of the rhythmic placement of solids and voids," carefully structuring his composition so that "the caesurae between his figures play a role fully as important as the figures themselves."[48] In Carpaccio's arrangement of figures the spectator experiences a caesurae between forms that recall the "gap" or imagined space of action created by the broken sequence of camera shots that introduces the procession at the beginning and end of Welles's *Othello*. Welles's multiple fragments interpret cinematically the sense of movement and form that Carpaccio creates through association of forms and space.

However, in Carpaccio's painting the defining rhythm of the funeral procession is jarred by the rapid and violent tempo of the events adjacent to it. Brown observes:

> In the proleptic sequence of *The Martyrdom of the Pilgrims and Funeral of St. Ursula,* the narrative action unfolds across the front plane, and the most significant events are no longer deliberately obscured in the background. Another violent act is about to happen right before us. But the descriptive details remain to draw away our attention.[49]

The ponderous and ritualized movements of the funeral in Carpaccio's painting act as a visual "reference point to clarify and organize a confusion of competing events and objects," in which simple, ritualized gestures are used to measure the explosion of violence within the frame.[50] Welles employs a similar strategy of contrasting rhythms in his filmed funeral sequence, using the ritualized movement of the procession as a means to measure the frenzied violence of Iago's capture.

In *The Martyrdom of the Pilgrims and Funeral of St. Ursula* the spectator's gaze travels from the slaughter of the virgins to the soldiers poised for violent action in the foreground of the painting, and finally to the funeral procession as it appears to be leaving the borders of the painting. Similarly, in Welles's film we witness angry soldiers drag the tethered Iago through a turbulent crowd and shove him into a cage, which swings wildly as it is hoisted above the tower (figures 2.16–2.17). However, moments later, the details of the funeral procession again draw the audience's gaze away from the violence of Iago's capture (figures 2.18–2.19). In the solemn funeral procession, shot from the perspective of the tethered and caged Iago, we witness "the film's first reversals of the expected relation between spectator and character."[51]

Particularly in the opening sequence, in which Welles intersplices the funeral processions of Desdemona and Othello with shots of Iago dragged by chains through a crowd of onlookers, we sense the temporal and spatial fragmentation that is the dominant experience of this film.

FIGURE 2.16. Soldiers drag Iago through the crowd in *Othello*. (Courtesy of Castle Hill Productions, Inc.)

FIGURE 2.17. Iago dragged past the funeral procession. (Courtesy of Castle Hill Productions, Inc.)

FIGURE 2.18. Iago gazes from the cage. (Courtesy of Castle Hill Productions, Inc.)

FIGURE 2.19. The funeral procession below. (Courtesy of Castle Hill Productions, Inc.)

Lorne Buchman observes that Welles uses "the dominant rhythms of the processions to establish a sense of coherence and order early in the film," which is then shattered by Iago.[52] The alternation between rhythmic coherence and confusion, so significant in Carpaccio's *Martyrdom of the Pilgrims and Funeral of St. Ursula,* is the central experience of Welles's *Othello,* in which the viewer experiences "an ambiguous sense of time—ordered and chaotic, constant and fragmented."[53] In fact, the opening scene of the film establishes the pervasive camera technique in this film. The spectator sees the action through a subjective camera technique, which is immediately followed by a shot that reveals whose perspective the spectator has shared, in this case, Iago's. Jorgens has termed the unrelenting oscillation of point of view in these opening scenes as the "Iago style" of an oppressive consciousness conveyed through dizzying perspectives, tortured compositions, grotesque shadows, and mad distortions. Davies observes that Welles frequently places Iago in an elevated position to characters around him, from which to view "the world whose collapse he has wrought."[54] In the final moments of the film the spectator discov-

ers, however, that he has shared in the brutality of Iago's gaze as eyewitness to the tragedy unfolded below him.

Although one might expect the circular structure of the film to unify
its narrative, the final effect of having the viewer share Iago's perspective
is fragmentation. The formal procession that begins and ends the film
underscores Welles's interest in the way the viewer experiences the plot,
so that "the way the plot unravels takes precedence over the surprises of
narrative."[55] Iago's piercing gaze upon his victims below conveys to the
viewer the oppressive consciousness of the "Iago style" as a sense of
imprisoned space, in which the barred angle shots of Iago's face remind
the viewer of Roderigo's savage murder in the Turkish bath. Davies notes
that "the film becomes increasingly enclosed" as those around him
become a victim of Iago's "style" or perspective.[56] By repeating this
sequence of shots at the end of his film, Welles comments on the perverse
voyeurism of the spectator, who shares Iago's "style" of perspective,
imprisoned by his desire to see the forbidden and left only to gaze.

The "Iago" style of perspective has its counterpart in Carpaccio's *The
Martyrdom of the Pilgrims and Funeral of St. Ursula*. In this painting the narrative action is divided spatially between the martyrdom and the funeral.
As the spectator's gaze moves from left to right, from the martyrdom in
the front left plane to the funeral on the far right side (figures 2.20–2.21),
one notices three central figures suspended in the space between the two
events: a knight withdrawing his sword from his scabbard, an archer
directing his arrow at the heart of a kneeling virgin, and a trumpeting,
turbaned Moor on horseback. The caesura in the rhythms of the narrative created by their presence, and their pivotal placement within the
strict geometric patterns of the painting, encourage the spectator to view
these figures in connection with the two major events flanking them.

The controlled demeanor of the knight in the center of this group
contrasts with the romanticized, albeit greatly diminished, figure of the
Moor on horseback in the background of the painting. The knight's central position and his controlling gaze over the events in the left of the
frame convey the impression that this knight, like Iago, has orchestrated
the slaughter before him. He surveys the frenzied communal destruction
of countless female victims, even as the trumpeting Moor signals an

FIGURE 2.20. "The Martyrdom of the Pilgrims," detail. (Courtesy of Gallerie dell'Accademia, Venice)

impossibly idealized image of the same event. These two figures reveal the narrative pattern of the composition as the presentation of two perversions, the one suggesting an idealized image of heightened emotion and suspended desire, the other featuring the mechanistic destruction of female victims.

In the immediate foreground and to the right of the knight stands a bent archer. His relationship with the other two figures is obscure. He is suspended in violent mid-gesture, and faces away from the viewer, his body tilted forward, bow bent and arrow poised at the virgin who kneels quietly before him. The effect of slightly inclining the archer's form conveys a sense of his precariousness and transitional existence, captured on the brink of

FIGURE 2.21. "The Martyrdom of the Pilgrims," detail. (Courtesy of Gallerie dell'Accademia, Venice)

murderous violence. The virgin's calm resignation contrasts sharply with the aggressive male figure who directs the phallic shaft at her body. However, the viewer finds himself turning from the murderous spectacle to a fetishistic disavowal of that knowledge, the spectator's gaze arrested momentarily by the archer's bent form. The archer's buttocks, displayed toward the audience, announce the male body as spectacle and fetishized object, and enable the viewer to momentarily suspend his awareness of the slaughter. His gaze captured by the objectified image of the male body, the spectator discovers himself caught in the morally ambiguous position of looking.

As the spectator's gaze moves from the center to the right of the painting, the alignment of the image moves diagonally from lower left to upper right, from the archer's buttocks to the column that separates the narrative to the stairs upon which mourners and holy men mount to the bier and body of the martyred saint. The composition directs the gaze of the spectator from the eroticized male body to the passive, cold, and denying form of the martyred woman, and couples sadistic violence with narrativity within the same composition. In doing so, Carpaccio underscores the connection between voyeurism and sadistic impulses explored by the gaze of the spectator in *The Martyrdom of the Pilgrims and Funeral of St. Ursula.*

"Look on the tragic lodging of this bed"

Welles intended that his *Othello* would have the "atmosphere of violence . . . of Venice . . . in the heyday of Carpaccio."[57] By the same token, the "atmosphere" of Carpaccio's world that determined Welles's conception of his *Othello* was informed by the circumstances of life in Renaissance Venice. Carpaccio's paintings capture the reciprocal relationship between the artist and the environment that influenced his art. The popularity of the "eyewitness style" in Quattrocentro Venice "developed its particular artistic profile in a precise cultural setting and with precise perceptual habits, tastes and literary models, echoed in a precise artistic tradition." That is, Carpaccio's work is "a symptom of a whole complex of cultural concerns."[58] As Patricia Fortini Brown observes, the eyewitness style of documentary evidence and detail provides a clue to the perceptual skills and values of the Venetians, who believed that the objects themselves could provide an index of truth and "a full account of men and places unseen."[59] Artists rendered a detailed and faithful accounting of their world, for in Renaissance Venice "truth" rested on "prevailing standards of evidence and proof."[60] Yet the distracting power of objects to avert our eyes from truth is central to the tragedy of *Othello*. It takes only one piece of evidence, only one "theatrical property," the handkerchief spotted with red strawberries, to distract the protagonist from the vision of his "saint," consuming him with his own blighted speculations and dark misgivings. In the context of such a world we begin to understand the rich allusiveness of Carpaccio's "eyewitness style" and its link with Welles's treatment of voyeurism in his film *Othello*.

Carpaccio's Venice, like the Venice of Shakespeare's play, is one characterized by surveillance and the grisly aftermath of its justice. Venice was a city whose very existence seemed predicated upon surveillance, where "every merchant, every priest was expected to spy for his country's good."[61] In Venice the fragmented truths discovered through spying and surveillance were sometimes enough to condemn an imagined malefactor. It was a world ominously policed by every citizen, where whispered innuendo served the purposes of dark justice. On the knowledge supplied by spies, Venice's governing body, the Council of Ten, effectively policed the city of Venice:

> So voracious was their desire to pry that, throughout Venice, they set up the famous Lions' Mouths, by which Venetians could inform the Council anonymously of their suspicions of their neighbors. On this knowledge the Council acted swiftly and silently, for no public trials enlivened the Venetian scene, and there were no appeals. Once found guilty, the prisoner was sometimes quickly and efficiently strangled in the dungeons; or thrown into a part of the lagoon reserved for the purpose, where no fishing was allowed; or hanged by one leg from the pillars of the Doge's Palace; or quartered and distributed about the city; or buried upside down in the Piazzetta, legs protruding; or beheaded — as a public spectacle . . . But most traitors went silently in the night, their broken bodies sending a shiver of horror through the waking city as dawn gilded the palaces and churches.[62]

The habits of justice as practiced by Renaissance Venetians and the Council of Ten would have pleased Iago, who by mere appearance of truth condemns Desdemona to a silent and swift sentencing. It is a justice that also satisfies Othello's wounded narcissism, replete with the irony that Desdemona be strangled on "the bed she hath contaminated" in the secrecy of the night: "Good, good, the justice of it pleases, very good" (IV.i.204–5).

The courts were capable of violence and bloody public spectacle, as acknowledged by the Duke who hears Brabantio's charges against Othello when he promises that "the bloody book of law / You shall yourself read, in the bitter letter" (I.iii.67–68).[63] Yet, as Guido Ruggiero points out, cases tried by the Avogadori of the Commune and reviewed by the Council of Ten were tried with "generally little reference to the law."[64] Venetian justice prided itself on being "individualistic and personal rather than fixed upon an abstract concept of justice embodied in the law," scrutinizing the details of a crime as well as the life of the accused perpetrator.[65] Courts were careful to gauge penalties to the crime and took special care to consider the status of the criminal and victim and the particular details of their history. Ironically, when the crime of eloping with Brabantio's daughter is weighed against the circumstances of Othello's immediate usefulness to the state and Desdemona's testimony of their courtship, the Duke and Senate react much as Ruggiero claims Venetian courts often did — they decide his case without reference to the thirteenth-century law code *Promissio Maleficorum* that concerned "sexual crimes" such as elopement. The circumstances and methods of Venetian justice were not lost on the Venetian artists of the period, who frequently depicted images of Venetian Justice with its eyes open. On the Ducal Palace one of the sculptures on the capitals represents Venetian Justice without a blindfold, for "Venetian law removed the blindfold from justice by asking judges to evaluate each case with their eyes open, mindful of the character and condition of both culprit and victim."[66] Yet if Venetian justice studied the accused malefactor with open eyes, its punishments were secret and hidden, in which condemned criminals were dispatched in silence and hidden by the night. The habits of justice in Renaissance Venice give topical relevance to Ludovico's injunction at the close of *Othello* to both "Look on the tragic lodging of this bed" and "Let it be hid" (V.ii.364, 366), his responses alternating between the evidentiary nature of establishing "truth" (the bed and its contents) and the guilt that accompanies scopophilic impulses, even those sanctioned by law.

The bed and its "lodging" ("loading" in the Folio) as lamented by Ludovico, luridly described by Iago, and anticipated by the theater audience, might well be considered the imaginative center of Shakespeare's play. It is the object within Shakespeare's theatrical tableau that establishes the evidentiary "truth" of a crime ("Look on . . . this bed") and provides the focus for luridly imagined scenes of sexual explicitness and degradation. Yet in his film Welles allows his audience to view the bedroom well before the play's catastrophic end. Those glimpses of the wedded pair in the bedroom ominously foreshadow Desdemona's death, but are curiously devoid of the lurid and voyeuristic pleasures one might expect Welles to explore. To understand Welles's particular treatment of the bedroom scenes, we must again turn to Carpaccio's *Life of St. Ursula,* which also provided the director with the visual inspiration for this scene. The "first interior ever painted in the Renaissance," Carpaccio's *Dream of St. Ursula,* c. 1495, evokes the serenity of a graceful, domestic interior familiar in seventeenth-century Flemish paintings. However, like the bedroom scene in Welles's *Othello,* Carpaccio's domestic interior, as Philip Brockbank observes, has the unsettling effect of "a death-vision, an intimation of martyrdom."[67]

The domestic interior revealed in Carpaccio's painting depicts a large canopied bed with a simple rounded footboard (figure 2.22). The bed, which contains the sleeping saint, occupies all of the left half of the composition. On the right a winged angel enters the doorway and gazes upon the sleeping woman. This painting bears an interesting resemblance to the bedroom setting created for Welles's film (figure 2.23). In one of the film's earliest glimpses of the bed, Welles presents a view of the room and its contents from a perspective slightly to the left and behind where the angel stands in Carpaccio's painting. However, the figure that stands in the doorway in Welles's film is the darkened figure of Othello himself. He gazes upon Desdemona, whose luminescent form stands before the bed upon which she shall be sacrificed. Barber and Wheeler have suggested that Shakespeare's tragedy has its roots in the "gay gazing sights" of the old religion and the visual representations of Christ on the Rood, saints, and the Virgin Mary so often lambasted in the sermons and religious homilies of Shakespeare's England.[68] Similarly, in this scene Welles invites his spectator to view Othello's love through Othello's eyes as an anguished type of worship, as he searches for the visible embodiment of divine perfection in a "saintly" and luminescent Desdemona. It is appropriate to Welles's configuration of Othello's tragedy that the spectator be privy to the bedroom, for it proclaims the martyrdom of Desdemona as necessary to Othello's fantasy of affections and desires. The film's first glimpses of the bed anticipate the final death scene and its grim parody of sexual desire.

FIGURE 2.22. Carpaccio's "Dream of Saint Ursula." (Courtesy of Gallerie dell'Accademia, Venice)

The repetition of the bedroom scene in Welles's film effectively undercuts the film's narrative action by substituting images of regressive preoedipal visual pleasures, because, instead of narrative movement, the spectator discovers pleasure in a repeated return to the moment of loss. The film's strategies for depicting Othello's repressed desires concurs with masochistic repetition in film as delineated by Gaylyn Studlar, in which masochism "aestheticizes the erotic into cold suspense" and "diverts sexuality from orgasm to an erotic contemplation at once frustrating and pleasurable."[69] In masochistic repetition, scenes are reenacted "in a sort of frozen progression," so that the desiring female agent becomes frozen into positions "that identify her with a statue, a painting, or a photograph."[70] Similarly, Welles's film represents Othello's desire as prefiguring Desdemona's death, freezing her desire like the painted image of Carpaccio's martyred saint or a statue of monumental alabaster.

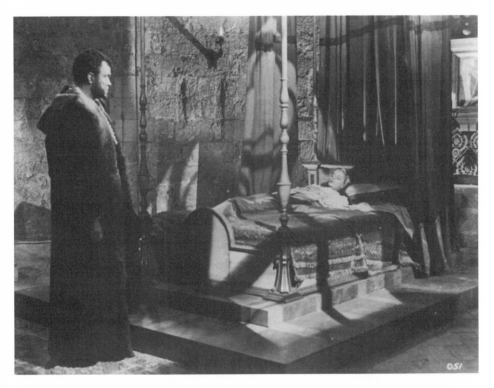

FIGURE 2.23. The bed in Welles's *Othello*. (Courtesy of The Academy of Motion Picture Arts and Sciences)

The film's return to the domestic interior frustrates the narrative impulse operative within linear time, its masochistic aesthetic conditioning the spectator's voyeuristic pleasure of viewing the bedroom by the punishment and death that inevitably follow it. In this way Welles signals to his audience the collapse of conventional cause-and-effect action, reconstituting cinematically the effect achieved in Carpaccio's paintings. Desdemona's martyrdom is anticipated and predicted in the same way that the viewer of Carpaccio's *Dream of St. Ursula* recognizes that Ursula's

dream is part of a closed narrative in which her sacrifice has been anticipated. The return to the bedroom also allows Welles to give cinematic
expression to mechanisms rooted in disavowal and fetishism, the need to
"Look upon . . . the bed" and "Let it be hid." Like the funeral procession
that begins and ends Welles's film, the repetition of the bedroom scene
reflects the repetition of loss that erases time and brings the frenzy of
sadistic violence back to the beginning—to death. The film imitates the
repetitions of masochistic ritual, fetishistically returning again and again
to the point of loss and charting "the regressive movement toward the
fantasy goal of a return to the beginning, to the womb of rebirth and
nothingness."[71]

Welles's *Othello*, like Carpaccio's narrative painting of *The Martyrdom
of the Pilgrims and Funeral of St. Ursula*, alternates the display of masochistic repetition with the sadian frenzy of activity. Welles's camerawork
captures the sadistic impulse for constant motion and perverse movement
in the activities and perspective of MacLiammoir's Iago, while Carpaccio
measures the sadistic actions of the soldiers by the vast numbers of victims
who darken his landscape. Both artists alternate their violent images with
funeral processions. The circular structure of Welles's film and Carpaccio's narrative painting expresses the constant dialectic between stasis and
perverse motion that is so central to Shakespeare's play, described by
Jonathan Dollimore as "an arrest of mobility which at the same time
intensifies it."[72] The passive return to loss that marks masochistic repetition ultimately serves to mobilize the constant activity indicative of sadistic repetition. The final scene of the play, as Dollimore observes, reveals
that Othello's attempts to displace masochistic reparation onto another
must ultimately circle back upon himself, the "turban'd Turk" whom he
must kill. So, too, Welles conceives Othello's tragedy as exploring the
experiential polarities expressed in psychic conflict, in the interplay of
the masochistic aesthetic with sadistic impulses.

Welles demands in his *Othello* that the spectator create a coherent
narrative from the oscillating perspective of the camera, and so must the
critic reconstruct the visual and imaginative framework upon which
Welles created his masterpiece. Through glimpses of intention and imagined relationships one begins to recognize the associative richness of

Welles's visual imagination. Welles's film is powerful precisely because it synthesizes the visual experience of Renaissance Venice with the voyeuristic impulses of his own life and art, in which the spectator gleans significance from the richness of detail and inferred truth from imagined relationship. Tracing the connections between Welles's artistic imagination and voyeuristic impulses, one discovers the visual inspiration of Vittore Carpaccio in Welles's filmic expression of the "voyeuristic pleasure of pain."[73] Welles's film unites the director's personal vision of the dangers and enticements of voyeuristic excitements with Carpaccio's "eyewitness style" in re-creating Shakespeare's scopophile tragedy. The director captures the play's concern with regulating disordering and disordered sexuality by subjecting it to the gaze of his camera, but, like the Venetian art that inspired his film, Welles's camera reveals the dangers implicit in spectatorship.

Chapter Three

Framing Ambiguity

Kenneth Branagh's *Henry V*

As Kenneth Branagh says of his role as King Henry in the Royal Shakespeare Company production of *Henry V,* "I had no desire to beg an audience's forgiveness for a man who had invaded another country on dubious pretexts and with enormous loss of life. They had to make up their own minds about the fascinating, enraging conflict between the ruthless killer and the Christian king."[1] In Branagh's summation of his role he envisions his audience with conflicted and opposing views of King Henry, straddling perceptions based on the carnage and the charisma. Branagh brings a similar ambiguity to his portrayal of the character of Henry V in his 1989 film of the same title, whose charismatic resourcefulness also keeps at bay the audience's condemnation of the king's trumped up invasion of France.

Critical readings of Shakespeare's *Henry V* underscore the play's ironies and ambiguities, and challenge the celebratory and unambiguous cinematic representation of the king in Laurence Olivier's 1944 film. Yet in *Shakespearean Negotiations* Stephen Greenblatt questions whether "in the wake of full-scale ironic readings" *Henry V* is not playable for modern audiences: "it is not at all clear that *Henry V* can be successfully performed as subversive," for "the problem with any attempt to do so is that the play's central figure seems to feed on the doubt he provokes."[2] Indeed, critics such as William Shaw find that ambiguity is notably absent from Branagh's creation of an "uncompromised, heroic figure" who is more "sensitive" than Shakespeare's character in the play.[3] Those critics who do trace ambiguity in Branagh's treatment of individual scenes, as

Sarah Munson Deats does in the hanging of Bardolph, or as a paradox of character in the king himself in what Donald Hedrick describes as a process of "whitewashing chiefly by means of mud," argue that the film's interrogation of Henry's actions is a far cry from Greenblatt's subversive reading of the play.[4]

Hedrick's insistence upon the essential "neutralizing" character of the images in Branagh's film, however, brings up the issue of what framework the viewer applies to the meaning of Henry's actions in Branagh's film. In "unpacking" Branagh's ambiguity, Hedrick looks to sources other than Shakespeare—in mud, Dirty Harry, and capitalism's multinational corporate stage—and emphasizes that historical contexts distinguish the "kinds" of ambivalence the viewer experiences. Hedrick concludes that Branagh achieves his own version of "glorifying charisma" through a "knotted ambiguity in which one implied critique or political interrogation is paired up with a different one, a pairing which effectively cancels out both of them."[5] In other words, if the "muddiness" of war serves as Henry's excuse, then Henry's dubious motivations exonerate the character of war, and all ambiguities rest comfortably, without anxiety, in the film spectacle.

But Branagh's *Henry V* also raises the question of whether the viewer recognizes that facts have been misaligned when distinguishing the fundamental organization of an activity, and how a viewer might respond when it is perceived that the film's belief system is epistemically defective or ambiguous. Hedrick suggests that there are all kinds of ambiguities, some "resolved by the audience" and others "resolved for one part of the audience and not for another part."[6] However, although narrative films are not arguments, their intelligibility does rest upon the linkages that audiences make between the ideas that comprise the narrative, which are reflective of the logic of practical inference. The viewer will "piece out" the story of Henry V, as the Chorus bids him, but the narrative will be intelligible only if the viewer can understand the film's events and characters in terms of the practical reasoning the viewer applies in his own life. Here we account for Hedrick's analysis of extratextual material in the film in terms of the viewer's reading formations of popular culture. However, I also suggest that the film's categorical frameworks, or what Noël Carroll describes as "ways of carving up phenomena," uphold distortions that implicate the viewer's ways of addressing ambiguity.[7] In that the film poses more than one clearly possible explanation, the process of choosing implicates the viewer in the social and political dimensions of misframing by tempting one to select between what Erving Goffman calls "a reduced responsibility and full responsibility perspective."[8] In other words, the viewer rationalizes an explanation for behavior that accords with his assumptions about King Henry, assumptions that are manipulated by the narrative so that the viewer supplies the missing premises that explain certain ideas about the king's conduct. The viewer's choices function in consort not only with the practical reasoning applicable in the viewer's own life but with what the viewer believes to be the fundamental structures of Henry's psychic displacements, enabling the viewer subliminally to displace errors that may bear on the film narrative's principles of organization.

Perspective is crucial, in that the film employs strategies of purposeful and organized deception that "contain" the audience's expectations, and replicates the thematic issues at stake in the play by constructing the perfect icon of royal authority based upon strategies of manipulation and display. Ironically, by inviting viewers to "make up their own minds" about a "ruthless killer" and "Christian king," Branagh employs a juxtaposition of competing frameworks that reconfigure Henry's actions as political mystification. Branagh's *Henry V* rigorously polices the boundaries of its own representation, in that in scene after scene the film faithfully reproduces a grammar of expectations upon which Henry's image is visually articulated as a mimetic mixture that both incorporates and resists. The film's frame disputes are resolved not because the viewer perceives and thereby "neutralizes" ambiguities, but because the viewer embraces an interpretation of events that allows Henry to detach himself from misaligned events and attach it to others, notably Falstaff, the Eastcheap gang, the executed rebels, and the French. The film carefully establishes the viewer's directional track in the opening scene, in offering explanations of behavior that allow the audience to disregard elements that fail to conform to evidential boundaries, with strategies that embrace a process that Linda Woodbridge describes as "magical politics," in that the conjuration of ambiguity enables its dispersal, even as the application of violence has the paradoxical effect of subduing violence.[9]

As Norman Rabkin first pointed out, the audience's dilemma in determining the character and actions of King Henry is similar to that of distinguishing between a "rabbit/duck" picture.[10] However, in attempting to account for the apparent instability of the rabbit/duck, the viewer grounds his perspective in one unambiguous fact—that what he sees is an unambiguous *picture* of something. Similarly, Branagh's film draws the audience's attention to the unambiguous fact that what it views is a film, reducible to the mechanisms of its own enactment. Peter Donaldson suggests that the Chorus is a crucial device in demystifying the filmic apparatus and its issuing authority, but also contends that by unmasking its own cinematic pretensions the film tries "to be honest about its own relation to power."[11] However, the viewer's awareness of the film as a representation (in exposing the mechanics of its own production) and the viewer's involvement with what is represented in the three-dimensional, represented space are mutually exclusive perceptions. Just as there "is no 'flip-flop' effect of the duck-rabbit figure," as Murray Smith observes, in that there is no conflict between the projective illusion and the viewer's awareness of the image as photographic reproduction, Branagh's film does not disengage the audience from the events represented on the cinematic screen simply because it alerts the audience to its status as representation.[12] The film's claims to self-exposure are like the hyperbolic claims made about the illusory powers of cinema, in that the audience is able to sustain a simultaneous involvement with the screen narrative and an awareness of the distancing signaled by the Chorus. What Murray Smith says of the audience's awareness of cinematic conventions is equally true of the story bracketed by the Chorus, in that "we are moved by what we know not to be real."[13]

The Chorus invites the audience to participate in its concentrated focus on the fissures of historical resemblance. From the opening moments of the film, when the artistic and ontological ambiguity of the Chorus invades the darkness of the sound studio, to the Chorus's closing epilogue, the film constructs a time-bound fiction of Henry V founded upon the repressed terrain of culture. Yet the film also performs a shift in Henry's identification and cultural reinforcements by revealing the king's struggle for power as a lack of patriarchal confidence, in which Falstaff's irreverent presence diverts Henry's rhetoric into valorized images of inner structures and sublimated energies of displacement and figuration. Branagh admits that he created the world of Eastcheap and its inhabitants as if "they belonged to a quite different movie, so marked was the change in tone."[14] Falstaff appears as a reconstituted memory that disrupts the flow of the narrative, like a "different movie" in its provocative time-space reorganization of Henry's story. The film links cinematic space and time to experiences distinct from that of Henry's situation and space-time vision, so that Falstaff hovers like a fantasy and forgotten phantom, less defiant than resigned to the deadening numbness of Henry's psychic struggle. Falstaff functions as one of several emotional motifs throughout the film in which a memory of the past underscores the recollector's distance from it, and provides a basis for registering the changes the viewer uses to develop interpretations of character and action.

However, the film manages the memory of Falstaff, like the exploitative fabrication that leads to the traitors' self-condemnation, so that the evidential boundaries of the scene persuade the viewer that Falstaff's rejection is not Henry's responsibility. Hal's softly spoken, non-diegetic utterance seems strangely at odds with the presence of this stalwart youth who is, with Falstaff, bathed in the warm glow of memory. Unlike Olivier's *Henry V,* in which Olivier's voice-over sharply upbraids a startled, dying old man, Branagh's Henry quietly renounces a vital and slightly inebriated companion in a solemn face-to-face interaction. The scene is constructed to make Henry's rejection of Falstaff seem forthright, until one recalls that it is Falstaff who intuits meaning from the expression on Henry's face, since the intoned "I do, I will" occurs as non-diegetic sound. The voice-over also reminds the viewer that this so-called flashback reveals the distortions of Pistol's memory, not the realistic recording of events, and that his memory of experience remains ambiguous and undefined with regard to the meaning the viewer should associate with it. In this sense, these recollected traces imposed upon the tissue of the film, although of a particular emotional intensity, are as "honest" as the Chorus in demystifying the authority of the unfolding narrative, in that what the audience sees does not disengage it from conceptions of character and action it already was disposed to embrace. The film dramatizes the view that ambiguity in the king's actions, if "read" with the assumption that the king's virtues are real, will be ignored by the viewer. Even if the viewer perceives ambiguity at any given moment in the film, and considers that his beliefs may be epistemically defective, the organizational premises of the unfolding drama will not necessarily be "cleared."[15]

In the play Henry literally commands a spatial or geographical distance between Falstaff and himself, and from himself and what he was, though that space threatens to collapse in the confused and comic comparisons Fluellen makes between King Henry and Alexander the Great. Fluellen marks the commonplaces that unite the two conquerors by mapping their topographic similarities of origins and comparing their tactics for eliminating companions, in which Falstaff stands as the half-recollected "fat knight with the great-belly doublet," who was "full of jests and gipes, and knaveries, and mocks" but whose name Fluellen has forgotten (IV.vii.47–48). In the film Falstaff also exists in the exiled borders of memory, in a fabricated scene drawn from exchanges between various characters in *Henry IV, Parts I* and *II*. However, in order to be made intelligible in terms of what the audience believes to be Henry's character, the memory of Falstaff requires that the viewer, like Fluellen, draw upon tenets of rhetorical positioning that the film seems to justify. The viewer is disposed to conclude, as does Fluellen, "O, 'tis a gallant king!" although Fluellen's statement reveals how an entire set of expectations will not work when uttered in the same breath as "the King most worthily hath caused every soldier to cut his prisoner's throat" (IV.vii.9–10). However, the viewer, like Fluellen, overcomes these obvious distortions in categorical frameworks with commonplaces such as "sacrifice is necessary for the safety of the kingdom," and variations on this idea mouthed throughout the play that justify the rejection of Falstaff. As Noël Carroll observes, "When confronted with situations, we will often grasp for whatever heuristics—such as commonplace generalizations—are available to us for the purpose of rendering the situation intelligible."[16] Like Fluellen, the viewer believes he has reached these conclusions himself, although, as Carroll emphasizes, film narratives dispose the audience toward mobilizing commonplace generalizations as part of the rhetorical operations of the film.

The rhetoric of the play, of course, turns on detaching evil actions from the king and placing the blame upon others. Working with the rhetoric of the text and its adroit manipulation of commonplaces, both those overtly stated by characters like Fluellen and those elicited from the audience by contriving situations in which the audience tracks the action by employing these beliefs, Branagh exploits the viewer's acceptance of ideological commonplaces in contending with ambiguity, as we see in this fabricated scene in which Henry rejects Falstaff. Because commonplaces function in conjunction with the plot, the viewer's presuppositions seem to be supported by the events on the screen, which thereby acquire the status of an unassailable paradigm. Add to this the fact that film narration, in general, has a compelling momentum that encourages the audience to respond to what it sees as if it had an aura of inevitability. Of course, the driving force with which Branagh's film dramatizes events suits the dramatic construction of Shakespeare's *Henry V* as the inevitable unfolding of authority, or what Leonard Tennenhouse calls "a piece of political hagiography."[17]

However, as Hedrick points out, Shakespeare's ambiguity is not Branagh's. Nor, as Linda Woodbridge argues, is Shakespeare's drama transhistorical material upon which we see a reflection of our own age's concerns. Yet in exploring the historical parameters that defined Shakespeare's drama, we often overlook how its concerns remain subliminally operative. The structures of experience in Shakespeare's drama, particularly in the play's interest in magical thinking as sublimated scapegoating, continue to have substance in the collective anxieties of our century. That is not to say that film audiences today harbor magical beliefs, any more than Shakespeare's audience did. Even in Shakespeare's drama, Woodbridge cautions, "magical thinking" is not the same thing as belief in magical or supernatural agencies, although the plays do reveal "the unconscious residue of such belief, which remains to structure experience even though true magical belief has atrophied in the individual psyche."[18] The "residue" of magical thinking adheres to the audience's responses to King Henry's behavior in the play, in that the audience externalizes and alienates discontinuous aspects of Henry's personality from the rest. As Woodbridge points out, "discontinuity of personality is

a precondition" for magical thinking that allows Hal to transfer to scape-
goats undesirable attributes attached to himself.[19] Appropriately, Branagh
conceived of the initial scenes of the film as though they were "a dark
world beyond" that had the "feel" of a "documentary," suggesting how
the structures of magical thinking can attach themselves to the realism of
contemporary cinema.[20]

The operations of the film's opening scene reveal how "magical
thinking" implicates the viewer in misframing gaps in the film narrative.
Branagh's mythmaking is more than expansive stylization, for it develops
Henry's image within a network of ideals and values that have an aggres-
sively visceral effect on the audience's collective consciousness. The opening shot of Henry's darkened form as it emerges from the distanced and
blazing light of the doorframe establishes the audience's relation to frame
by placing Henry on a mythic level.[21] The king's indistinct form alerts the
viewer to the film's quasi-mystical lionization of masculine kingship, as
signaled by a magically protective circle of young noblemen who immediately rise to meet the monarch. The viewer responds to this king as to a
myth, in that he never questions the hero's origin or existence because he
feels that it is the same as his own. In this sense, the issuing image of the
king reinforces the effect of the play's rhetorical structures, in imbuing his
story with an aura of truth. As Biró observes, "Myth lends the severity of
law to the fictional image" and "makes whatever exists appear to be axi-
omatic: reality equals truth."[22] Whatever gaps exist between Henry's idealized image and his human identity are inevitably completed by an
audience who finds in the king its own completeness.

Joel Altman observes that the play's King Henry produces responses
in the theater audience that transform it "into a polity whose mind, filled
with Harry, is historically coextensive with Harry, sharing both the hero-
ism and the savagery."[23] Branagh's mobile camera has the benefit of con-
tributing to the narrative by surveying the faces of the nobles before it
completes our identification with the hero's consciousness. By means of a
ritual of approbation, the ranks of nobles signal their respect to an audience that has already identified with the figure who stands before them.
The reaction shots link audience and bowing nobility in an experience
similar to what happens to Henry's audience in the play, by forging an

alliance of positive response and identification, an experience Altman describes as "an honorable fellowship transcending time and space."[24]

Altman's observations regarding the play's rhetorical technique of "amplification" have relevance in this scene, for Branagh manipulates the audience's awareness of space, inducing identification with the king through visual tactics that are similar to Shakespeare's verbal ones. In the play Henry acquires the audience's identification through amplification, which Altman describes as having "the oxymoronic capacity to enlarge something by cutting it up. It consists chiefly in two activities: dividing and presencing."[25] Similarly, in the film Branagh fragments images in order to "presence" Henry's image. For example, he introduces the approving nobles in a series of close-up reaction shots well before the audience views Henry's diminished figure. The reaction shots serve a function similar to the play's rhetorical technique of "serving him [Henry V] up in bits and pieces of various shades and lusters."[26] As Robert Lane points out, the "persistent pattern of reaction shots to Henry's speeches" convinces the viewer of the audience's "appreciation of, respect for, and deference to Henry," in that the viewer's experience of fragmentation creates the visual equivalent of the play's verbal interplay of revelation and mystification.[27]

Branagh refers to the cinematic technique used in the reaction shots of the English court as "crossing the line," a process he recalls as difficult to learn. The young director discovered that "unless one is extremely careful it's very easy to lose track of who's looking at who, and when. If you don't get it right, then it can make editing impossible." The confusion stems from the fact that the actors are "appearing to look one way and sometimes looking quite the other," which, as Branagh confesses, "was an unfathomable mystery to me. I understood the principle of it but no element of its practice."[28] The technique Branagh struggled to learn reveals how compositionally indeterminate point of view shots affect the spectator's construction of space in a relationship similar to how the play employs ambiguities in its principles of organization. Although this particular scene manipulates the audience's responses through the camera's fragmentation of space, it also subjects the audience to a heightened experience of ambivalence through the camera's elucidation of space. Fragmenting the body of the aristocratic audience into individual facial expressions makes the viewer cognizant of the film's arrangement of space in that it demands that the viewer work to complete the picture of the king. As a result, the viewer also becomes aware that the visual linkages made may be completely contingent and fully interchangeable. Paradoxically, even as the scene urges the viewer's emotional participation in presencing the king, its construction of space also forces the viewer to engage in a process of testing spatial hypotheses, since the camera's mobility, which apparently tracks in a linear path, works against the moment-by-moment oscillations in point of view and reaction shots. This technique also succeeds in intensifying the viewer's shock-oriented responses to associative relationships, as when the viewer first sees the young king seated upon the throne. For when the audience has been prepared to identify with the towering figure of a king, the camera reveals a boy-king dwarfed by the exaggerated size of his throne, his figure seated slightly off-center, and clearly no presence before the camera's critical eye. In a reversal of audience expectations, Branagh visually underscores the contradictions that sustain the poles of audience expectations—of the king's imagined power and what the audience actually sees of the king's person, a diminished figure seated upon the exaggerated greatness of his throne. As Branagh writes of his stage performance, nothing else could have carried off the "emotional impact of our production," which, as all the reviewers seemed to agree, "was distinguished by the sight of Branagh looking all of twelve in the title role."[29]

The film also tempts the viewer with choices that the spatial positioning of characters offers as false or ambiguous cues. Branagh's personal notion of religion has some relevance to the opening scene's spatial articulation of choice, when Henry sits upon his enormous throne flanked by the darker forms of Ely and Canterbury, who whisper in his ear and tempt him by declaring his invasion just. The profiles of the holy men slither into the space that contains the king, forming a geometrical composition that suggests the conflicting forces impinging upon Henry's will. Branagh claims that his screen performance was derived from an understanding of Henry's character as depending upon "his faith," but one has to ask what kind of confidence Branagh brought to that role when his personal response to religion was "various forms of resentment," so that "to this day I dislike churches, which make me feel physically ill."[30] His visceral response stems, so he claims, from the choices his religious education afforded him, conceived as a fork in the road where the soul arrives when one dies:

> I had been transfixed by the information that when we died we arrived at a fork in the road. One long, straight road led to heaven, the other—narrow and winding—to hell. In my astonishment at this geographical gem, I had paid scant regard to which road was which. I spent a sleepless week certain that I would die early and would not remember which road to take. I cursed the church for not supplying me with some easy-to-read chart, a kind of Tube map for purgatory.[31]

Henry's character charts the same divide, straddling two representations or choices. Similarly, the audience lacks an easy-to-read chart or map to understand the choices that are spatially articulated, in that the scene establishes the paradox of Henry's assertion of moral right by composing his image as if it were pulled in two directions. As in Branagh's dream of indecipherable choices, the positioning of the clergy implies that the king has reached a sort of fork in the road, whether he might with right and conscience invade France. But, in truth, either choice—for the viewer, at least—transverses the limits of doubt and guilt. The king's real choices are unclear or unavailable to the viewer, as are his motives for the invasion, and the two religious men who crouch beside the king compound the viewer's quandary, since they admit in an earlier scene that they are eager to promote a war that will protect the church's considerable financial interests.

The film tends to externalize and concretize abstractions, persistently physicalizing ambiguous regions of Henry's inner self so that the audience is able to embrace an interpretation that alienates discontinuous elements from the king and attaches them to others. For example, the character of Exeter illustrates how the film externalizes the audience's fear of tyranny and insecurity about Henry's invasion. In his autobiography Branagh calls Brian Blessed "a wild anarchic presence" on the set, but one notices that Blessed's screen character has this quality as well.[32] At Agincourt Exeter's presence is a striking reminder of the bloody aggression and dubious claims that motivated this war. His face speaks with cruel joy when the numbers of the dead are read aloud after the battle as he sits beside Henry. At this point Exeter symbolically replaces Fluellen in the king's company, as reflected in Henry's absorption in tallying the numbers of French dead rather than harkening to Fluellen's questions about law and justice. Fluellen loses focus as the camera moves from deep focus to a shallow focus upon the king and Exeter, implying Henry's shift in alliances from the man of conscience and law to the warrior who celebrates the slaughter.

Similarly, when Ely and Canterbury approach the king with arguments opposing the Law Salic, Exeter's knowing nod to the archbishop to continue his long and tedious recital of Henry's dubious claims to the French throne underscores the scene's darker meanings. Exeter is a dramatic presence, saying little but enormous in his suggestiveness, his nod signaling to the audience what has not been said. Branagh creates in the character of Exeter another fat companion for Hal, an alter ego to the fat knight whose heart he kills. Exeter's resemblance underscores how the psychology of perception operates reflexively in allowing the audience to apprehend the new in terms of the familiar. We are reminded, when we see Exeter dressed in his armor and challenging the French nobility or gleefully hurling his mace against some unseen foe during the Battle of Agincourt, of a parody of Welles's Falstaff in *Chimes at Midnight,* himself a parodic version of chivalry and knighthood. However, this armored fat man loves the fire of battle and the clang of war, not sack. In creating this visual reminder of Falstaff, Branagh reminds us of the knight's anarchic presence upon which Hal could blame the offenses of his youth, and invites the audience to misframe Henry's relationship to the bloody victory over France, in that Exeter's presence reduces Henry's responsibility for the carnage of war. For example, immediately after the Governor of Harfleur capitulates to the English forces, when the sound of Henry's gruesome threats still resonate in the audience's ears, the scene presents the audience with an opportunity to rationalize Henry's behavior and reduce his responsibility. When Henry commands Exeter to remain in

Harfleur and fortify it against the French, Exeter's eagerness is gently checked by the king, who, with a look of weariness and concern, cautions Exeter to "Use mercy to them all" (III.iii.54). The close-up reaction shots between the two men convey the impression that Henry must exercise constant vigilance in keeping Exeter's bloodthirsty impulses in check, and that his own vivid rhetoric of "mowing like grass / Your fresh fair virgins and your flowering infants" (III.iii.13–14) is compelled upon him, no more than a role he plays that chafes against his character.

Falstaff's and Exeter's anarchic energies suggest the importance of a surrogate in the play's configuration of heroic identity, which the film harnesses as a process of scapegoating that drives confusing ambiguity to the borders of Henry's cinematic representation. Branagh underscores the sacrificial nature of that process by having the Chorus introduce the traitors at Dover Cliffs, which the English regard as the source of the nation's genesis and an infamous spot for suicides. The location evokes the expansiveness of Henry's legend and its temporal limits: "From this day to the ending of the world, / But we in it shall be rememberèd" (IV.iii.58–59). The traitors perch precariously on the brink of spatial openness, as if balanced on the cliff's edge, momentarily suspended in medium shot within the antitheatrical medium of cinematic naturalism. The location is a significant choice, as Graham Holderness points out, "for the enactment of a particular ritual; the cleansing of the English body politic by a sacrificial execution."[33]

The Chorus introduces the traitors with the exaggerated solemnity and ponderous movement of sacrificial ritual, yet the scene in which the king exposes and apprehends the three men explodes with sudden violence in an exaggerated male-on-male encounter that links violence and intimacy. Branagh had wanted the set "very cramped" for "the Hitchcockian underbelly of this sequence," in a scene that would prove to be "fast-moving, tense and violent."[34] By treating this scene as "Hitchcockian" suspense (escape is usually a staple of the suspense genre), Branagh gives the capture of the traitors a psychological urgency. And, true to Hitchcock's emphasis upon the importance of the viewer's having knowledge for suspense, the Chorus's introduction of the traitors and Exeter's discussion of their fortuitous discovery allow the viewer to consider what is at stake in the scene. However, what's at stake is complicated in the suspense genre because of the audience's awareness of the dyadic structure of morality and probability outcomes. According to Noël Carroll, suspense normally offers two logically opposed outcomes, one in which a morally correct outcome is unlikely and the other in which an evil outcome is unlikely. However, one curious aspect of Hitchcock's structuring of his films that has relevance here is that Hitchcock, by his own testimony, frequently sought to involve his audience with the success of an immoral action. As Carroll points out, Hitchcock created scenes "where the audience worries because the success of some immoral action—'immoral' even in terms of the film's point of view—is imperiled. That is, Hitchcock has made, and, if he is to be believed, he has intentionally striven to create suspense scenes where immoral outcomes are improbable—scenes where there is suspense even though the moral outcome appears likely."[35] The significance of this theoretical problem for this discussion is that Branagh creates a suspenseful scene in which the desired outcome and its moral implications remain ambiguous. The audience already knows that the traitors' attempt to escape is futile. Therefore, if suspense in the film is contingent upon the desirability of an *unlikely moral* solution, does that then imply that the audience desires that Scroop, Cambridge, and Grey escape? Or, does this scene follow the alternative Hitchcockian pattern, in which suspense occurs because the audience desires that an improbable *immoral* action be successful, and that the traitors escape? The problem is that Branagh constructs this scene so that, either way, the audience's sympathies are with the traitors and not with the king who ensnares them. The suspense elements in the scene allow Branagh to place in sharp focus the oppositions that face the viewer, and, like Hitchcock, to show his audience "that the line between being moral and immoral is slim and easily crossed."[36]

Once the king overpowers Scroop and throws him down upon the table, however, the notion of moral culpability as a functional basis for the action takes another turn. Lying prone, silent, and stripped of his weapon, Scroop is entrapped visually and verbally, limited to fragmented reaction shots and edited lines while Henry narrates his crimes, and denied the violent excess that defines the masculine image so that his passive position defines him as body-object, typical of the cinematic treatment of the female form. Samuel Crowl observes that the intimacy of this scene is intensified by the close-up shot that permits the audience to view the "mixture of tenderness and revulsion as Henry's hand caresses Scroop's brow even as his words lash out at his betrayal."[37] Indeed, Henry's suppression of the conspirators, at once violent and curiously intimate, instigates frame disputes that lead some critics, such as Michael Manheim, to interpret the scene's encoding of the personal as superseding the political: "The emphasis in the scene is clearly more on Henry's rage at Scroop, his erstwhile 'bedfellow', than on making a political point."[38] Manheim's impression that rage motivates Henry's actions falls within the scheme of frame debates. In this case, the viewer (Manheim) makes claims of inadvertence (the king simply lost control because he was personally offended) rather than charge Henry with blameworthy action (tyranny and abuse in a drama that is calculated and staged). Hedrick detects this strategy when he contends that Branagh "portrays all the key actions of Henry as being spontaneous."[39] The result is that the apparent outburst of personal rage reduces the king's culpability in the eyes of the audience, turning sympathy in his favor when he registers a mixture of emotions, caressing Scroop's face while his own distorts in anger, and bitterly denouncing the man who "didst bear the key of all my counsels, / That knew'st the very bottom of my soul" (II.ii.96–97). Henry's behavior allows the audience to indulge in claims of blameless action and to rationalize its responses to a king who condemns men to death without mercy after having orchestrated the scene that tricks them into self-condemnation. In accepting his claims of diminished responsibility, the audience embraces the rhetorical commonplaces that are echoed in Henry's claim that "we our kingdom's safety must so tender, / Whose ruin you have sought, that to her laws / We do deliver you" (II.ii.175–77). The viewer's acceptance of this oft-repeated commonplace contributes to the impression that the traitors' guilt is an inexorable "fact" rather than a presupposition, abetted by the Chorus's ritualized introduction of the men. The scene demonstrates how frame debates work in conjunction with the play's appropriation of magical thinking to obfuscate political and social issues. For when Henry condemns Scroop, Cambridge, and Grey to death, he renames them "English monsters" to distinguish them from the masculine community that their scapegoating protects. The rhetoric of the play underscores the insider/ outsider paradox that prevents the generative violence that could ensue from the murder of a victim not designated as "cruel, / Ingrateful, savage, and inhuman" (II.ii.94–95).

The film's Battle of Agincourt is arguably one of the most stirring battle scenes found in Shakespeare films, and for some of the same reasons that make King Henry's character so compelling for film audiences. For the Battle of Agincourt Branagh wanted to convey "the brutal, savage scrum" of battle.[40] The barbarity of the battle scene is undoubtedly indebted to Welles's *Chimes at Midnight,* particularly in the symbolic implications of shooting the scenes at eye level and in slow motion, with the camera's concentrated focus on the mud, fallen men, and the clash of battle. The variegated sameness of the slaughter and the lyricism of the soldiers' choreographed death dance strike the viewer as a single, continuous action in a spellbinding panorama of destruction. The individual components of the scene—close-up shots of horses' eyes and hooves, clashing swords, and fallen bodies—condense into a single and oft-repeated ritual in which human conflict crystallizes into its most essential form. However, Branagh intersperses in the chaos of the battle individual moments that are poignant and heroic, such as a momentary shot of the mud-splattered king running toward the camera when he hears the scream of murdered boys or a medium shot of Pistol caressing the slain Nym. These shots, when investigated closely, contribute to the viewer's errors that bear on the frame. For example, when the French murder the English boys, the screams of the slaughtered boys resound through the air as the camera cuts to a long shot of a distraught Henry pushing past the forms of men and horses and moving directly toward the camera, as if he were struggling to come to the rescue of the boys. The shot only lasts several seconds, but while the spirited music plays and we see Henry's desperate movement toward the camera and (we believe) the boys, it is a convincing vision of the king's heroic efforts and his empathy for the smallest and least. However, in the next scene only Fluellen and Gower appear, as Fluellen holds the dead boy in his arms and Gower sadly looks on. The disjunction between the previous image and Henry's late appearance in the scene is forgotten, however, in the spontaneous outburst of emotion in which the king throws Mountjoy to the ground, which allows the viewer to disattend the gap in the narrative.

Branagh's *Henry V* also substantially departs from Welles, and from Shakespeare, in his cinematic concentration upon particular individuals whose deaths evoke images of blood sacrifices and ritualized slaughter. Pistol's pietà-like cradling of the slain Nym, who is stabbed and left hanging outstretched upon a gnarled limb, suggests the powerful relevance of the surrogate in a way that Nym's offstage hanging leaves unexplored. Similarly, the film endows the death of York with a ritual aura, as if his murder by a faceless mob of soldiers is an act of deliberate mystification that assimilates brutal bloodletting to the world of sacrifice. His death is dramatically different from what we see in the play. He dies alone and unwept, without Exeter's teary testimony to chivalry and "noble-ending love." Instead, the terrifying lyricism of York's slow death in medium shot, his body "all haggled over" (IV.vi.11) and slightly elevated above the heads of his killers, in unison with the haunting musical underscoring, give the scene the aura of a crucifixion and the piety of a human sacrifice. The dynamic between the reduction of physical action and time slowed down lifts York as a symbol into a magical-mythical level, where isolated objects and events can achieve what Yvette Biró calls "an atmosphere of superplus-experience" that allows the image to approach abstraction.[41] In the impersonal scrutiny of the camera the audience searches the components of the film narrative that make time-space structures and their situational context metaphoric. York's death demonstrates how Henry V shifts guilt from his own shoulders to others, in that it signifies a beneficial blood sacrifice that inoculates him against the bloody crime of invading another country. And although York had begged the honor of leading the charge for a cause of questionable honor, this irony is largely lost on an audience who emotionally responds to York's butchering and "the brutal, savage scrum" of battle.

Branagh has said of the long tracking shot that concludes the Battle of Agincourt that "there would be no question about the statement this movie was making about war."[42] Branagh's confidence is ironic considering the range of opinions this scene has generated and the contradictions it has elicited in audience responses, which Michael Manheim describes as

part of "our eternal schizophrenia about wars and heroes."[43] In a continuous tracking shot Branagh carries the body of the dead boy to a cart
filled with the bodies of slaughtered boys, pictorially elucidating the terms
of Henry's victory after the battle of Agincourt as a seamless and unified
surface upon which we read the terms of our own complicity, protest, and
acquiescence. Its surface retraces Henry's journey through a visual reas-
sessment and analysis of the film's ways of reading and mapping, in which
the angry women who attempt to assault the king play a crucial role in
alerting the viewer to the scene's construction as fantasy, in which the
viewer is shielded, as Mountjoy shields Henry, from getting too close.
Instead, the scene disavows its own mechanisms of incorporation or strategies of manipulation and display, in that it frustrates and avoids Henry's
entrapment by a negative legacy. As Henry slogs through the tableau of
fallen horses and bodies, the viewer distinguishes the intersecting paths
that trace the cultural and psychic markers of Henry's history, from Pistol's
mourning of Nym, to Williams's trudging past the king on the field of
battle, to the cart piled high with the bodies of dead boys upon which the
king stands at the close of the scene. The shot stands as a trenchant symbol
of the incorporations and resistances evoked by cinematic spectacle and
choric ritual in exploring the complexity of Henry's provocative-cathartic
ambition.

The "eternal schizophrenia" of the battle translates into the compul-
sory ambivalences of Henry's inner life as well. During the negotiations
between France and England, the victorious English king sits calmly at
the end of the table as a montage sequence of flashbacks of York, Scroop,
Mistress Quickly, the Boy, Bardolph, and Falstaff appears as Henry's
metadiegetic associations. The images seem as if subordinate links in a
chain, their ultimate meaning determined by their intensified significance as building-blocks in Henry's comprehensive mode of thinking.
Because Henry recalls those now dead at the moment of his greatest victory, the flashback seems to imply that the violence he inflicts upon others is also self-inflicted. The viewer is tempted to read these ambiguous
images as the suppressed material of Henry's unconscious, perhaps as
Henry's recognition of the "truth" of the play's rhetorical commonplaces
(sacrifice is necessary for the security of the commonwealth), or as a tacit

confession of having executed, scapegoated, and banished others in order to eschew blame himself. At the very least, the flashback throws into question the meaning of the victory at Agincourt and the means by which it was achieved.

It is worthwhile to consider briefly those scenes in Branagh's film that critics and audiences generally view as unambiguous, which happen to be those moments when Henry is at his greatest pitch of oratory and exudes his greatest personal charm — his Saint Crispin's Day speech to the troops and his wooing of the French Princess Katharine. These scenes are concerned less with action than reaction, and the psychological effects of Henry's winning oratory. The focus in both the Saint Crispin's Day speech and the wooing of Katharine is on the existential import of each situation and how it motivates the characters who listen to Henry to express their mental states. Whether in rousing despondent English troops to fight against overwhelming odds or in proposing marriage to a French princess who questions if it is possible to love "de *ennemi* of France" (V.ii.170-71), Branagh's king exercises a collective fascination over his audiences.

However, the ultimate impression that these scenes convey of Henry's inevitable momentum toward power seems suspect to critics. In particular, critics lament the ease with which the king conquers the "all-too-willing" Katharine and the fact that her apparent reticence seems "nothing more than wily coquetry," when current criticism of the play finds less romance than ruthlessness, less personal attraction than "national 'spousal.'"[44] Because the film seems to deploy its presuppositions in the service of eliciting certain ideological tenets (namely, those in service of political conservatism), Derek Royal contends that the director himself becomes "a victim of that very disturbing ideological presence he set out to critique."[45] If Branagh's political critique seems undercut by what Royal perceives as a loss of cynicism in the tone of the Chorus or in the concluding scenes' barrage of unambiguous images of Henry, one must remember that viewers easily reject ideological tenets with which they have little sympathy. As Sinfield and Dollimore caution about the play, "Whether the betrothal of Katharine appears delightful or oppressive depends on the framework of assumptions readers and audiences bring to

FIGURE 3.1. Henry V and Princess Katharine of France in Branagh's *Henry V.* (From the collection of the Museum of Modern Art Stills Archive, New York)

it."[46] Therefore, if film audiences find Branagh's Saint Crispin's Day speech and the wooing of Katharine effective, it is because the play couches its rhetoric in ideological commonplaces that still find acceptance in film audiences today. As Noël Carroll observes, "where viewers readily accept the rhetoric of the film, they probably already accept the ideological commonplaces, and the ideological operation of the film in such cases is probably best described as reinforcing existing ideology."[47]

Branagh's treatment of these scenes demonstrates how conflicting accounts of incorporation can be camouflaged by an apparently objective uniformity in stylistic patterning. Branagh tends to rely upon a strong symmetry in composition in developing the viewer's iconographical and perceptual codes, so that by the end of the film the stylistic patterning of the film seems so habitual and familiar that the viewer considers the compositions "natural," as in the triangulated images of Henry, the princess,

FIGURE 3.2. Henry V surrounded by his men. (From the collection of the Museum of Modern Art Stills Archive, New York)

and Alice that close the final scene. Henry and Katharine face one another in profile, while an approving maternal-surrogate, Alice, stands slightly above and between them in the background. This stylistic patterning is a purely cinematographic signifying feature, but it also has the potential to function ideologically. Viewers find what they see on the screen to be "believable" because of the way in which cinematic codes are tightly focused on individual characters who function as figures of identification. Alice's strategic placement enables a process of internal colonization that gives the scene a double vision, in that the viewer also approves of this (visually) balanced and matched pair.

Similarly, when Henry makes his speech to his troops before the Battle of Agincourt, each shot places the story interest in the center of the cinematic frame, and every aspect of camera technique is obedient to making bodies and faces the focal points of attention. The approving nods of the followers as they listen to the king underscore the national impetus behind him and link audience identity and allegiance in a heightened moment of community. Figure placement of the soldiers and their density of organization allow the viewer to make plausible hypotheses about the grouping of characters, particularly since the audience has come to "know" these ten or so characters from previous scenes, who can be identified in what appears to be a strict hierarchy of attention and tight causality. When the king names "Bedford and Exeter," the camera focuses upon the nobles as one composition, and when Henry predicts the future commemoration of Agincourt as a "story" that "the good man [shall] teach his son" (IV.iii.56), the camera reveals Nym crouched next to the Boy in a grouping of the surviving Eastcheap gang. The relations on screen strike the viewer as realistic because they seem immediate and universal, of father and son, and comrades-in-arms. The camera seems to confirm Henry's rhetorical positioning in terms of the narrative, and brings the viewer to certain conclusions even before Henry states them outright.

Yet the viewer remains capable of detaching himself from the film's materializations of the many contingencies of enunciation and their social conditions. Closer scrutiny of the scene reveals a tenuous linking of events and an inconsistency and indeterminacy in the scene's representation of ideological harmony that invites cynical appraisals of the film's ideological appearance of unity. The viewer sees the solemn Pistol and is reminded of the hanged Bardolph, and warily watches the glint in Exeter's eyes and is reminded of Harfleur. And, despite the camera's nostalgic interpretation of flashback sequences in Eastcheap Tavern, the viewer's knowledge of the characters tells him that Boy is not Nym's son. So, too, the fragmentation of the images into social groupings works against the rhetoric that deems the soldiers a "band of brothers," as well as the fact that the individuals upon whom the camera focuses when these lines are spoken are the same men who had threatened to kill one another at the Battle of Harfleur. The scene's patterning demands that the spectator construct form and meaning according to a process of knowledge, memory, and inference (linkages), and thereby reiterates the game of visual information and alternative hypotheses that has informed the whole film, in which exclusive and equally probable hypotheses about Henry's character and motives cheat the viewer of satisfying inferences, and arouse audience expectations only to frustrate them. In frequent close-up shots the camera focuses upon the personal charisma of the king, yet simultaneously raises the question of his personal motives. While the film advances ideological perspective by the persuasiveness and attractiveness of the king, its cinematic tactics expose the cynical ideological premises of the play — that Englishmen are "equal" only when they die on the battlefield or that dynastic rule requires nation-building on the bodies of women.

Although Brownell Salomon claims that it is the intent of heroic poetry in general and of *Henry V* in particular to transform the audience "from indifferent onlookers to partisan believers," the internal organization of narrative and pictorial elements in Branagh's film, while encouraging ideological beliefs in the viewer, also suggests the arbitrariness with which the viewer makes the linkages that are put in the service of soliciting ideological tenets.[48] If the viewer accepts the film's commonplaces, it is only because he is predisposed to do so. The viewer who yearns for the potentially regenerative conclusion that the final scene offers in the marriage of Katharine and Henry may be gratified by the spectacle and yet denied its certainty. Although the Chorus's final words of the play promise redemption through sacrifice that produces the boy-child, its triumph is diminished by the anxiety of English history, where ritual elements, as Linda Woodbridge admits, "turn out to be rhetorical ploys, manipulated by cynical politicians." However, as Woodbridge qualifies, "it is precisely their sacramental air, seeming to raise them above the sordid world of politics, that makes them so useful as rhetorical ploys."[49] Indeed, Branagh serves up the play's ideological tenets only insofar as they allow the audience to disregard the traumatic truth it knows lies beneath the story's surface. In the cynical backwash of our modern times, the film leaves its audience emotionally moved by what it knows not to be real.

Chapter Four

Breaking the Frame

Akira Kurosawa's *Ran*

In *Ran* Kurosawa explores the space of tenuous masculine constructions of identity within the cinematic frame and the powerfully subversive oppositional imaging of female identity. In a film that apparently is representative of the Jidai Geki genre, glorifying the bravery of the ancient samurai and his masculine code, *Ran* exhibits what Stephen Prince has called a "negative inversion" of the samurai code and a bursting of the cinematic frame in which that code is represented.[1] In the film the female emerges as the means by which the samurai sign-system is restructured and ultimately broken, and the experience of space becomes the locus of the male and female struggle for identity and domination. The social structure—and cinematic space—that rigidly frame the woman become the space of her rebellion, and the silence that contains the female expression of self becomes a subversive strength. When the frame breaks, Prince suggests, we find hell. More precisely, we find a collapsed system of encoded samurai behavior effectively challenged by the women who are entrapped within it. Yet the breaking of the frame in *Ran* also yields new worlds outside the main site of conflict and alternative spaces of identity beyond the samurai prescriptions of self. In the opening up of the diegetic space of the cinema screen, Kurosawa explores possibilities for the expression of self outside the classical narrative.

An incident from Kurosawa's childhood memories reveals, in a startling way, the strategies for spatial representation, gender, and identity that emerge in *Ran*. In his *Something Like an Autobiography* the director recalls a recurring dinner scene, in which his father, a man of "extreme severity," routinely chastises his wife for pointing the fishhead on the meal tray in the wrong direction. Having observed that his wife once again had failed to observe the "finer points of samurai etiquette," Kurosawa's father would berate his wife with "Idiot! Are you trying to make me commit suicide?" In remembering the passion of his father, Kurosawa attempts to understand the daily failure of his mother to appease her husband in this one simple detail:

> Apparently there was a special procedure for serving the meal that precedes a ritual suicide. It seems it extended to the position of the fish on the plate. My father had worn his hair in a samurai topknot as a child, and even at the time these scoldings occurred he would frequently take a formal sitting position with his back to the art alcove and hold his sword straight up to polish the blade with abrasive powder. So it's probably quite natural that he should have been angry, but I couldn't help feeling sorry for my mother and thinking it could hardly matter that much which way the fishhead pointed. Yet my mother continued to make the same mistake over and over again. And every time the fish on his tray was pointed the wrong way, my father scolded her. As I think about it now, it could have been that my father's fault-finding was so frequent an occurrence that she became deaf to it, as the saying goes, "like a horse's ears in an east wind."[2]

The spatial arrangement of the fishhead in the frame of the meal tray inflames Kurosawa's father to a display of samurai histrionics, and to an assertion of male identity and power before the mother's silent, unrelenting, and subversive reorganization of the objects before him. The husband asserts himself with all the privileges and power of samurai tradition and male authority, sitting in a formal samurai posture, deriding his wife, and holding "his sword straight up to polish the blade with abrasive powder." The erect sword the father rubs compensates for his sense of male vulnerability to the power of his wife, as either threatened castration or feminization. Ironically, the husband frames his own body or physical presence as spectacle, constructing masculinity as an image, with the art alcove as theatrical backdrop for his erect and formal representation of self. In the husband's articulation of the threatened self—"Are you trying to make me commit suicide?"—he formulates the nature of the threat as the oblivion of identity. The apparent insignificance of the incident itself only makes more profound the father's tenuous sense of self, so easily displaced when boundaries dissolve or objects are displaced.

In Kurosawa's narrative the mother's obedience is tacit; yet she "continued to make the same mistake over and over again." The woman's silence, like the continual "accidental" displacement of the objects on the meal tray, suggests the unspoken and subversive desires of the wife. In cinematic terms, the woman's silence becomes what one feminist film critic calls the "site of a special resistance—a strength rather than a weakness."[3] In Kurosawa's narrative the mother's resistance is also registered in spatial terms—in the space of a meal tray—and her silence suggests the "opening up" of the space of the mother's inner life normally contained or repressed. The imagined desire of the silent wife is articulated in the husband's angry reproach—"Are you trying to make me commit suicide?"—and the silence that should suggest obedience and passivity reveals a threatening strength and resistance. As Kurosawa recalls this incident, he acknowledges that the spatial reorganization of the fishhead suggests behavior "no Japanese would ever think of" for it is the space of resistance and of imagined formulations of identity known only to one person—the mother.[4] The scene is heavily imbued with irony, the formidable presence of the threatened husband arrayed to meet the silent and subversive challenge of his wife to restructure the space of the meal tray.

Yet as Kurosawa narrates this incident he seems curiously oblivious to the significance of the scene played before him. He speculates that his mother's failure stemmed from ignorance of class distinctions, since she "came from an Ōsaka merchant family and was thus less sensitive" to the required forms of samurai etiquette, or (related to this charge of insensitivity) she had become numb to her husband's constant scolding. However, the son's sympathies are with his silent and oppressed mother; Kurosawa admits that he "pitied" his mother as she faced her formidable husband. The director struggles to explain a mother's behavior "no Japanese would ever think of," and to make sense of his father's demand in the little scene his parents played out daily:

> . . . when you are served a fish on a meal tray, usually its head
> points to the left and its belly is toward you to make it easy to
> reach. If you are going to commit suicide, I gather that it is
> served with its head pointing to the right and its belly away
> from you, because it would be insensitive to place a cut fish
> belly directly facing someone who is about to cut open his
> own abdomen. This is my assumption, but it is no more than
> an assumption.[5]

It is suggestive that this director ponders the relevance of the direction of the fishhead and dismisses the mother's motivation; in fact, he finds the visual representation of the object that instigated such extreme emotion more interesting than the quietly subversive woman who has disappeared within Kurosawa's own discourse. Her behavior, as he tells us, is un-Japanese, and thereby alien; so too the rebellion her behavior signals lies outside the bounds of the director's own narrative and representation.

In later years Kurosawa was to boast that he never used a production designer in directing his films: "It is always I who frame the shot, who design the movement."[6] As Kurosawa learned in his childhood, how an object is framed—in the space of a meal tray or in the cinematic screen—constitutes a struggle for identity and domination within that space. Framing conditions representational practices, and allows the viewer to witness the complex exchanges that rework boundaries between masculine and feminine identity. In particular, cinematic framing is the space in which oppositional discourses can also interpret social configurations of power and desire, oppression and rebellion. Kurosawa always frames the shot and designs the movement, but he contemplates within that frame an alternate space and design, the space of oppositional discourses, of fishheads and samurai swords, of the explosive rage of the samurai and the silent and subversive power of the female.

The samurai film, as David Desser has pointed out, offers iconic archetypes which enable the audience to explore the boundaries between "the permitted and the forbidden."[7] These boundaries between "permitted" samurai representation of identity and power and the "forbidden" subversive and oppositional representation of female identity are curiously mutable in *Ran*. Gender distinctions blur in Lady Kaede's vindictive and predatory sexuality, which links eroticism and violence, sex and politics; in Tsurumaru's effeminate posture that so effectively dramatizes the frustration and helplessness of those victimized by the samurai code; and in the sexually ambiguous presence of the Fool Kyoami. Kurosawa underscores the confusion of gender in casting "Peter," a popular transvestite star of Japanese film, in the role of the fool. He is Hidetora's guide, nurse, and companion through the ruined castles and wastes. Ironically, Kyoami's sexually ambiguous presence confirms the Great Lord's samurai identity. Early in the film we see Hidetora, greatly diminished under Taro's roof, his concubines forced aside by Lady Kaede's procession of servants and rerouted within the narrow passages along the castle walls, rise up angrily and defiantly to kill the man who threatens Kyoami's life. In a close-up shot of Hidetora, we see him slowly recoil into the narrow window of the tower that now inhibits his movement. The great bow he has just used to kill a man, and the fiery expression in his eyes, belie the restraint recently urged upon him and the narrowed space of his powers. In *Ran* the presence of a male who descends in the gender hierarchy has none of the threatening implications of the female who attempts to ascend in the same hierarchy. The presence of Lady Kaede, on the other hand, challenges Hidetora's samurai identity as Great Lord. She repeatedly challenges Hidetora's assertion of space and, ultimately, seeks the erasure of the entire Ichimonji family. Her subversive identity is effectively concealed for some time within her studied movements reminiscent of Noh drama and in her quiet and measured speech. Ironically, her hidden desires and rebellious identity emerge in her performance of designated female tasks and in the space of the traditionally structured female identity.

Japanese theatrical practice recognizes that the relationship between sex, gender, and sexuality is an arbitrary construction and subject to sociohistorical conditions. "Although the Japanese apparently recognize two sexes and two genders, 'female' gender (femininity) and 'male' gender (masculinity) are not ultimately regarded as the exclusive province of

Figure 4.1. Lady Kaede in *Ran*. (From the collection of the Museum of Modern Art Stills Archive, New York)

anatomical females and males. Sex, gender, and sexuality may be popularly perceived as irreducibly joined, but this remains a situational, not a permanently fixed, condition."[8] The Kabuki theater and the Takarazuka Revue (an all-female theater founded in 1914) demonstrate that "gender ideology, like most ideologies, functions to contain differences or antinomies by *setting up differences.*"[9] Significantly, the Kabuki theater sets the conditions for "acceptable" transformations of gender identity. But even within the theatrical space of the Takarazuka Revue the women who assumed male roles became alarming because they seemed to transform their roles from that of "male" gender to the stereotype of the "male" female. "For an anatomical female to assume 'male' gender is for her to rise in the gender hierarchy, which is subversive, from a patriarchal point of view."[10] As becomes increasingly obvious to Jiro's men, Lady Kaede assumes the "male" gender in her ability to rise in the gender hierarchy, a position that ultimately demands her decapitation and erasure. In this, cinematic representation in *Ran* of traditional theatrical gender roles and identities (like those familiar in both Kabuki theater and the less-celebrated Takarazuka Revue) opposes the "acceptable" transvestite to the destructive and threatening "male" female.

The film's pictorial emphasis upon a coded sign-system (family crests, armor, swords, banners, and carved scabbards) establishes the icons that entrap Hidetora in a rigid system of samurai identity. The first scene reveals the formal structures and sign system of the samurai world, represented in the rectangular structure Hidetora has erected on the expansive and sprawling lava fields of Mount Fuji. John Collick calls this a "sacred area" or enclosure, and the structure quite literally marks the dramatic space or performance area in which Hidetora will stage the formal abdication of his rule.[11] When Hidetora falls asleep, as Collick points out, the other sons leave this "performance space" except Hidetora—and even the camera leaves the enclosure—so that when Hidetora emerges, frantic, from the enclosure, claiming to have had a terrible dream, the viewer is already distanced from this enclosure.[12] In this scene Hidetora literally bursts outside the frame of the samurai enclosure. He does not reveal his fearful dream to his sons or the audience, but, visually, we connect his fears with the space that he is in a frenzy to escape. The flapping canvas that entraps Hidetora's feeble limbs as he thrashes wildly reinforces our visual association that it is the enclosure itself that frightens the old man.

In this scene the camera technique distances the audience from the space of the enclosure as well. In *Ran,* argues Stephen Prince, Kurosawa's filmic "strategy of withdrawal via the long take and the long shot" became necessary when "Cultural and historical spaces had become hostile to Kurosawa's investigation. . . . In its absence, montage, and the spatial analysis it proposed, became demonic and suited to violence and death."[13] The camera's assertion of space works against the presence of the samurai in the frame. As Prince recognizes, the eye of the camera is hostile to the "cultural and historical spaces" of the samurai. In this first scene the camera refuses audience participation or identification with the enclosed space of the samurai; instead, the camera reveals the singularity and isolation of the brilliantly colored rectangular enclosure staked out in the muted greenery of the expansive hillside. We are at once outside of samurai ritual and remote from it, so that the experience of the "negative inversion" of samurai ritual and form is prepared for the viewer in the first scene of the film.

Spatial arrangement in *Ran,* particularly in the enclosed spaces of the samurai, can be confrontational. The static and codified world of *Ran's* interior spaces provides the site of the rebellion of Lady Kaede as well as the site of her subordination. Claudine Hermann asserts that, for women, space "is by definition a place of frustration, whether physical, moral, or cultural. It is also the place of systematization and hierarchization."[14] The camera positions Lady Kaede within the frame of the cinema screen like the two-dimensional landscape against which she is photographed, thereby conveying subordination and inactivity. Yet within the limits of this space Lady Kaede asserts her identity, reorganizing the symbols of her containment in an experience of "negative inversion."

Lady Kaede retreats to the domestic space with which she identifies, in the reclaimed space of her family castle, like a living *muenbotoke* or *onryo,* a vengeful female spirit without living relatives. Lady Kaede's revenge against the Great Lord who has murdered her family is reminiscent of the female vengeful spirit familiar in Japanese folklore. Gregory Barrett describes the presence of the vengeful female as the "Japanese equivalent to rebellion sentiments, for the grudge borne one man could be extended to include a male-dominated society."[15] In fact, Lady Kaede's revenge extends well beyond the Ichimonji family to the entire society that has shaped her silent and rebellious desires. She makes these hidden and silent desires explicit when she realizes that Jiro's position as the new Great Lord may displace her from her family castle. From her silent and suppliant position before the seated Jiro she suddenly rises to defiantly close the screens of the room, laughing wildly as she does so. In the enclosed and narrowed space of that room she challenges Jiro's dominance by resisting the traditional roles assigned to women who have lost their husbands: "I won't be a widow with my hair cropped, or a nun with my head shaved! This castle was my father's. I won't leave it!" She resists the definitions thrust upon her, as widow or nun, and repositions herself within the Ichimonji family by threatening to expose Jiro's murder of his brother and then by seducing the frightened Jiro. She asserts her dominance within the domestic space that has shaped her identity, and effectively displaces Jiro's wife Sué in her struggle for that space.

Lady Kaede effectively employs the samurai codes to reorganize power within the Ichimonji family, a reorganization that sets the stage for the obliteration of the Ichimonji clan. She mounts her attack against Hidetora and his family within the reclaimed domestic space of her family castle. As Hidetora gazes from a tower of First Castle he observes the spatial reorganization of his concubines, who first freeze in position in the passageway of the castle and then move against the wall to make way for Kaede's women. Later, in private conference Lady Kaede upbraids Taro for failing to claim the emblems of the Great Lord. She tells Taro, her head bowed and body passive, that without the Ichimonji banner "you are a shadow." She demands the signs of samurai power and restructures Hidetora and Taro's relationship to those signs in the "family gathering" that follows. Lady Kaede and Taro invite Hidetora to a "family dinner" for the purpose of his humiliating written assignation of all power and properties to Taro. Hidetora is humiliated to sit below both Taro and his wife, and indeed, as Hidetora enters the room Taro's figure disappears off the screen, allowing a powerful and central Lady Kaede to be the focus of the camera with the bowed back of Hidetora well beneath her figure. Hidetora obliges his son and daughter-in-law in signing his retraction of authority with blood, but leaves the scene humiliated and disgusted, telling Taro: "The hen pecks the cock and makes him crow." When Hidetora leaves the room the man who has been his companion and advisor bows low before Lady Kaede. The camera moves closer to Lady Kaede, who dominates the cinematic screen, and the bowed figure of the man nearly disappears beneath hers. She says to him, "You have done well," and he is dismissed. In the strategic reorganization of loyalties and hierarchical space—including the prominent display of the family banner on the wall behind her—Lady Kaede appropriates the forms of samurai power and authority. The result, for both father and son, will be the obliteration of identity.

Lady Kaede quietly glories in her triumph over Hidetora and her confirmed possession of her family castle. The spatial arrangement of shots in the next few moments also confirms her separateness from her husband, and her domination in the separate space she inhabits. Taro and Lady Kaede both sit off-center in the cinematic screen and occupy opposite ends of their separate spaces, with the Ichimonji banner balanced in the space on the wall that separates them. For an uncomfortably long period Kurosawa focuses the camera upon the frame occupied by Lady Kaede, who sits frozen in her separate space and silent. However, in film, "woman's silence helps her to define a new relation to objects."[16] Indeed, when Lady Kaede does speak she reveals the result of her reorganization of space and repositioning of Hidetora. She is back in her family castle, she tells Taro, the castle she left to marry him. In halting and measured speech she quietly recalls Hidetora's crime: "My father and brothers, after the marriage relaxed their vigilance. Hidetora murdered them. I have longed for this day." The camera focuses upon Taro, who has remained passive while listening to Lady Kaede's narrative. He makes a slight movement in her direction, but his torso is arrested in its slow movement as she continues her narrative, spoken almost as if it were an internal monologue, since Taro's presence is scarcely noticed or recognized. "Right there," she utters, the gaze of the camera centered on the circular floor space contained within both their individual frames, "my mother took her own life." Taro remains silent and still, the conditions for their relationship reformulated by the circular space on the floor.

The body is the site of woman's oppression, but it is also the site of the battle between Lady Kaede and the Ichimonji family. *Ran* dramatically represents such a battle in Lady Kaede's "seduction" of Jiro. In this scene, Kurosawa manipulates traditional cinematic coding of sexual difference, displacing and dissolving the boundaries between the passive female object of desire and constructing the male body as the site of spectacle and desire. When Lady Kaede objects to Jiro's appropriation of his dead brother's armor, Jiro strips himself of these signs of samurai power. He begins to strip off the armor before the quietly bowed figure of the woman and tells her that if she stays in the room she will see a naked man. She leaves, and the camera concentrates on the ritual by which she picks up her fan and the carefully controlled and stylized movements by which she leaves the room. However, when Jiro next appears before Lady Kaede he is stripped of his emblems of conquest. He is now only the younger brother of the dead Great Lord. In the following scene the frame registers a series of complex exchanges that continually dissolve the boundaries of sexual difference. The seated Jiro watches as Lady Kaede rises and slowly closes each of the screens that enclose them both within the narrowed space of the room. In this restricted domestic space Lady Kaede redefines the power relationships between them, and, by the appropriation of symbols of masculine power, threatens Jiro's identity and existence. Lady Kaede wields the knife that threatens castration and feminization, slicing Jiro across the neck to create the "cut" that renders him passive. She also slices the sleeve of her restricting kimono, not only to threaten Jiro but to register the failure of codes of dress and behavior to contain her aggressive spirit or arrest her frustration. The seduction displaces the audience's traditional social and cultural locations, imagining new pleasures, terrors, and relationships in the reconstituted space of woman's desire and gender identity.

The camera always reveals the locus of Lady Kaede's identity and struggle within the space of her family castle. When Jiro's samurai warrior decapitates Lady Kaede with his sword, her blood splashes across the castle wall and dramatically registers her relationship with the space that has shaped her perceptions and articulated her will. However, Sué, unlike Kaede, is never limited or defined by domestic space. In fact, the small hut in which Hidetora seeks her encloses only a portrait of Buddha, but not the woman. The imaging of Sué within the camera's frame functions indices of negativity, a withdrawal or refusal to "continue employing the objects of the world in the traditional way."[17] The camera, in effect, "sympathizes" with the perspective of the female encoded by the samurai system, withdrawing or refusing, much like the female subject, to participate in the sacred enclosure of the samurai. Hidetora finds Sué perched on the castle wall, her slight figure seated before an expanse of sky. She has moved outside the home, and the camera demands a new relation between the character and her space. But, as Inez Hedges points out, such a new space in the creation of female identity "would break the frames of our normal perception."[18] Sué and Hidetora are seated before the vast nothingness of the sky, their figures within the cinematic screen suggesting an inner integrity or diegetic space outside the world of men that defines their physical space within the cinematic frame.

To break the frame is to threaten oblivion, signified as the literal bursting of enclosures that hurls Hidetora outside the sacred enclosures of the samurai code into a wasteland of ruined castles and desert spaces. Perhaps this is why critics fail to agree as to what the ending of *Ran* means, finding either spiritual escapism or a destructive engagement with reality in the final image of the tiny figure of the emasculated and blinded Tsurumaru before the expanse of land and sky. Is the ending optimistic, as Collick argues, or a "discourse on isolation and defeat"?[19] Certainly Kurosawa's father only saw the reformulation of space (even in a meal tray) as inherently threatening to identity. Yet Kurosawa's film has real sympathy for the imagined space beyond the boundaries of the cinematic frame. The experience of space in this final shot of Tsurumaru perched on the edge of the abyss liberates the viewer from the decorum of classical narrative, but that experience is threatening and liberating simultaneously.

As Shakespearean adaptation, *Ran*'s cinematic emphasis upon spatial struggle and representation is faithful to the conflict in *King Lear* over the charting of geographic as well as ideological space. For Lear, the charting of his daughter's duty and love lies within the province of patriarchal right, the right to enclose and limit the space of female will. The decided mapping of patriarchal space and power is destroyed by Cordelia's "nothing" and by the decorous fictions of love proclaimed by Goneril and Regan, just as Sué's sad smile and Lady Kaede's guileful manipulation of samurai decorum and codes disturb Hidetora's established self. "O indistinguished space of woman's will!" (IV.vi.275), Edgar utters, as he stands before the blinded Gloucester and slain Oswald, victim and instrument of unbounded female will. Hidetora might well say the same. Hidetora, like Lear, steps outside the boundaries of the sign-system that has defined and limited him and discovers the vulnerability of his own identity.

Ran, like Shakespeare's play, also develops this realm of "indistinguished space" as the quality of love that resists patriarchal categories, definitions, and limits. Love, too, in terms of this play, represents that "indistinguished space" that cannot be categorized, defined, or enclosed. No terms can be set, no tangible essence awarded, and no boundaries known to distinguish the quality of love that Cordelia and Sué feel. The measured and bounded spaces of masculine identity are repudiated by a woman's unconditional and hyperbolic love. The bursting of the frame might reveal a hell, as Prince suggests, but in the silence of Sué's sad smile and Cordelia's nothing we glimpse the imagining of identity beyond the limits of space and experience.

Chapter Five

Vivid Negativity

Richard Loncraine's *Richard III*

Richard Loncraine's *Richard III* (1995)
sets Shakespeare's play about a medieval tyrant's rise to power within the
material trappings of a 1930s fascist England, a transformation that troubles
some film critics, who call the film "a time-travel experiment gone wrong,"
with "Fascist regalia" that "seems oddly beside the point."[1] Even those critics
who are impressed with the film's fascist spectacle remain skeptical that it is
still Shakespeare. Richard Bowman, film critic for · *The American Spectator*,
praises the film's "consistent cleverness of its setting," finding that "in some
ways [it is] the best film adaptation of Shakespeare there has ever been." Yet,
paradoxically, he concludes that the film "is not Shakespeare."[2]

The film's varied collection of images from the Third Reich includes
some breathtaking visuals, most notably Richard's Nuremberg-styled
rally, but Hollywood's familiarization of audiences with the clichés of fascist spectacle has so trivialized their meaning that the representation of
Richard as fascist seems less historical than cinematic. That, of course,
may be Loncraine's point. As Thomas Elsaesser observes of Hollywood's
stereotyping of fascist imagery, "its very inauthenticity might be its truth
as history."[3] The question of how the film *ought* to represent sociopolitical and historical processes that constitute the historical rise of Richard
III, or even the spectacle of the Nazi past, is not this chapter's concern.
Instead, its interest lies in investigating the notion that cinema itself can
play the role of historical agent by conjuring images that reproduce the
fascination of the viewing subject. The film aligns the myths, sentimentality, horror, and spectacle of fascism with the film industry itself, so that

Richard's story is as much a part of cinema as cinema is part of the Nazi past.

Loncraine credits Ian McKellen, who plays Richard III in the film and who cowrote the screenplay, with setting the play in a fascist 1930s, but Loncraine admits that he had to change nearly everything in McKellen's original screenplay. Using what he calls "the grammar of film," Loncraine approaches Shakespeare's play "from the point of view of a storyteller."[4] However, as Marjorie Garber observes, Richard's history, like all history, is a "story that the teller imposes upon the reconstructed events of the past."[5] As the story of Tudor ascendancy, Richard's history bears the marks of reconstruction, a story told to justify the current regime. Loncraine's film illuminates how twentieth-century culture reshapes the vagaries of history and reconstructs its own villains, by showing the viewer that Richard's history is deformed from the outset, whether as a reconstruction that justifies Tudor orthodoxy or one that justifies our late twentieth-century political orthodoxies.

As Loncraine claims, "We tried, and I think we've succeeded, to do something different with Shakespeare. Something that's never been done before."[6] The film's difference lies less in its fascist-era setting than in the way the camera establishes the viewers' experience of the aesthetic frame. For Loncraine not only fills the frame of Richard's story with vividly negative anecdotal similitudes to a Nazi past but suspends those images — and the temporality of Richard's story — within the timeless absence of historicity of the Hollywood gangster film. The transformation of Shakespeare's *Richard III* to a form recognizable within twentieth-century political *and* cinematic experience allows the audience to perceive Richard's history as an act of retroactive reconstruction and mythologizing similar to our cinematic reconstruction of twentieth-century criminals and tyrants. The film engages the audience through analogies to a tyrant in recent history to demonstrate how the audience participates in its culture's mythmaking. The key, according to Loncraine, is to "forget you're watching Shakespeare."[7]

"And frame my face to all occasions!"[8]

Certainly McKellen's is not the first fascist Richard. Ever since the 1930s, when the public became aware of the threat of fascism, theatrical practice transformed Richard into an unheroic Hitler-styled schemer. Even Laurence Olivier admitted that his stage performance of *Richard III* was shaped by such an awareness: "One had Hitler over the way, one was playing it definitely as a paranoiac, so there was a core of something to which the audience would immediately respond."[9] But when Olivier claimed that audiences "immediately respond" to the Hitler characterization, what did he mean? For when one scans theatrical performances of the role, it becomes clear that conceptions of Hitler changed over time — and so, consequently, did characterizations of Richard III.

In 1942 Donald Wolfit played Richard in a "blood-and-thunder" approach that accorded with current perceptions of Hitler as an old-fashioned and unself-conscious tyrant, which appealed to London audiences "bracing against nightly bomb attacks."[10] As the public's knowledge of Hitler's regime grew, however, its idea of the tyrant altered, so that by the time McKellen assumed the role on stage in a 1990 production, Hitler had become "one of us." As one reviewer said of McKellen's performance, "there is no missing the Sandhurst accent. . . . He comes stiffly across the bare, black stage in his general's uniform and talks of 'wintah' and 'myajestea' in a blend of drawl and blimpish staccato. It is one of our own."[11] The theatrical production suppressed Richard's deformity and emphasized the self-mythologizing quality of fascism. Similarly, reviewers of Loncraine's film detect in McKellen's Richard "a Sandhurst-trained man's man, well versed in the terse, fraternal idiom that gives him equal access to hired thugs like Tyrrel . . . and backroom politicians like Buckingham."[12] The recognition that McKellen's Hitler-esque Richard (figure 5.1) "is one of our own" resonates with the ironies of history, for Goebbels concluded Hitler's 1933 birthday address with a similar phrase: "We give you our hands and vow that you will ever be for us what you are today: 'Our Hitler!'"[13]

In fact, Loncraine's film's fascist context coincides with how Shakespeare scholars discuss the play, in political terms that reflect his vision, describing Richard as "the play's resident (and Tudor historiography's requisite) monster fascist."[14] But just as significant to the play's investigation of the soul of a tyrant and the darker side of human nature is the connection between audience and villain. As Morton Frisch speculates, "It is even

FIGURE 5.1. Richard III as Hitler-figure in Richard Loncraine's *Richard III*. (Courtesy of MGM/United Artists and Bayley Paré)

conceivable that the gulf which separates Richard Plantagenet from the rest of the world is not as great as might be imagined at first appearance."[15]

The problem of an audience's relationship with its historical villains has, not unexpectedly, been a hotly contested topic among Germany's traditional cultural elites, who have been distressed to find that televised American versions of German history, such as Marvin Chomsky's series *Holocaust,* generated more national reflection than German films on the subject. Attempts in German films and television drama of the 1960s to deal with the subject of Germany's fascist past had failed to awaken dormant responses to the Nazi regime, largely because the narratives seemed conceived primarily to unburden the younger generation of inherited guilt while indicting the parent generation. On the other hand, the American television series *Holocaust* concentrated on the complementarity of terror and civilized behaviors that gave German society its illusion of normalcy. That a product of popular and commercial culture awoke long dormant responses to the Third Reich suggests, as Anton Kaes wryly observes, that the German people only recognized themselves "in the mirror held up by Hollywood."[16]

The efforts of current German cinema to abandon "Papa's Kino" and its participation in what Thomas Elsaesser describes as the "binary lines and exclusionary formulations of the postwar period in politics," affords an interesting comparison between Loncraine's and Olivier's versions of *Richard III*.[17] Olivier's *Richard III* also works to prevent ruptures between the viewer and the past by visualizing Shakespeare's protagonist as legend, a manufactured thing. The film blocks the process of history by creating a rhetoric of binary oppositions that split the past from the present, thereby polarizing Richard as a monster in a bygone era. This point is confirmed in the film's opening scene, in which the viewer sees a two-dimensional drawing of a crown, beneath which appears the announcement of the film's intention — to portray a "legend." The film's frequent processionals and orderly stream of victims also suggest order and pattern in the chaos that is history, while a variety of distancing techniques separate the audience from its enjoyment of Richard's crime, including the theatrical sets that allow the audience to perceive Richard's crimes as performance, the incorporation of the exaggerated qualities of a cartoon character (the Big Bad Wolf) in Richard's portrayal that reduce the serious implications of the play, and the camera's manipulation of spatial depth, which, as Davies observes, "invariably" consigns Richard's victims "to the depth of the frame."[18] The overall effect of the film's imaginative framework is to dislocate the film from the historical burden of responsibility in its depiction of tyranny, and to distance the viewer from the past that is Richard's story.

Yet the fascist past in which Loncraine's film establishes Richard's story is every bit as much a stylized, self-invented, and replicated history as the theatrical "medievalism" that Olivier conjures. In fact, at times Loncraine's film seems to be little more than an unstable play of costumes and settings that fail to connect the viewer to any clearly realized past or to establish any real historical grounding. Loncraine's film transcodes its fascist spectacle within the seamless moment of Hollywood's reductive historicism, in which the structures of history are replaced with representations that do not represent. For despite the film's twentieth-century dressing, Loncraine presents the viewer with a fantastic and overdramatized spectacle that erases its own representation as historical present.

Loncraine's *Richard III* makes vivid the problem of representation, in which fragmentation and alienation make unintelligible historical events as recent as the rise of fascism and a Nazi past. As Erving Goffman warns, "issues which turn on events that occurred in the distant past are especially vulnerable" to the viewer's misframing; so are historical events that are charged with a "vivid negativity."[19] German historian Ernst Nolte underscores that "the vivid negativity of a historical phenomenon represents a great danger for the discipline of history. A permanent negative or positive image necessarily has the character of a myth, which is an actualized form of a legend."[20] When the past assumes powerful negative representations, it threatens to become legend. And "without doubt," Nolte adds, "the Third Reich is cut from the cloth from which legends are made."[21] The only corrective to misframing, Goffman asserts, is by reexamining the meaning of our experience, and by rupturing the distance between ourselves and the mythologized past.

Interestingly, when German historians recently debated how to physically represent the artifacts of German history in a museum, they too resisted chronological or linear models of representation.

> Around a central space, which has as its theme a historical nodal point or the explanation in depth of the selected historical problem, other rooms can be arranged, which are devoted to comparisons, flashbacks or flashforwards, the presentation of controversial points of view or the connections with non-German history. The architectonic form might be conceived of as a "serpentine," "spiral," "honeycomb" . . .[22]

The design reflects the problem of how to confront "vivid negativity" in historical representation. The model is especially intriguing in its conception of history in cinematic terms, as "flashbacks" or "flashforwards," cinematic devices that work against linear or chronological models. The visitor to this museum would experience history as subjective truth, perceived according to one's experience of the architectural design or aesthetic frame of the building itself, and disconnected from temporal constructs that link it to a German past or present.[23] However, the museum's critics note that the spatialization of German history creates ossification and distance between the observer and the objects of history. As Eric Santner laments, the Deutsches Historisches Museum may end up being a "house of mirrors, an enclosed space in which Germans may go to see themselves reflected and thereby reinstated in an imaginary plenitude and wholeness."[24]

The issue of how cinema reflects history, particularly the vivid negativity of German history, is the concern of Hans-Jürgen Syberberg's 6-hour 45-minute film *Hitler, A Film from Germany* (1977), later retitled *Our Hitler,* which announces itself from the start as *not* a historical film nor a historical construction of the Third Reich, but as history as theater. Of Syberberg's film Susan Sontag observes that "historical reality is, by definition, unrepeatable. Reality can only be grasped indirectly—seen reflected in a mirror, staged in the theatre of the mind." In an ironic insight, Syberberg's film suggests that all history is cinematic, for it is "one of the film's conceits . . . that Hitler, who never visited the front and watched the war every night through newsreels, was a kind of moviemaker. Germany, a Film by Hitler."[25] Syberberg's film makes clear that Hitlerism cannot be contained within a single thesis but, as Anton Kaes observes, is "a subject that becomes concrete and comprehensible only in the distorting mirror of others, a hollow center that is filled to the degree that we project ourselves into it."[26]

Loncraine also formulates Richard's story on the ruins of modern history, in a world that is not a model of history but a reflection of the cinematic experience that is history. As Loncraine's set designer maintains, "We were creating our own world and our own sort of history; we had the flexibility to take the reality and heighten it. . . . Obviously, we didn't slavishly stick to the 30s."[27] The time period is nebulous, the locations seem uncertain. The film's visualization of place suggests how the problem of continuity and discontinuity in history, of recurring cycles and the return of the repressed in opposition to humanity's desire for new beginnings and breaks from the past, constitute the material of Richard's story. These concerns are illustrated in the play itself, in that Richard's story is absorbed within the history of the Tudor ascension and the process of providential history that conceals contradictions. Loncraine's film also positions Richard's story at a symbolic moment of social transformation which absorbs the abnormal back into a sense of order. The film traces the process by which Richard's story moves from a period of liminality to incorporation by portraying Richard's journey to power as a literal movement of the liminal outsider through a threshold.

In the opening scene of the play Richard signals to his audience that his presentation is a mode of acting that breaks through the play's self-contained illusionist frame. In the film, that scene begins with Richard's opening address to the large formal gathering of Yorkists and moves to the viewer's claustrophobic encounter with Richard in the repulsive intimacy of the toilets, where we hear him detail his bodily deformities and planned villainies. The camera follows the movement of Richard's speech as it travels from the political and social sphere to the personalized space of his body. The camera movement works in unison with Richard's mode of direct address, moving from public space to private musings, puncturing the boundaries of outside and inside, just as in the play Richard's rhetorical asides puncture the play's dominant rhetorical style and its conventions of theatricality. The camera is central to the viewer's experience of Richard, in that the viewer enters Richard's inner space through the camera, subject to his own proportions and projections.

Richard addresses the first lines of his famous opening soliloquy to a ballroom filled with elegant aristocrats. As he speaks to the crowd through the microphone, the camera dollies forward and focuses in tight close-up upon McKellen's face, drawing closer and closer to the gnashing and yellowed teeth until the camera seems to enter into the maw of the fascist monster himself. The film then cuts from a close-up of Richard's hard mouth to a private space that he inhabits alone, where being "rudely stamped," "deformed," and "unfinished" take on specific sexual overtones when he stands before the urinal. When Richard admires his image in the mirror and descants upon his deformity, he acknowledges his audience for the first time, although there is no other reflection in the mirror than his own. Richard discovers his audience when he spies his "shadow in the sun," suggesting that the audience is necessary to the image he projects, and signals the possibility that he may reconstruct himself as a projection in terms of showing himself showing himself.

"Put on some other shape. And not be Richard"[28]

The film's stylistic indebtedness to the gangster film of the 1930s and 1940s has led film critics such as Richard Corliss to call the film "Hitler as Scarface" and "all movie."[29] In specifying the historical rise of a particular film genre (the gangster film), Corliss touches upon an intriguing aspect of this film's realization, in that its representation of history is ultimately cinematic, and enables Loncraine to achieve a blend of popular entertainment and historiographic inquiry that Shakespeare's *Richard III* also accommodates. Since viewers are largely interested in the real crimes of real criminals, Leo Braudy observes, "the crime film has constantly maintained an effort to connect in *some* way with a real and contemporary social history."[30] Arising from the same period of financial and political crisis that created fascist Europe, gangster films emphasize the historical realities of crime while celebrating the criminal protagonist. Not surprisingly, gangsters and fascist thugs bear certain similarities to one another, in that the Freicorps and Hitler's Brown Shirts were versions of the same malaise, the violence of the antisocial. Weimar Germany witnessed gangsterlike assassinations of public figures such as Walter Rathenau, Germany's brilliant foreign minister, who was murdered Chicago style (machine-gunned and hand-grenaded) in 1922.

However, as Bertolt Brecht warned, "too close a coupling of the two plots (gangster plot and nazi plot) — that is, a form in which the gangster plot is a symbolic version of the other plot — would be unbearable, not least because people would constantly be looking for the real-life model for every figure."[31] Brecht's reservations alert us that, like Richard himself, the film gangster is not contained by the specific historical moment that occasioned the criminal's rise to prominence in journalistic headlines or on the cinematic screen. On the contrary, the film gangster exists in what Eugene Roscow calls "kairotic time," those propitious moments that mark the deeper meaning of time.[32] Contemporary audiences' continuing fascination with the gangster arises, according to Roscow, not from interest in the historical moment that spawns the criminal but in the social dislocations that characterize his rise. The gangster's story, like Richard's, flourishes in the subjective space of popular fantasy. As Susan Bennett observes, Shakespeare's popularized historical theater should not be confused with historical representation, for "unlike History, the history play can perform the discourses of the past as fantasies, posing characters and events in the realm of 'what if?'"[33] McKellen echoes Bennett when he claims that in *Richard III* Shakespeare "was creating history-which-never-happened. Our production was properly in the realm of 'what might have been.'"[34]

The result of recording Richard's story with an ensemble of reality effects that satisfy Hollywood cinematic conventions of the gangster film is that the film takes the traumatic material of twentieth-century history, as inscribed within the well-established images of the Third Reich, and makes it into an old movie. The film ironically reflects upon the Third Reich's unshakable belief in the demagogic power of images and upon Propaganda Minister Goebbels's prediction that "in a hundred years' time they will be showing a fine color film of the terrible days we are living through."[35] The Nazi era, memorable to audiences in photographs of Nazi rallies, gas chambers, mass murders, is reduced to mere iconography, "a set of disposable, interchangeable, dehistoricized images that can be inserted into any historical narrative, no matter how trivial, to give it a simulated authenticity and a sense of tragic depth."[36]

The fascist spectacle is only one aspect of the multilayered cultural strands that label this film cultural fantasy. Yet even in its stylized and hybrid representation, the vivid negativity of the images associated with a Nazi past gives special prominence to the role of subjectivity in the film's historicizing. For in a story in which the tyrant's demise is certain and without suspense, Loncraine turns to familiar and formulaic scenarios and images that seduce the audience by their affect. Loncraine knows about seduction, for he has made his career in the world of television advertising for over twenty years. Loncraine admits, "I really enjoy the discipline [of advertising]. I do a lot of car ads."[37] The director's familiarity with the seductive powers of the advertising medium made his alliance with Royal Shakespeare Company actor Ian McKellen an unlikely but appropriate one for the film they were to produce together. As Loncraine recognizes, "I feel the version we came up with is absolutely the product of both of us."[38] Their union suggests a fluidity between mercantile values and cultural perspectives, imported from the world of television advertising, and the genre that is Shakespeare, enshrined as an artifact of moral and cultural instruction. Loncraine claims this melding of approaches to Shakespeare is also an aspect of his cultural and family inheritance, having descended from a family of "traveling show people. Half gypsy, half Jewish," who "had the last franchise to do Shakespeare in Regent Park's open-air theatre in the '50s."[39]

Shakespeare's *Richard III* bears witness to the shifting material conditions and social relations of a new market economy from which Richard emerges as the central figure of Shakespeare's play. As Linda Charnes observes, Shakespeare situates the figure of Richard III within the marketplace of the new relations between "literary genres devoted to moral instruction and social description" and those resonant with the new money-based economy, a "moveable, fluid activity" that invaded both the social and spatial surfaces of social interactions.[40] Loncraine situates Richard's rise to power as an effect and symptom of the materiality of the early 1930s, and emphasizes the bankruptcy of society at a palpable, material level. At the beginning of the film the song that resonates throughout the gathering of the victorious Yorkists — "Come live with me and be my love and we will some new pleasures prove" — is Christopher Marlowe's materialistic vision of love set to a melody befitting the mood of easy self-indulgence indicative of a period eager to forget the trauma of war. The smooth melody and glib sentiments of the lyrics, along with the camera's invitation to imbibe the dazzling visual spectacle of a nation embracing a period of sensual gratification after the experience of war, suggest to the viewer that Richard's world is one that dwells upon the beautiful surfaces but fails to perceive its inner deformities. Marlowe's lyrics translate naturally into the material opulence of Loncraine's set, as the queen's family arrives to join in the Yorkist victory celebration. This scene also emphasizes social anxieties that Shakespeare's contemporaries would have understood as moral ones, in that the gathering represents a blurring of boundaries in social space between mercantile interests (in the guise of American interlopers to royal prerogative and power) and aristocratic forms. The play interrogates this problem in its characterization of Queen Elizabeth's family and in its repeated references to Mistress Shore, a mere burgher's wife and the king's mistress. But it is in the character of Richard himself that the issue of boundaries becomes detrimental.

In the film's opening sequence at the Battle of Tewkesbury, the fragile forms of civilized behavior collapse when confronted with Richard's raw aggression. In the battlefield war room of the reigning king's camp, a large black dog quietly chews his bone before the fireplace, a fire roars in the hearth behind him, and the lighting creates a warm glow on the bookshelves lined with volumes on either side of the fireplace. A large pastoral painting hangs on the wall behind Prince Edward, and a grandfather clock stands beside it. However, these vestiges of civilization conveyed through the prince's leisurely meal (wine poured into crystal glasses and food artfully prepared on the plate, a picture of his wife, Anne, nearby) are suddenly shattered when Richard's tank abruptly and violently penetrates the wall of the prince's headquarters, emerging with its gun erect and pointed at the audience from the space directly behind the fireplace (figure 5.2). The entrance effectively destroys any sense of civilized engagement with war, for, as the film makes vivid, Richard threatens to overrun all boundaries. The succession of events that follow rapidly upon this dramatic entrance underscores Richard's challenge to civilized codes: the murder of the prince, with a brief cut to his blood splattering on the painting behind him, and the non-diegetic execution of an old, white-haired king at his prayers, registered in the loud crack of gunfire as Richard's name appears on screen in large red letters. Only then does Richard remove his gas mask and reveal the man behind the monster.

As the film's opening sequence makes clear, Richard's monstrosity is political, not providential. The film does not stigmatize Richard's bodily deformities as God's mark upon the sinful any more than it suggests that the murder of innocent babes is an act of divine retribution. In the film's

FIGURE 5.2. Richard's tank in the film's opening sequence. (Courtesy of MGM/United Artists and Bayley Paré)

twentieth-century context, audiences reject the rationalization that attributes physical abnormalities or the sufferings of innocent people as a sign of God's justice. Hence the erasure of the play's ghosts who appear to judge Richard in his dreams in Act V, and to applaud Richmond in his. No divine judgment or supernatural explanation can justify the tyrant's rise to power, any more than Tudor moralizing could sufficiently explain the slaying of the princes in the Tower.

Although film critics decry the film's "swanky costumes and decor" for creating "more distractions than revelations," style and costume are important elements of Loncraine's portrayal of Richard III.[41] Loncraine presents a Richard who, in the context of his world, is its best dresser and smoothest talker. The film presents the elegance of dress as its central symbol of the surfaces that hide the body and give the illusion of wholeness, just as Richard's deformed arm is always plunged deep into the front pocket of his pants, an erotically suggestive gesture that gives his body an uneven swagger of masculine bravado. In this film Richard's physical abnormalities are well disguised by the civilized veneer of his elegant dress and only noticeable when he calls attention to them in abrupt and perverse ways, such as when he singles out Hastings for a bloody example to others who may block his path of power. When Richard gestures obscenely at Hastings with his deformed arm, and smacks him across the back of the head with it, we see how he employs his deformity as hidden weapon against the truth. Richard uses his deformity in a number of ways, as erotic object, as weapon, and as instrument of obscenity. In the superficialities of the world of the film, his deformity is his mode of dress, an outward sign that tells us little of the inner man but much about the people and society he controls with it, through his manipulation of the signs of what the body means.

Richard assumes various roles as if he were assuming another mode of dress, his performity itself like another sort of clothing, which McKellen emphasizes in Richard's rise to power as projections of an image, much as Hitler's public appearances were contained within a cultural frame that was highly theatrical and cinematic. As German historians point out, "Hitler, in reality a master of the art of the theatrical, was profiled [by Goebbels] as a man 'whom it was impossible to imagine posing.'"[42] Historians agree that the "Hitler myth" was consciously devised as an integrating force by a regime acutely aware of the need to manufacture consensus, in pursuit of which the German cinema was an important tool. Hitler's descent from the clouds in his propaganda film *Triumph of the Will* reveals how self-dramatization was a crucial element in his control of the state, much as Loncraine's film depicts Richard watching a film of his own coronation as he mandates the deaths of the princes. Sitting in the dark projection room, Richard watches his black-and-white image assume the robes of royal power again and again, tirelessly performing his ascent to the throne on the cinematic screen. The film record of the coronation represents the past as a projection of the image Richard wishes to appear, even as Riefenstahl's documentaries projected Hitler and his war in images Hitler wished to appear, blurring the boundaries between Richard's past and the myth he becomes, enabling him to deceive the audience through seductive similarities.

Deformity can also be performative in *Richard III* in that Richard's deformity becomes projected upon others. As the play reveals, Richard's image escapes its own borders to contaminate the viewer's perspective of others, as when Richard accuses Queen Elizabeth of witchcraft or blames the tardy cripple for failing to deliver Clarence's pardon on time to forestall his execution. In Loncraine's film, not only does the audience become a projection of Richard's self, but Richard's perversity finally infects an entire nation, in which the condition of deformity is transferred to the diseased polity itself:

> The noble isle doth want her proper limbs;
> Her face defaced with scars of infamy,
> Her royal stock graft with ignoble plants,
> And almost shouldered in the swallowing gulf
> Of dark forgetfulness and deep oblivion.
>
> (III.vii.125-29)

A striking instance in which the film reworks the other characters' relations to Richard is in the death of Rivers (Robert Downey, Jr.). Decidedly unlike his offstage death in the play, Rivers's eroticized death in Loncraine's film is a completely fabricated scene. Rivers's right arm is tied to the bed as he passively enjoys erotic pleasures in non-diegetic space, while the camera remains focused upon his face and naked torso. Rivers shares similarities with Richard at this moment, in that the outward sign of Richard's erotic proclivities—his useless arm—is replicated in Rivers's representation, and reminds the viewer, at least subliminally, of Richard's deformity.[43] When he suddenly registers a startled cry, the viewer is almost as shocked as Rivers to discover that he cries out not from pleasure but from the deadly thrust of the bayonet that protrudes from his belly.

Rivers's death is confusing in that it seems to be caused by a mysterious internal source. It is unlikely that Richard or his henchman is lying beneath the bed awaiting this particular moment to murder him, though we know that Richard and Buckingham are later credited with the murder. The scene is more symbolic than realistic, for it perpetuates the myth of Richard's murderous aggression in a way that replicates the viewer's experience in the opening moments of the film, in which Richard's unruly masculinity bursts through the walls of Prince Edward's headquarters. The method of Rivers's destruction in some ways resembles a perverse birth, of which Richard is the play's outstanding example (born too late and too soon). In the visual logic of the film, death and birth are the same sign, a blurring of boundaries that Richard understands when he proposes an incestuous marriage to his niece. He tells her mother, Queen Elizabeth, whose sons he has also killed, "If I have killed the issue of your womb, / To quicken your increase, I will beget / Mine issue of your blood upon your daughter" (IV.iv.296–98). In Richard's logic, the womb is source of both life and death.

Projecting his own deformities upon others is essential to Richard's strategy for acquiring power through the scapegoating of others. In terms of the play, Richard is most successful in scapegoating women, invoking the differences of gender to cloak his own physical (and moral) difference from other men.[44] This becomes quite clear in the scene in which he condemns Hastings to death when he refuses to join with Richard and the other men in blaming Queen Elizabeth for Richard's physical deformity, for Richard, like the women he excoriates, is aware of what bodies can be made to mean. Tellingly, Phyllis Rackin comments that "the power that Richard takes from women is not only the power to curse and seduce; it is also the power to transcend the frame of historical representation."[45]

Richard's infamous wooing of Anne also poses the question of blame and responsibility, when Richard asks her who is "the causer of the timeless deaths / Of these Plantagenets, Henry and Edward, / As blameful as the executioner?" (I.ii.117–19). The scene represents an act of scapegoating that reminds us of the play's earlier account of the circumstances surrounding Clarence's murder, which, as Michael Mooney points out, "is in an important sense symbolic of the moral state of England, a land in which everyone wishes to be 'guiltless.'"[46] Loncraine underscores how the nation actively flees from responsibility in Clarence's death in a stunning visual moment at the sun drenched seashore. When Richard breaks the news of Clarence's execution, King Edward is so overwhelmed that he collapses. Although Richard blames the death on a tardy cripple who delivered the pardon too late, the film reveals how the group staves off guilt. Looking diminished and insignificant, together they scurry toward the exotic and massive edifice of Brighton Pavilion that looms ahead, the low-angle shot capturing their desperate flight toward a symbol of their material opulence and away from their moral culpability. It is an image that shares elements of the fantastic one associates with Dorothy's flight with her entourage to the gates of the Emerald City, to an impossible illusion of wholeness and escape from the dangers behind them.

If a fantasy of wholeness and plentitude is the landscape toward which they flee, Richard's encounter with Anne in the morgue makes explicit how Richard stands as a distorting mirror of their putative lack. The film sets Anne's capitulation in a morgue, a scene imbued with the ghostly quality of a nether world as light filters through the basement windows behind her (figure 5.3). When Richard descends the stairs to this grisly underworld, the numbers of bleeding bodies and corpses that strew the halls emphasize that his crimes extend well beyond the murder of one man. Consequently, Anne's position as mourner becomes less exclusive, more representative, when she walks past the multitudes who claim the bodies of their loved ones. Her yielding therefore seems less singular, less the weak capitulation of an inexperienced and frightened young woman than the commingling of fascination and revulsion. The setting implies that Anne cannot condemn Richard without blaming herself. For although she excoriates Richard for "infecting" her eyes, Richard ruptures the boundaries between guilt and innocence by proving Anne a murderer: "Thou wast the cause and most accurst effect" (I.ii.123).

Even as the film reveals how Anne's capitulation is an evasion or even an erasure of critical thought by her acceptance of Richard's distorted representation of events, the film's depthless, historical grounding in some imaginary fascist England, and in the dehistoricized style of the Hollywood gangster film, similarly "infects" the viewer's perspective of the complexities of history. In this regard, Richard's story replicates the pattern of myth as the intertwining of history and fiction as a way out of responsibility, "as though one could be indemnified by regret for once-upon-a-time acts of struggle in phrases such as 'the end of an era.'"[47] And although at the end of Loncraine's film we witness Richard's defeat, the viewer's experience of Richard's death keeps his story open and unre-

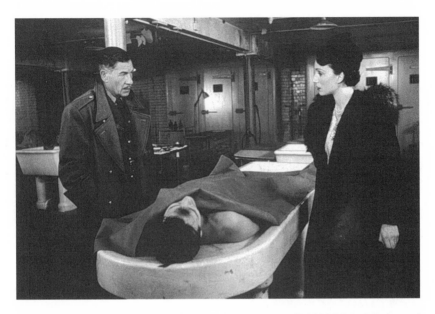

FIGURE 5.3. Richard and Anne in the morgue. (Courtesy of MGM/United Artists and Bayley Paré)

solved. Loncraine's camera opens the surrounding context by underscoring the contradictions that propelled Richard to become king, and reveals the film's distrust of narrative closure. Loncraine, indeed, may agree with the young prince who declares "Methinks the truth should live from age to age, / As 'twere retailed to all posterity" (III.i.76–77).

The final scene of the film is staged as a version of the siege of Berlin, as Richard attempts to flee the burning and bombed out city (figure 5.4). Pursued by Richmond, Richard grasps whatever weaponry lies in his way and indiscriminately fires upon friend and foe. At one point he seizes upon an enormous gun and holds it erect as he fires off volley after volley in an image almost comically suggestive of critical assessments that Richard's masculine aggression as "perpetually engaged in erecting himself."[48] Yet for all these monumental images, Richard is a figure greatly diminished at the end of this film, almost grotesquely so. When his jeep becomes stuck, McKellen weakly moans "My kingdom for a horse," and shoots the driver who urges him to safety through the head. With Richmond in hot pursuit, Richard finds himself trapped upon the outermost reaches of metal

FIGURE 5.4. Richard at the Battle of Bosworth. (Courtesy of MGM/United Artists and Bayley Paré)

scaffolding atop a ravaged building, when he turns and faces Richmond and extends him his arm. Yet almost in the same gesture, Richard flings himself backwards into the flaming depths below, a mesmerizing final glimpse of the man who went laughing to hell.

Richard's fantastic end is the film's most conspicuous homage to the gangster film genre, specifically Jimmy Cagney's fiery end in *White Heat* (1949).[49] Just as Cagney's unrepentant Cody Jarett triumphantly shouts "Made it, Ma! Top of the world!" amidst an apocalyptic explosion of chemical tanks, McKellen's Richard gleefully plunges to his fiery end to the tune of "I'm sitting on top of the world."[50] In evoking Cagney's now-famous ending from the gangster film genre, Loncraine underscores the moralizing impulses evident in Shakespeare's play, in which Richard's story fulfills the pattern of a cautionary tale. Richard, like the gangster, climbs the ladder of success only to plunge (literally) from great heights back to his place of origin, his descent into a flaming abyss an appropriate (symbolic) end for a man dominated by what Ian Moulton calls a "surfeit of masculine heat."[51] Yet the moralizing impulse of Richard's fiery end strains hard against the tendency of film audiences to identify with the criminal who lives out the dark side of our dreams of power, wealth, and ambition. As Bob Sklar observes, Depression-era audiences "identified with the movie gangsters, despite printed prologues in *Scarface* and *The Public Enemy* reminding viewers of how evil the characters were."[52] McKellen's portrayal of Richard carries with it a similar double view of the film's central figure, in that viewers both identify with and morally disdain the murderous villain whose violence fuels the action of the film. In consciously invoking past cinematic forms that recall the histories of bizarre and dangerous men, Loncraine involves the viewer in a complex awareness of how our own dreams contribute to the imaginative landscape in which Richard rises and falls. If Cagney's character's end, as one critic suggests, presents an "unsettling metaphor of the derangement of our nuclear age," in which the demise of a remorseless, psychotic killer with grandiose dreams reveals similarities with the madness of our modern age, then perhaps in Richard's end we witness the failure of the late twentieth century to liberate itself from a complex, contradictory, and fascinating mythology that indemnifies a culture from the pain of recognition.[53]

Richard's end leaves the viewer asking, like the Scrivener, "Who is so gross / That cannot see this palpable device? / Yet who's so bold but says he sees it not?" (III.vi.10-12). For if Shakespeare writes history backwards, Loncraine projects Richard's end as our future. That future, of course, lies in the sudden awareness and startling directness of Richmond's expression as it now addresses the camera that had been dominated by Richard. The viewer's fascination with Richard as a figure both intimate and external, both inside and outside, is transferred at this moment to Richmond. The film cuts the long epilogue that gives the play its illusion of closure, leaving the viewer to ponder the meaning behind Richmond's expression and its implication for an historical narrative that seems incapable of advancing "politically into a new terrain."[54] The final shot resists the polarizations that divide the past and the future by implicating the viewer when Richmond turns and addresses the camera with a look that punctures the boundaries of inside and outside. The viewer experiences not simply the unreality of

Richard's end but also a disruptive face-to-face interaction with Richmond, an experience of the interpenetration of frames that is what Goffman calls the "manufacture of negative experience."[55] Jarred from a protective psychological distance when Richmond squarely faces the camera, the viewer, at least momentarily, grasps the connection between the circumstances of Richard's story and his own ambiguous context as viewing subject.

In his demonic laughter Richard also breaches the psychological distance between the audience and himself, in that in his fantastic end, recorded by the camera as a long distance shot into an inferno, he bursts the boundaries of realistic representation. When the viewer discovers inherent weaknesses in the framing process, as in Richard's laughter or in Richmond's enigmatic smile, it follows that the viewer's sense of what is going on will also be found vulnerable.[56] Richard's laughter, like Richmond's look, denies the viewer's need to exclude and totalize, in that it forces the viewer retrospectively to reassess the continuity of the present with the past.

Leah Marcus observes that "our recovery of the past is always interpretation and self-interpretation."[57] In the mirror held up by Hollywood we begin to understand our relationship to our monsters, but only when the materials of the film's imaginary style and "past" break down. The logic of the cinematic form itself liberates the viewer from an interpretative closure that brackets the past from the present. "Only by facing the past," writes German historian Richard Leicht, "can we be free. We are our own past."[58] Loncraine's film gives us a view into the experience of that past, not as a realistic record of life in fascist Europe in the 1930s, but as the cinematic experience of history. Richard's story is a projection of that which the civilized world demonizes as monstrous and perverse, in that what the viewer sees is not the image itself but what exists in the "space between image and viewer, a meeting point of desire, meaning, and interpretation."[59]

Chapter Six

Utopian Revisioning of Falstaff's Tavern World

Orson Welles's
Chimes at Midnight and
Gus Van Sant's
My Own Private Idaho

Gus Van Sant's 1991 film *My Own Private Idaho* is a "popular" reworking of the story of Shakespeare's Prince Hal, and, as critics have noted, an homage to Orson Welles's 1966 film *Chimes at Midnight*. Van Sant's conception of the Shakespeare sequences in his film is largely indebted to Welles's film, particularly the early scenes in the Boar's Head Tavern, in which we are introduced to Hal and Falstaff, and the scene that comprises the Gadshill robbery (which Anthony Davies argues is visually an extension of the tavern world in Welles's film).[1] The so-called tavern scenes in *My Own Private Idaho* are nearly frame-for-frame imitations of those in Welles's earlier film. Yet Van Sant savagely degrades the tavern world revealed in *Chimes at Midnight,* and situates it within the contemporary urban squalor of Portland's and Seattle's homeless street hustlers. Such a metamorphosis is licensed within the *Henriad* itself when Poins bids Hal "put on two leathern jerkins and aprons, and wait upon him [Falstaff] at his table as drawers." Hal describes his transformation as that "from a God to a bull? A heavy declension! It was Jove's case. From a prince to a prentice? A low transformation! That shall be mine, for in everything the purpose must weigh with the folly"(*2 Henry IV,* II.ii.165–

168). Hal's purpose—to expose Falstaff—justifies the "low transformation," much as Van Sant's reframing effectively subverts and exposes the
nostalgia established in Welles's film for "Merrie England" and the world
of Falstaff's tavern.

In part, the success of Van Sant's *My Own Private Idaho* as a "popular"
film informs our perception of the film as a "low transformation." The
film's modernized language, in which all traces of poetry or elevated language are omitted and substituted with vulgar and colloquial language
(Keanu Reeves's "Valley-speak," for example), achieves an anti-intellectual
and therefore "popular" tone that works against the perceived elitism commercial culture associates with objects of "high culture," such as Shakespeare's drama and the auteur cinema of Orson Welles. The stars of the
film, Keanu Reeves and River Phoenix, guaranteed a certain marketability
with mass audiences at the theaters and video stores, many of whom pre-
sumably remain unaware of its relationship to either Shakespeare's play or
Welles's film despite Van Sant's conscious use of both. Recasting Shakespeare's play and Welles's celebrated tavern scenes within the seedy tene-
ments and urban landscapes of Portland and Seattle, emphasizing
homosexuality merely implicit in the play's "male bonding," and translating the taking of purses as the peddling of sexual favors complete the
"heavy declension" of Falstaff's tavern world in modern drag. However,
even Van Sant's "low transformation" of Shakespeare's play met with opposition from film distributors, not because his tavern scenes were unsavory
degradations of Shakespeare's play but because they yet retained some vestiges of "high" culture that might make the film unsalable. In an interview
Van Sant lamented that the film was subject to the control of the movie system with its emphasis upon commodity production: "There was a whole
contingent of people at New Line—the domestic distributors—who were
totally against the Shakespeare scenes and wanted us to cut them all out."[2]
The distributors feared that the Shakespeare scenes—even "degraded" as
they are in Van Sant's film—would be "unpopular" and therefore unmar-
ketable, a conclusion that seems reasonable when one considers Welles's
Chimes at Midnight.

Welles's film never received any attention from popular audiences,
and only meager and not entirely favorable attention from film critics at

the time of its distribution. Lacking financing from the Hollywood studios, Welles pieced together the fabric of his film with a limited budget and under a constrained shooting schedule. His failure to achieve institutional validation within the Hollywood movie system perhaps affected the success of *Chimes at Midnight* with popular audiences, for the film lacked the substantial powers of Hollywood to market and distribute it. Certainly financial and budgetary concerns affected how Welles shot his film, and perhaps the final quality of the film. There are critics such as Michael Anderegg who argue that the poor audio quality of *Chimes at Midnight* was intentionally engineered and is an indication of Welles's art—his mumbled speech serving to emphasize the linguistic deflation apparent in Falstaff's lines.[3] However, one cannot ignore the dire effect of budget problems on the shooting of the film. Having shot an entire reel with actors whom he could not afford to pay to return for another shooting, Welles discovered that a technical blunder had ruined much of the work he had done, so that "the entire first reel had come back from the lab slightly out of sync."[4] To what extent Welles was forced to work with those initial blunders is unclear. However, the result, whether intentional or not, furthered the public's perception of Welles as an artist who exhibited a reactive resistance to the commodification of his art, developing in his film what Fredric Jameson calls "an aesthetic language incapable of offering commodity satisfaction."[5]

Jean Renoir believed that Welles's failure at the box office stemmed directly from his "aristocratic" tendencies as a filmmaker. Commenting on the connection between "popular" film and its audience (which Renoir defines as working class and, in America, middle class), Renoir declared that "Orson Welles is one of a handful of aristocrats. And his films are aristocratic works. It is probably for that reason that they often are not financially successful."[6] And so it was with *Chimes at Midnight,* since an audience ignorant of Shakespeare's *Henriad* has difficulty following the film. The sophisticated demands that Welles's *Chimes at Midnight* makes upon the viewing audience may, in fact, account for its neglect by mass audiences. Welles nevertheless attempted to work within the Hollywood studio system for years and even wrote a script of *Henry IV* in an American context for the Hungarian producer Alex Korda.[7] The project never materialized, and perhaps never could; Welles was notoriously unskilled in dealing with the movie studios and distributors. Ironically, *Henry IV* in an American context—perhaps not quite as Welles envisioned it—would become the project of a man who, although decidedly antiestablishment in sentiment and subject, could work within the movie system to produce and distribute a film greatly indebted to Welles's *Chimes at Midnight*.

However, according to Jameson, the marketing of a film to a mass audience does not make it a "popular" film. Under the current circumstances of film production, so Jameson argues, popular culture and thereby the popular film (as understood in terms of looking back toward historical origins, folk art, and festivity) simply do not exist. Jameson suggests that our definitions of what constitutes "high" and "low" culture need scrutiny, and he contests the binary system that renders mass culture as "popular and thus more authentic than high culture" and high culture as "autonomous and, therefore, utterly incomparable to a degraded mass culture."[8] Instead, Jameson suggests that "we read high and mass culture as objectively related and dialectically interdependent phenomena, as twin and inseparable forms of the fission of aesthetic production under capitalism."[9] The achievement of Van Sant's film is its interpenetration of high and low culture, in which Shakespeare's play and Welles's film cannot be regarded as the "fixed point or eternal standard against which to measure the 'degraded' status of mass culture."[10] Although Van Sant intentionally and obviously degrades the tavern scenes from *Chimes at Midnight,* his point is not to emphasize his own film's degraded status as a "popular" film. On the contrary, by writing Shakespeare's play into the center of his script, and by imitating Welles's celebrated tavern scenes, Van Sant breaks down the binary opposition between high and low culture to reveal the vitality of the Shakespearean text given an American context. Mass audiences, unaware that the play was structured on the story of Shakespeare's Prince Hal, did not stigmatize the film as an object of high or hermetic culture (there is no mention on the video cover that Van Sant's film bears any relation to Shakespeare's *Henriad* or Welles's film). *Chimes at Midnight,* called "inaccessible" to mass audiences, even modernist in its reactive stance to its own commodification, in Van Sant's "low transformation" reaches a mass audience hitherto unknown.[11] Van Sant, rather than problematizing the relationship between art and commodity production, grasps the connection between them, and uses the historical and aesthetic material of Shakespeare's play and Welles's film to explore the aesthetic possibilities that lie at the convergence of mass culture and art.[12]

Van Sant signals his interest in the commodification of art in the scene that begins the "tavern" sequence in *My Own Private Idaho.* As I stated earlier, this scene reframes the tavern scene in Welles's *Chimes at Midnight.* In Welles's film the tavern scene immediately follows Hotspur's wish that Hal be "poisoned with a pot of ale" (*1 Henry IV,* I.iii.232). On that cue Welles introduces Prince Hal with a close-up of his face (figure 6.1), which is partially obscured by the rounded bottom of the pot of ale from which he drinks, visually heralding the repetition of rounded forms—casks of ale, the roof of the tavern, and Falstaff's own rotund figure. This shot emphasizes what Anthony Davies calls the "muted subtlety of the relationship of character to spatial context" in *Chimes at Midnight,* in which characters are realized in the dynamic between things and characterized space.[13] In this

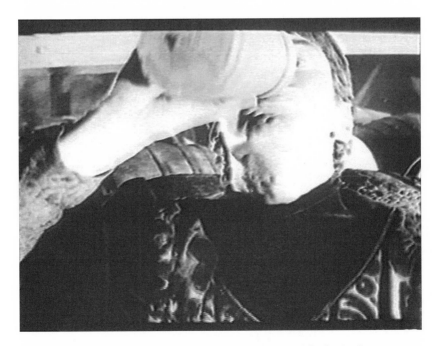

FIGURE 6.1. Hal drinking a pot of ale in Welles's *Chimes at Midnight.* (Videotape copyright permission of Aruthur Cantor Film Collection, New York)

shot Prince Hal (Keith Baxter) visually announces his intimate connection with the rounded and maternal forms within the tavern—the rounded shape of the casks behind him and the bottom of the pot of ale before him—and prepares us for his intimate acquaintance with Falstaff himself, whom the prince immediately begins to seek after he takes his gulp of ale.

In contrast, a similar shot from the tavern sequence in *My Own Private Idaho* signals Van Sant's intention to demonstrate new spatial relationships between his Prince Hal, played by Keanu Reeves, and Falstaff's tavern. Although clearly derived from the scene just described in *Chimes at Midnight* (figure 6.1), this Hal drinks his ale or beer with a difference (figure 6.2). Here the Prince Hal figure (called "Scott Favor" in the film) appears in a striking profile, John Barrymore-like, signaling the film as a Hollywood star-vehicle, as he takes a swig from a bottle of "Falstaff" beer. Hal's relationship to this Falstaff is that of a consumer of the commodities of capitalist production, signaling the degradation of the appeal of Falstaff to

FIGURE 6.2. Scott Favor drinking "Falstaff" beer in Van Sant's *My Own Private Idaho*. (Courtesy of New Line Cinema)

an item of mass-produced merchandise. In this one shot we see simultaneously the commodification of the Hollywood star as vehicle for the film and of the reduction of Falstaff from the mythic figure of Welles's film to a mere by-product of mass culture. The composition of the shot also signals a change in the character's relationship to the space and forms around him. Just as Van Sant has reshaped the relationship between Falstaff and Hal to that of lovers, so too the shape of the bottle in Keanu Reeves's hand is decidedly phallic compared to the rounded shape of the bottom of the pot of ale held by Keith Baxter in Welles's film.

The differences in the way the camera frames the two Hals also signals a change in the direction of the story. When Welles's camera introduces us to Hal in *Chimes at Midnight,* the viewer's first sight of the prince is obscured by the rounded bottom of the pot of ale, announcing that this film's interest lies with Falstaff and not the prince. Although Shakespeare's Hal may promise to "imitate the sun, / Who doth permit the base contagious clouds / To smother up his beauty from the world" (*1 Henry IV,* I.ii.191–93), Welles's Hal never fulfills that promise. *Chimes at Midnight* mourns the loss of Falstaff and does not celebrate Hal's transformation. In contrast, in Van Sant's version, Hal/Scott is never obscured by the presence of the Falstaff-character. Reeves's profile is clearly visible in this shot, and the film never compromises that vision with the competing attractiveness or visibility of Falstaff. In *My Own Private Idaho* the Falstaff character is every bit King Henry IV's parodied nightmare of a "villainous abominable misleader of youth" (*1 Henry IV,* II.iv.457), without the compensating wit and charm that distinguishes Welles's performance. Van Sant specifies this Falstaff's unattractiveness as well as his universality. The film captures Falstaff's dark side; he is an angry and degenerate man, who is every bit as manipulative and predatory as the politicians he eschews. However, the name Van Sant gives him in the film, "Bob Pigeon," suggests more vulnerable aspects of his character, including his dirty, urban origins and commonality. When the police invade the dilapidated h·.el that serves as Falstaff's tavern, they comment on the stench of the place, and question whether they should just grab another fat man from under the bridge instead of looking for this particular one. In this American context Falstaff becomes another commodity, one that is easily disposed of or replaced. The jokes about Falstaff's waist/waste take on new significance — Falstaff's overabundance of flesh implying not the dangerous wastes frequented by vagabonds and highwaymen in Shakespeare's day, nor the scatological humor of the chamber pot emphasized in Welles's film, but suggesting instead the economically and erotically marginalized in a disposable culture. In Van Sant's film the world of Falstaff's tavern retains its ability to stir our anxieties, concerns, and deepest fantasies of social life, revealing that the inhabitants of the wastes of Shakespeare's culture have become the wastes of our own.

The "aristocrat" in Welles espoused the values of "high culture" and repudiated the values of the marketplace. His response as an artist was the reactive protest of the isolated artist against a system that reduces art to formula and repetition. This attitude is reflected in Welles's conception of Falstaff and his tavern, in which historical and socioeconomic realities are all but eliminated, and replaced with psychological and sexual issues. As Welles indicates, his conception of the film was that of a psychological "triangle: the prince, his king-father, and Falstaff, who's a kind of foster father. Essentially the film is the story of that triangle."[14] Political, historical, and socioeconomic realities, such as those conveyed through the concerns of common men in Shakespeare's *1 Henry IV* — who complain about their ailments and the fleas that plague them in the inn, and who cease to smile when the price of oats rises (II.i.1-31) — are supplanted by the emotional and psychological triangle of the son and fathers. Welles saw Falstaff as an embodiment of "that lost Maytime" and dismisses the unsavory and compromised characteristics of Falstaff and his tavern world: "All the roguery and the tavern wit and the liar and bluff is simply a turn of his — it's a little song he sings for his supper. It isn't really what he's about."[15]

For Welles the myth of the tavern was an image of recuperated utopian fantasy rather than historical reality: "I'm interested really in the myth of the past, *as* a myth [and not as history]."[16] *Chimes at Midnight* conveys what Jack Jorgens has called a "muted pastness," and Anthony Davies points out the expressionistic emphasis given to the tavern scenes, which are "enlarged beyond probability, in much the same way that a childhood haunt is enlarged in one's memory."[17] Such observations naturally have led to speculations regarding Welles's personal history and the creation of this film. Barbara Leaming suggests that in casting his daughter Beatrice (who looks amazingly like the young Orson Welles) as the page who earnestly mourns the passing of Falstaff at the end of the film, Welles recreates the moment of his own father's passing, a man who succumbed to "heavy drinking, coupled with gambling, opium smoking, and whoring" which "considerably impaired his physical and mental health."[18] Certainly the notorious Dick Welles had certain Falstaff-like elements about him; Welles describes his father as a "great wit and great raconteur."[19] Leaming reports that Dick Welles had been "living in a defunct hotel he had bought in rural Grand Detour, Illinois," cultivating "the friendship of an assortment of dubious vaudevillians whom he'd liberally invited to stay with him."[20] Leaming speculates that the triangular relationship in *Chimes at Midnight* replicates the one in Welles's own life between himself, his father, and headmaster Roger Hill (with whom Welles wrote four textbooks on Shakespeare); however, Jack Jorgens sees in Welles's elegiac portrayal of Falstaff's world a lament for Welles's own frustrated and failed career. It is the richness of the film's presentation that it collapses together lost relationships and present sorrows in a utopian fantasy of recuperation. Welles had said, "Even if the good old days never existed, the fact that we can *conceive* of such a world is, in fact, an affirmation of the human spirit."[21] Welles finds his utopian past by creating it: "you must find a new period, you must invent your own England, your own epoch."[22] Yet history does finally intrude into Falstaff's tavern world in *Chimes at Midnight*. Although Welles creates his utopian past in his vision of Falstaff's tavern, he is painfully aware that that world is rejected and lost: "Almost all serious stories in the world are stories of a failure with a death in it. . . . But there is more lost paradise in them than defeat. To me that's the central theme in Western culture: the lost paradise."[23] Welles ends his film with the newly crowned Henry V rejecting the old man and their past relationship as a dream from which he has been awakened. In the final scene, Welles's camera records Falstaff's enormous coffin outside the tavern walls, the tavern now sadly emptied of its carnivalesque energy. Welles's elegiac portrayal of Falstaff's death contrasts sharply with the irreverent, ambivalent, and sometimes violent carnivalesque laughter of the "mourners" at the funeral of Van Sant's Falstaff/

Bob Pigeon, who mark the passing of their companion by beating their fists against his coffin, alternating laughter with tears, and mocking the solemnity of death with a raucous display of pan-sexual pleasure on the coffin itself.

My Own Private Idaho explores the space of Welles's resistance to historical and socioeconomic forces and draws on the audience's awareness of socioeconomic realities in degrading the utopian fantasy of Falstaff's tavern world. In signs and images familiar to consumer society, Van Sant relentlessly exposes the sentimentality and nostalgia in Welles's tavern scenes, and belies any hope of utopian recuperation within his revisioned urban context. The gritty realism of *My Own Private Idaho* emphasizes the gulf between rich and poor that divides the world of Portland's urban hustlers and the privileged suburbs. It works to demystify the ideological function of Falstaff's tavern world in Welles's film, in which Welles looks back to the precapitalist society of the past and the "family" that constitutes Falstaff's tavern community. Van Sant exposes the ideological content in Welles's film and betrays its roots; in doing so he is able to disengage his own art from the myth of the family. The reconstituted "family" in *My Own Private Idaho* inhabits a ruined hotel, the terms of its survival and destruction predicated on drugs, sex, and violence. Van Sant's film constitutes what Fredric Jameson describes as a "degraded Utopian content of the family paradigm," which "ultimately unmasks itself as the survival of more archaic forms of repression and sexism and violence."[24]

Van Sant's revisioning of Falstaff's tavern world is critical of Welles's fantasy of utopian recuperation, but his approach is not dystopic.[25] Satiric or parodic revisionings do not necessarily dismantle the utopian project. Utopian revisioning is always a critical process because it repudiates conventional views of utopia, particularly as formulated in the models of its predecessors. Similarly, Van Sant's critique of the ideological content in Welles's film does not preclude *My Own Private Idaho*'s own assertion of an oppositional ideology of the oppressed. Whereas the nostalgia in *Chimes at Midnight* for a preindustrial past may appear unremittingly conservative, Van Sant's utopian revisioning looks toward the future and takes the form of a degraded and democratic carnival. Jameson argues that the oppositional ideological perspective "is in its very nature Utopian," and, indeed, Van Sant's revisioning of Falstaff's tavern world as social transformation is ultimately just as unstable and ambiguous as Welles's conservative and nostalgic representation.[26]

Ironically, Van Sant "degrades" Welles's tavern scenes to assert his connection with the Shakespearean text. *My Own Private Idaho* suggests Shakespeare's own technique of presenting his plays as destabilized and degraded history. On the Elizabethan stage the *Henriad* as play text was subject to frequent alteration in performance, and would have been acted in various locales with various actors in various ways and for different audiences. The sense of social degeneration and disintegration in Van Sant's film is not incompatible with how contemporaries viewed Shakespeare's theater: "a disreputable place where common players draped in the discarded clothes of aristocrats impersonated their betters for the entertainment (and the pennies) of a disorderly, socially heterogeneous audience."[27] Van Sant's film degrades the "superior" auteur cinema of Orson Welles by parodying it; the transformation is ultimately destabilizing, leading viewers to question their nostalgia for the past represented in *Chimes at Midnight*. So, too, the audiences of Shakespeare's history plays, Phyllis Rackin argues, were cast in the role of historians, "viewing the events from a variety of perspectives, struggling to make sense of conflicting reports and evidence, and uncomfortably reminded of the anachronistic distance that separated them from the objects of their nostalgic yearning."[28]

Van Sant captures a similar spirit by revisioning Welles's celebrated tavern scenes, an act of utopian anarchism every bit as uncompromising as Falstaff's demands for freedom without limit. Van Sant stated, "I tried to forget the Welles film because I didn't want to be plagiaristic or stylistically influenced by it, even though it had given me the idea. So I referred to the original Shakespeare."[29] Ironically, what Van Sant discovered in "the original Shakespeare" was the irresistible energy and infinite possibility of popular drama. The power of Shakespeare's play as it is revisioned in *My Own Private Idaho* resides in its connection to popular drama — the clowning and the parodic — in re-creating "the delight of a world re-made in the image of fantasy."[30]

Van Sant's delight in the parodic becomes apparent if we compare the relevant scenes that imitate those in Welles's film's Boar's Head Tavern (figures 6.1–6.12). Keanu Reeves bears an uncanny resemblance to Keith Baxter, the Hal of Welles's film, but his performance, unlike Baxter's, emphasizes artificiality, his Valley-speak suggesting a false eloquence and his wooden performance underscoring his superficiality. Welles understood Hal as "a complicated young man with a curious, rather spooky internal coldness,"[31] but in Reeves's portrayal we see only the emptiness of his character, pursuing the life of a street hustler merely to bide his time before he inherits his fortune. The film heralds the arrival of the Falstaff character, Bob, with the sound of Renaissance music similar to the leitmotif used to introduce Falstaff in the tavern scenes in *Chimes at Midnight*. Van Sant's film music in this scene directly engages the nostalgic function of Welles's film music by parodying its utopian properties.[32] Van Sant's camera reveals in a long shot two tiny figures, "Falstaff"/Bob and "Shallow," as they stride across a flat and barren lot, surrounded by the spiraling overhead bands of interstate highway that cross through the urban landscape. The flat and barren wastes visually correspond to the wintery and barren terrain that characterizes the audience's introduction to Falstaff and Justice Shallow in *Chimes at Midnight*. As Van Sant's camera pans the bleak urban terrain inhabited by this Bob/Falstaff and his "tavern" companions, he alerts us to historical and ideological conditions that subvert the nostalgia generated by the film music.

In the dilapidated hotel that parodies Falstaff's tavern Van Sant imitates Welles's tracking shot of Hal's progress up the stairs (figures 6.3 and 6.4), winding his way through the narrow passages to discover Falstaff "snoring like a horse" in bed. In both films Hal greets the awakened Falstaff by leaping on his bed (figures 6.5 and 6.6). However, the intimacy only suggested in Welles's film is made explicit in Van Sant's. In *Chimes at Midnight* Hal and Falstaff face the camera and are sitting rather than lying in bed. There is no physical contact between the men, although the scene is undeniably intimate, whereas Van Sant's version of this scene parodies the frustrated intimacy of the two men. However, even as Van Sant impresses upon his viewer the sexual intimacy of his Hal and Falstaff in this particular scene, he emphasizes that these characters inhabit separate spaces and different social worlds (figures 6.7 and 6.8). Welles's film also employs landscape and environment as a means of indicating Hal's competing psychological forces—the worlds of the tavern and the court—but in Van Sant's film the space that separates his Hal and Falstaff is the garbage-strewn alley of an abandoned and ruined hotel. Falstaff, discarded like so many of the other objects in that alley, is visually diminished and physically degraded (figure 6.8). Van Sant's Hal does not need to inform his audience that he intends to "re-create" himself and leave the life of the urban hustler; the visual emphasis in this scene makes it clear that this Falstaff has long since been discarded, first by society and now by Hal himself.

In "degrading" his cinematic inspiration for these scenes in *My Own Private Idaho,* Van Sant bids the viewer reconsider the source, the play itself, and the sacrosanctity of the "original Shakespeare." The authentic or traditional world of Falstaff's tavern (as revealed in Shakespeare's *Henry IV, Parts I* and *II,* and in portions of *Henry V*) borrows from the popular culture of its own time by centering the story of the profligate prince and his relationship with Sir John Falstaff within the tavern world of the late sixteenth century, a world that engages popular beliefs about the tavern as site for Saturnalian release and liminal excesses. In general, as Robert Elliot has argued, utopian discourse has ancient links to Saturnalian rituals and the carnivalesque.[33] In his revisioning of Falstaff's tavern world Van Sant recovers the play's links with its carnivalesque origins.

However, the tavern that constitutes the heart of Falstaff's kingdom would have been unrecognizable to the historical Henry IV and his son Hal, since it was an anachronistic element in Shakespeare's drama.[34] Scanning medieval records, historians find relatively few alehouses; it was not a medieval institution, since the parish church and churchyard furnished the community with its social center. Significant historical and social circumstances in the late sixteenth century reshaped English popular culture and created what we recognize today as the tavern world of Eastcheap.[35] An upsurge in poverty, urbanization, and mobility were factors that contributed to the rise of the tavern in the sixteenth and early seventeenth centuries, and the decay of established religion as a focal point for community activities allowed the tavern to develop as an "alternative society." Rather than signaling the return to festive communal traditions alive in the medieval villages that Welles's film invokes, the alehouse and tavern were instead products of a developing and urbanizing society. In this

FIGURE 6.3. Hal ascending the stairs to the tavern in *Chimes at Midnight*. (Videotape copyright permission of Arthur Cantor Film Collection, New York)

FIGURE 6.4. Scott ascending the stairs in the abandoned hotel in *My Own Private Idaho*. (Courtesy of New Line Cinema)

FIGURE 6.5. Hal and Falstaff in bed in *Chimes at Midnight*. (Videotape copyright permission of Arthur Cantor Film Collection, New York)

FIGURE 6.6. Scott and Bob Pigeon in bed in *My Own Private Idaho*. (Courtesy of New Line Cinema)

FIGURE 6.7. Hal rejects Falstaff in *Chimes at Midnight*. (Videotape copyright permission of Arthur Cantor Film Collection, New York)

respect, Van Sant's revisioning of Falstaff's tavern world is more true to the circumstances of Shakespeare's experience of the tavern and alehouse as an aspect of popular culture than Welles's nostalgic perspective.

Popular beliefs in Shakespeare's day held that taverns and alehouses were run by the poor for the poor, sheltering criminals, vagrants, drunks, and the destitute. Susan Amussen asserts in her study of early modern England that approximately 38.7 percent of the petitions submitted during quarter sessions by local constables were complaints for being drunk, an alehouse haunter or an alehouse keeper, or both.[36] Contemporaries spoke against the alehouse and tavern as a threat to general order, and "there was a broad consensus of opinion among the middling and (to some extent) the upper ranks of society in Tudor and early Stuart England: that alehouses were a new and increasingly dangerous force in popular society."[37] Fears of the rootless poor, without visible ties of kinship, whether to families or masters, were connected with unenclosed wastes and the taverns

FIGURE 6.8. Scott rejects Bob Pigeon in *My Own Private Idaho.* (Courtesy of New Line Cinema)

that the poor frequented and where they sometimes took lodgings.[38] Contemporaries connected the dangers of the wastes with the communal world of the tavern, and associated "leveling" impulses with utopian longings. For example, contemporary "complaints in enclosure-riot cases in the Court of Star Chamber" alleged "that the defendants had hired vagrants out of alehouses for the work of leveling hedges."[39] As taverns came to be patronized almost exclusively by the poor and scorned by the more respectable members of the community, they came to be viewed as havens for vagrants and seditious elements in society.[40]

Much as the tavern in Shakespeare's *Henriad* partakes in the period's fears about the crime, disorder, and drunkenness of the tavern, Van Sant's cinematic translation of the tavern world of Eastcheap in modern dress underscores our own anxieties concerning the social alienation of the poor, homeless, and drug-addicted. In looking back to the original Shakespeare, Van Sant revisions Falstaff's tavern world as the alternative society of the urban poor of contemporary America. He resists depicting Falstaff's tavern world as the festive voice of the entire community, instead capturing the carnivalesque energies of Shakespeare's characters from what Peter Stallybrass describes as a "perspective of *below.*" To do otherwise, Stallybrass cautions, "is to adopt a nostalgic perspective which mystifies the conditions which determined the fair's [or tavern world's] existence."⁴¹ If Welles's film adopts the "nostalgic perspective" that Stallybrass warns against, Van Sant's film relentlessly takes its focus *from* the "perspective of below," from the perspective of the sexually and economically marginalized.

Although Van Sant parodies Welles's nostalgia for a lost world, his film exhibits its own nostalgic tendencies. Susan Bennett qualifies Van Sant's nostalgia as "profoundly and determinedly queer, a fracturing of History which generates contrary (oppositional and perverse) ways of seeing."⁴² As an oppositional fracturing of nostalgia, *My Own Private Idaho* pointedly critiques Welles's neutralization of the potentially homoerotic energy of male bonding within the Falstaffian world of Eastcheap.⁴³ In Shakespeare's *Henriad* the rite of passage Hal undergoes from homosocial adolescence to a heterosexual manhood is prepared for in the temporary freedom of sexual desire suggested by the tavern world. *Chimes at Midnight* mutes the sexual license and energy associated with these aspects of the carnivalesque, though critics have remarked that the scenes in the Boar's Head Tavern exude a "rough excremental atmosphere, filled with spontaneous, pansexual displays of affection," and have noted the "ungratified sexuality" and "innuendos of homosexuality between Poins and Hal" in *Chimes at Midnight.*⁴⁴ In Van Sant's "low translation," the homoerotic impulses only suggested through innuendo and atmosphere in Welles's film are subjected to Van Sant's anti-idealist, materialist, and historicizing vision.

Turning once again to the original Shakespeare, Van Sant emphasizes elements within the play that suggest the homoerotic energy of male bonding implicit in the sexual license of the carnivalesque and in the tavern itself. In the play Falstaff underscores this connection with the festive inversion of Morris dancing and Whitsuntide festivals when he tells the Hostess, "There's no more faith in thee than in a stewed prune, nor no more truth in thee than in a drawn fox; and, for womanhood, Maid Marian may be the deputy's wife of the ward to thee. Go, you thing, go" (*1 Henry IV,* III.iii.113–16). In these lines Falstaff recalls the origin of Morris dancing as a rite of male bonding, in which transvestite boys danced the part of Maid Marian.[45] Shakespeare's contemporaries also understood that the communal circumstances of the tavern, inn, or alehouse might advantage strong bonds with other males. Notable examples from the period are from trials, which may not represent usual activities within the tavern but nonetheless gained popular attention and contributed to perceptions that the tavern functioned as a bawdy house and contributed to promiscuity. In one case, Evans ap Rice of West Ham was charged in 1584 with "lodging strange men and women together in one chamber and lodging strange men in his bed with him and his wife."[46] In another, more spectacular, case a yeoman from Somerset offered court testimony against an innkeeper named Dowdeney. The yeoman was sharing a bed with the innkeeper when about midnight Dowdeney grabbed him "by his privy member or secret parts and said . . . 'What? Are they no better? . . . Mine are better than thine!' And with that Dowdeney kissed him . . . about the cheek and culled him about the neck and with violence."[47] Both cases underscore the sexual licentiousness associated with the alehouses and taverns in contemporary discourses.

Using a range of deconstructive devices that defamiliarize traditional approaches to Shakespeare's text, Van Sant explores the limits of adaptation. Linguistic deflation is chief among these. Van Sant confirms the challenge of Shakespeare's carnivalesque discourse, which levels distinctions between the "Prince" and other men by privileging carnivalesque language and meanings over practices of literary signification, such as the high culture of Shakespeare's text and Welles's auteur cinema. For example, Van Sant targets the following lines for revisioning:

> What a devil hast thou to do with the time of the day? Unless hours were cups of sack, and minutes capons, and clocks the tongues of bawds, and dials the signs of leaping houses, and the blessed sun himself a fair hot wench in flame-coloured taffeta, I see no reason why thou shouldst be so superfluous to demand the time of the day.
>
> (*1 Henry IV,* I.ii.5–12)

In *My Own Private Idaho* Van Sant's Hal derides Falstaff's query after the time in the vulgar and colloquial language of contemporary America: "What do you care? Why, you wouldn't even look at a clock, unless hours were lines of coke, dials looked like the signs of gay bars, or time itself was a fair hustler in black leather."[48] Whereas Shakespeare's Hal's references are decidedly rooted in the conditions of a sixteenth-century tavern world, "cups of sack," "capons," "bawds," and "a fair hot wench in flame-coloured taffeta," Van Sant alters the constellation of meanings surrounding the materiality of Falstaff's desires, and translates the cultural and ideological circumstances of the scene to illuminate contemporary conditions of social, sexual, and linguistic exchange. The low transformation of Shakespeare's language emphasizes that marginalized figures stand at the convergence of sexual and social oppressions, where issues of sexual dominance intersect with issues of social stratification.

In an interesting reading that implies Van Sant's revisioning is performative in nature (forward-looking rather than backward-looking), Jonathan Goldberg glosses Shakespeare's lines as a thinly veiled locus of self-identification between the fat knight and his desire for a cross-dressed Hal: "To Falstaff's irrelevant question about the time of day, Hal replies that the time would be of interest to his fat companion only were the 'blessed sun himself' to appear like a 'fair hot wench in flame-coloured taffeta' (I.ii.9-10). Hal, we know, thinks he is the blessed sun, and in this line the sun is male; Hal imagines himself as cross-dressed."[49] If we accept Goldberg's reading of the Shakespearean text, then Van Sant's revisioning merely removes the boundaries between the desire and its articulation, between merely imagining Hal as cross-dressed to the embracing of the hustler in black leather. Although Van Sant's modernized street-slang degrades the Shakespearean poetry, its parodic transformation revives social and political meanings lost or dormant. The low translation reveals that carnivalesque meaning "is made and remade in the contested domain of social practices."[50] It is in the performance of desire, as Van Sant's revisioning implies, that utopian longings are realized.

In framing the tavern scenes in imitation of those in *Chimes at Midnight* (figures 6.9–6.12), Van Sant alerts the viewer to the central concern of his own utopian revisioning—the revival of carnivalesque meaning in the Shakespearean text. The visual framing of the scenes remains the same as in Welles's film, but its degraded verbal expression revives subversive social and political meanings lost to modern audiences. For example, in a scene from the Gadshill robbery Welles frames Falstaff and his accomplices as hooded pilgrims in feigned prayer (figure 6.9). Van Sant's film parodies this moment in Welles's film by identifying the pilgrims as their modern equivalent, "Rajneesh," an eastern religious sect entrenched in the Seattle area who have been accused of sacrificing religion for an abiding interest in worldly things (figure 6.10). In another scene from the Gadshill robbery, Falstaff and Hal struggle to put on Falstaff's disguise (figure 6.11). As Hal assists the fat knight, he asks Falstaff: "How long is't ago, Jack, since thou sawest thine own knee?" (*1 Henry IV,* II.iv.324–25). In a parallel scene that closely imitates this one in *Chimes at Midnight,* Van Sant frames Falstaff/Bob, Hal/Scott, and Poins/Mikey in a triangulated composition, visually articulating the significance of the Poins character and making explicit the joke that hovers over the Shakespearean text by changing "knee" to "dick," and charging the exchange with the crude energy of the popular idiom (figure 6.12).

Van Sant degrades the carnivalesque language of the Shakespearean text in order to liberate it. As Richard Lanham observes of the *Henriad,* "Shakespeare makes the language of parody into the only genuine high style, the only authentic sublimity, the play permits."[51] Like its debased formulation in Van Sant's film, Shakespeare's play explores the linguistic margins and subcultures of its contemporary world, and participates in the carnivalesque discourse of the audience's own present. The speech of Falstaff's tavern world, as Steven Mullaney observes, is alive in the "idiomatic expressions drawn from local dialects, and phrases of popular jargon, many of which would have gone unrecorded if they had not appeared in these plays, the richest in Shakespeare's corpus for popular speech."[52] Like the vulgar, popular speech of Van Sant's characters, in Shakespeare's play "the English that Hal acquires . . . [is] the native yet alien element of country dialects and 'rude' words with which Shakespeare's dramatic language abounds," discovered "in the inns and alehouses of London."[53] Logically, since the tavern is a product of Shakespeare's developing society and its popular element, the language that is born of that environment is also

FIGURE 6.9. The disguised thieves feigning prayers in *Chimes at Midnight*. (Videotape copyright permission of Arthur Cantor Film Collection, New York)

FIGURE 6.10. The disguised thieves feigning prayers in *My Own Private Idaho*. (Courtesy of New Line Cinema)

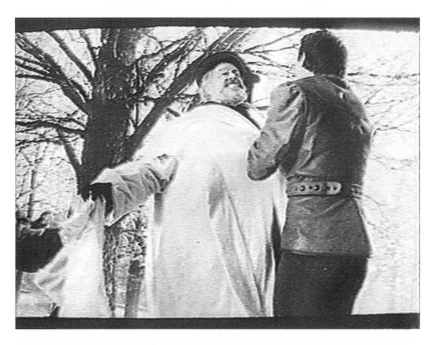

FIGURE 6.11. Hal helps Falstaff with his disguise in *Chimes at Midnight*. (Videotape copyright permission of Arthur Cantor Film Collection, New York)

FIGURE 6.12. Scott and Mike Waters help Bob Pigeon with his disguise in *My Own Private Idaho*. (Courtesy of New Line Cinema)

anachronistic to the historical world of Henry IV. Shakespeare's play not only spoke to contemporary anxiety about the displaced and marginalized but spoke about it in the vulgar carnivalesque discourse of its time. In a very real sense the play offers a critique of contemporary anxieties in a degraded and popular guise not dissimilar to Van Sant's own agenda. Yet, as Van Sant's film implies, subversive expressions become absorbed by the culture they criticize. Today the play's carnivalesque language is enshrined within the "official" linguistic codes that the play itself mocks and parodies. Within this context we begin to understand that Van Sant's project in revisioning the language of Shakespeare's play is, in effect, an attempt to bring it into accord with the energies of the "original Shakespeare."

Van Sant explains that the significance of the inclusion of the Shakespearean material in the film is an attempt "to transcend time, to show that those things have always happened, everywhere."[54] Yet in examining his filmic and Renaissance antecedents, including Shakespeare's plays, Van Sant understands his preoccupation as distinctly American: "America has a certain culture that's always reverting or trying to figure out where it came from. So we are always going back to the origins of different styles from the Renaissance through different movements in Europe."[55] In order to transcend time—to perceive the utopian dimension within his own world—Van Sant looks back to Falstaff's tavern world and the filmic stylization that Welles accords that world in *Chimes at Midnight*. The respective fantasy messages are encoded in the films' titles: *Chimes at Midnight* as a recovery of lost time in which "space vanquishes the hero," and *My Own Private Idaho* as a space in which time vanquishes the hero.[56]

The contrasting ways in which Welles's and Van Sant's films express utopian impulses suggest opposing perceptions of carnivalesque time, or what François Laroque describes as the difference between "impatient expectation" and "anxiety."[57] Laroque defines "impatient expectation" as a "a tendency to idealize the past and regard the present as a degraded image of the Golden Age now inaccessible, while never quite relinquishing the hope of it returning one fine day," whereas utopian time experienced as "anxiety" derives from a perception of time "as something concrete and material."[58] This distinction clarifies the directors' contrasting expressions of utopian recovery. Whereas *Chimes at Midnight* illustrates utopian time as a longing for an idealized past, *My Own Private Idaho* revises Welles's utopian experience as an expression of anxiety over the conditions of our modern and material existence.

The death of Falstaff illustrates the differences in the directors' understanding of time. This particular moment in *Henry V* (II.iii) is one that straddles two perceptions of Falstaff's death, as both comic and pathetic, realized through the fragmented and confused report of Mistress Quickly. Since Falstaff remains outside the audience's purview, one can only speculate whether his deathbed reformation has been complete; the scene itself remains an unfocused and contradictory memorial, captured in half-truths and dubious recollections, much like the man to whom the scene pays tribute. Welles realizes Falstaff's death, as does the play, only in the fragmented and ambiguous recollections of Mistress Quickly, in which the dead man himself is never seen. Yet in his film Welles nostalgically reminds his audience of Falstaff by the huge wooden coffin that stands in the courtyard. He also eliminates all bawdy and comic elements from the scene and converts Mistress Quickly's reporting of the death into a sentimental eulogy. Van Sant renders this scene in a different guise altogether. In the film Mistress Quickly's memorial loses its sentimentality when the audience is allowed to observe the dying man. *My Own Private Idaho* reveals a sweating Falstaff in a close-up shot, uttering "God, God, God" directly into the lens of the camera before he expires. There is no sentimentality here, and no wandering tribute to Falstaff's memory. Instead, the focus is unremittingly on the face of the sick and homeless man. The man who has counterfeited dying now dies in earnest. As Hal's mockery of Falstaff's query "what's o'clock" implies, utopian figures only gesture at time. However, Van Sant's revisioning robs Falstaff of his utopian function by stripping his death of its distance and ambiguity. In Shakespeare's play, as Paul Cubeta astutely observes, Mistress Quickly offers a "memorial to a real and mythic character whose essential ambiguity remains as mysteriously allusive in dying as in living."[59] But in Van Sant's film Falstaff unambiguously succumbs to time and death, impoverished and alone.

In Van Sant's materialist and historicizing vision, "redeeming time" does not entail spiritual and moral reformation, or even economic recovery. Instead, *My Own Private Idaho* attempts to recover the popular sense of time in the Renaissance as that of a "mysterious space" rather than "an undifferentiated interval."[60] As the film's "Mike Waters," a waif-like Poins equivalent, scours the Idaho landscape in search of his lost mother, we discover that although the past is unrecoverable (as demonstrated in the grainy home-movie style recollections of Waters's childhood, which his voice-over commentary invariably misinterprets or misremembers) there remains the "mysterious space" of recovery through the memory of the body, as prefigured in the Idaho landscape.

My Own Private Idaho is least imitative of Welles's film and Shakespeare's *Henriad* in exploring the utopian aspects of the Poins character. In those scenes Van Sant employs his most startling filmic techniques — time-lapse photography (essential to a sense of "timelessness" in the film) and the gritty realism of home movies with an inaccurate voice-over commentary. Mike Waters/Poins collapses the boundaries between memory and the present, and demonstrates a utopian disregard of time and order. As Laroque observes, "festival is the exact equivalent of sleep: a non-time in which awareness of duration and existence is wiped out. . . . and makes it possible to shake off, or at least relax, the binding grip of time."[61] Tellingly, Van Sant introduces his Poins (actor River Phoenix), whose narcolepsy makes time meaningless, within the first scenes of *My Own Private Idaho.* Just as Hal, who embraces his political destiny in linear time, wakes from his despised "dream" of a "surfeit-swelled" old man to become king, the film's Poins, who exists outside time, embraces the healing balm of forgetfulness, sleep, and narcolepsy.

All utopias are constructed as liminal states, and are situated somewhere beyond the boundaries of consciousness and memory. Van Sant's film anticipates utopia as a memory enacted by a return to Idaho. It is to the mysterious space of "my own private idaho" that the Poins character finally and always returns. Van Sant confirms the fantasy-element within the Idaho landscapes, whose "settings . . . were unfamiliar enough to me that they seemed like fairytale land."[62] Similarly, in *Chimes at Midnight* Welles creates a mythic landscape that reflects the character's values and relationships in spatial terms. Welles's Falstaff exists in congruence with the teeming vitality of life in the tavern. However, once outside those environs, in the sterile and empty landscapes of war and political struggle, his enormous bulk disappears. Van Sant specifically recasts the space that threatens the utopian figure as the vast and empty Idaho landscape, which emerges as the place of physical memory and material/maternal origin. To contemplate this space invites narcolepsy, forgetfulness, and oblivion. Whether Mike Waters/Poins gazes upon the Idaho landscape or gazes into the face of an attractive aging woman, the results are the same.

The landscape in which Mike Waters/Poins conducts his search is infused with a significance conditioned by historical and cultural variables, upon which the utopian fantasies of daily life are expressed. The film shatters assumptions of the natural innocence of landscape and reveals its profound ideological implications, pointing to the instability of signs by which the Poins character interprets landscape as buried in the unconscious memory of his own body. In this respect he functions as Falstaff does in Shakespeare's *Henriad,* appealing to the sensuous facts of his own body in deflating ideological illusion. The erotic signification of the landscape signaled by the Poins character's bodily responses makes material our own subjective responses and utopian longings projected upon the horizons of the American landscape.

However, the landscape's demystification simultaneously accords it a signification that transcends historicity by grounding it in the space of the mother. "The lost memory of the mother's body," as Laura Mulvey observes, "is similar to other metaphors of a buried past, or a lost history, that contribute to the rhetoric of oppressed people, in a colonial, class or even sexual context."[63] Utopian longings, grotesquely reimagined in Van Sant's film as the sexual appetite of the material/maternal body, are fulfilled by rejecting the authority that polices the boundaries of our desires. In his materialistic and demystifying critique of utopian longings for family, Van Sant rends the boundaries between production and consumption, between the mother who produces the male child whom she "consumes" sexually. Ultimately, the space that becomes both Idaho and mother resists closure by abolishing the distinctions between mother and child, father and brother, friend and lover. *My Own Private Idaho* revisions Welles's landscape as the ultimate recuperation of the forbidden and repressed.

Like the salmon that swim upstream in the film's initial frames, Mike Waters/Poins plays out a ritual regeneration within cyclical time, so that his story ends where it began—collapsed mid-journey in the vast Idaho landscape. As he gazes at the landscape, he experiences yet another narcoleptic seizure and collapses on the road. Oblivion is his only defense against remembering, when the pain of existence comes painfully close to connecting past and present. These last moments of the film reverberate with the oddly elegiac sounds of a hushed-pedal steel guitar musical underscoring of "America the Beautiful," music that connects nostalgia for the myth of an American past with the Poins character's search in the empty Idaho landscape for the fragmented truths of his origin. The final scene of the film reflects upon the character's utopian urge to "return home" (the Greek *nostos,* the root of "nostalgia") by essentially returning to the film's point of origin, on the road in the middle of an empty Idaho landscape. In pursuing the memory of mother and home, the Poins character discovers the degraded utopian promise of the American dream.

As Robert Stam reminds us, "All carnivals must be seen as complex crisscrossings of ideological manipulation and utopian desire."[64] Van Sant captures the unpitying nature of carnivalesque art, capable of unmasking sentimental attachments of "home" and "mother" and of ridiculing the conventional ethical hierarchies of "success" and "money." *My Own Private Idaho* reveals the prevarications that lie behind these hierarchies, so that "selling your ass" is acceptable, but giving oneself for love makes one a "fairy," degenerate, and inferior. The film's emphasis upon the physical, material, and carnal, revealed in forms parodic and hyperbolic, illuminate social truths. Although Van Sant shares with Welles the avant-garde impulse toward social and libidinal rebellion, his reformulation of carnivalesque impulses couples cultural critique with a degraded expression of the mass-mediated pleasure of the consumerist utopias of modern America. As Stam observes, "in a political culture, and a commercial film industry, where radical alternatives have been more or less ruled 'out of bounds,' it is not surprising that 'subversion' often takes the apparently apolitical form of comic aggressions that violate respectable decorum and decent standards of bodily behavior."[65]

In the imagined space of Idaho and within the context of a new and distinctly American history and identity, Van Sant tells the story of *Henry IV,* employing the aesthetic representation and figuration of Welles's tavern scenes in order to present a model of filmic transformation and an authentic utopian vision of liberation. Unlike Welles, who reads utopia backwards against its source (Shakespeare's play and his own imagined recuperated past), Van Sant reads his utopian vision forward or against performance.[66] Although, as Van Sant attests, his film looks back to its origins in Shakespeare and Welles, its articulation is an unsentimental view of the unreality of social existence in twentieth-century America today, what Jameson identifies as "the haunting and unmentionable persistence of the organic — of birth, copulation, and death."[67] In *My Own Private Idaho* the family itself is the object of utopian longing, but one that has been degraded, so that, ironically, the film's utopian fantasy of recuperation is imagined within the very discourse it criticizes. In rewriting Welles's *Chimes at Midnight* in terms of the myth of the family, Van Sant underscores the utopian dimension of his own film, in which class antagonisms between rich and poor are substituted by a new, but illegitimate, kind of fraternity. Together these films pose the question as to what is the best way to recover utopia — as a recovery of original meaning or as exploration?

Chapter Seven

Playing on the Rim of the Frame

Kenneth Branagh's *A Midwinter's Tale*

Written, directed, and produced by Kenneth Branagh, *A Midwinter's Tale* (1995) highlights an actor's engagement with Shakespeare's dramatic art, in which "working on Shakespeare," asserts Branagh, "is the search for meaning."[1] Branagh's *A Midwinter's Tale* reveals the variety of expression available to Shakespeare's drama when the viewer is permitted to concentrate on the critical intervals and asides, and on the mistakes that occur in the midst of the textual enactment. The film does not so much introduce restrictions as to what can be meaningful as it opens up variability and guides its audience in viewing variability without investment in *Hamlet*'s fixity of meaning, production, or moral order. As Branagh confirms, "In rehearsal, what works works. I think you ought to try everything."[2] Because the viewer discerns Shakespeare's *Hamlet* through multiple layers of framed activities identified as "play" or rehearsal, one learns not to invest meaning in the actors' proficiency of lines and interpretation of character, or in the stage business of blocking, timing, or costuming. Instead, Shakespeare's *Hamlet* is only a starting point for the film's prolonged rehearsal, and its attendant cultural, theatrical, and psychological investigations. Even the opening night performance that is the climax of the film is a rehearsal of sorts, for in those final, confused moments of the film the audience continues to entertain unexplored textual possibilities. What if Ophelia were to strike Hamlet in anger? What if Hamlet could be played by both a male and a female? Branagh's film demonstrates that Shakespeare's text is radically incomplete in itself.

As Branagh reveals through the film narrative, textuality is just another apparatus that participates in the production of meaning, but not the monolith that structures meaning. Although the film manifests Shakespeare's text at various levels — its rehearsal, the actors who perform it, its cultural world of theatrical and cinematic history, and the pressures of market considerations (as articulated by Joe's agent and the Hollywood producer who sees their production) — the viewer comprehends that no one level encompasses all the others. We witness multiple images imbedded in other images, in an infinite regress of self-enclosed representation that deconstructs the competing representations at work within textual, theatrical, and cinematic forms.

In openly parodying the conventions of theater and cinema from which the film's production of *Hamlet* is derived, *A Midwinter's Tale* renders explicit the intrinsic process of textuality. What had been on the margins of textual discourse — the instability and transience of the Shakespearean text — becomes the focus of *A Midwinter's Tale*. As we watch the actors struggle with the problem of mimetic art in *Hamlet,* we discover that there is no antecedent reality on which the artistic text is modeled.[3] The quest for "meaning," for what "works" in production, as the film reveals, is merely a critique of representation dependent upon arbitrary signs that cannot be systematized into any sort of hierarchy. Like the actor in Branagh's film who randomly makes words fit in the spaces of a crossword puzzle without adherence to the meaning assigned by the clues, *A Midwinter's Tale* explores the possibilities that "fit" dramatic action without adherence to meaning assigned by the textual clues. The audience witnesses multiple strategies of performance that deny the actors or viewer any inevitable strategies of containment, so that any word, scene, or character may experience a hybrid field of meaning without signaling any boundary. As a consequence, the film spectator becomes the sole organizer of the patterns he perceives, as he accepts the changes in *Hamlet*'s organizational premises and compensates for differences. Yet it is possible, as the film demonstrates, that these changes may still be meaningful, even as multiple perspectives and performative possibilities are played out in a sort of parallel universe of theatrical *Hamlet*s. In fact, Branagh's film makes the startling point that postmodernism may be a way of getting at Shakespeare.

A Midwinter's Tale releases latent meanings in the Shakespearean text through rehearsal, a process of discovery that sometimes takes the form of irreverent carnivalizing. Branagh participates in Hamlet's mirror of representation in deflecting Shakespeare's play from its customary locus of decorum by having the actors assume an "antic disposition" of dramaturgy. By calling attention to theatrical artifice and operations, *A Midwinter's Tale* burlesques traditional and formulaic aspects of *Hamlet*'s theatrical and cinematic history, from Shakespeare to Henry Irving to Laurence Olivier, and exposes layers of critical imagination, extending from Hollywood to Shakespeare's stage to the very actors who comically struggle with their roles. The film, as a consequence, embodies both the positive and negative postmodernisms of recent cultural theory, by imagining the relativity of Shakespeare's drama within our culture while pointing out its place within the development of late capitalism and its proliferation in the production of cultural "signs." For though the film demystifies those aspects of the play's production that render collectivity precarious, it also envisions, within the degraded process of the present, the hope of a future "golden age" where the actor can finally be free from depression, oppression, and alienation.

The Frame's the Thing

What is not framed within the play *Hamlet* is implicitly larger than the play's frame, in that it contains the processes and assumptions of the art contained. Leo Braudy observes that "to place an art within another art therefore creates an aesthetic perspective," in that it leads the viewer to an "inner space" or "history" that supplies "a depth in time to what might otherwise be only an individual work."[4] Branagh's film is a critique of representation that fills in *Hamlet*'s blank spaces and reveals how the strange can in fact be familiar, how the remoteness of a four-hundred-year-old play about a "depressed aristocrat," as Joe Harper's sister complains, can, in fact, reflect parts of the self in a late-twentieth-century postmodern world.[5] As Braudy observes, "Frames, like criticism, domesticate what they help us to discover. They protect us from disruption even while they teach us to cope with it."[6]

The frame of *A Midwinter's Tale* includes not only what is contained within Shakespeare's *Hamlet* but elements external to the play's borders. The actors' rehearsal of *Hamlet* constitutes the rim of the frame through which the audience expects to perceive the innermost activity, Shakespeare's drama, although the film frame never sustains the play in its entirety nor do its fragments have a stable form. Instead, the rim establishes the status of the theatrical frame in "reality," within which are further layerings, or untransformed events and their keyings. *Hamlet* itself illustrates the possibilities of multiple layerings within the dramatic frame, in that the play highlights differentiated levels of transformational framing, of which *The Murder of Gonzago* constitutes the play's innermost point. Similarly, in Branagh's film the play *Hamlet* is the innermost point that exposes the histories and motivations of the individual actors, and provides the perspective from which Branagh burlesques twentieth-century film and culture. Yet the film challenges the function of frames to protect the viewer from disruption, for in viewing the framed activities of *A Midwinter's Tale* the viewer experiences the ease with which the boundaries between frames are penetrated. Rather than taming what the viewer sees, the layers of framed activities have a revolutionary effect in that their confusing multiplicity and interpenetrability liberate the viewer from static conceptions of the play. As a consequence, what appears to be merely on the rim of the frame becomes, in fact, a competing representation of what lies inside.

Whereas *Hamlet* adds some dozen or sixteen lines to the original script of *The Murder of Gonzago,* thereby transforming "the theatrical keying into an exploitative fabrication," Branagh introduces multiple variations of Shakespeare's text at the center of his film, as well as embellishing upon the audience's expectations as to what lies *outside* the frame of Shakespeare's play.[7] Joe Harper's story forces the viewer to recognize that those elements normally considered outside the frame of Shakespeare's drama—the actors' experiences and values, theater and film history, genre conventions, and social contexts—are essential elements in comprehending Shakespeare.

The story that lies outside the frame of Hamlet's story—Harper's efforts to produce *Hamlet* for the Christmas holidays—not only highlights important distinctions between levels of fictionality but also suggests that these multiple layers of artistic fiction are crucial versions of *Hamlet* itself, in that the lives of the actors—in their existential situations—illuminate aspects of the reality of their theatrical situation. Terry's overwhelming guilt for having abandoned his son informs his tearful performance as Queen Gertrude, as does Nina's loss of her husband when she mournfully sings Ophelia's mad song, and even Joe Harper threatens to walk away from the production because "it's too personal for us all. It's a big play and we keep running up against it and hurting ourselves."[8]

Branagh's film, like Shakespeare's *Hamlet,* challenges the differences between a play's inner and outer frames of reference, or the interface of art and life, by highlighting the distinctions between Joe Harper's representation of himself as an actor and the role he plays in *Hamlet.* As Joe Harper's story illustrates, "art" and "life" are simply competing representations. Harper (Michael Maloney), the depressed, unemployed actor who directs, produces, and plays the lead in *Hamlet,* demonstrates the unsettling indeterminacy of the boundaries between the fictitious roles he plays and the "real" ones that define his life. The two spaces of representation—the actor and his role—reveal the dual capacity of dramatic art to recognize simultaneously the material realities of "this unworthy scaffold" (what Robert Weimann calls the "nonfictional site of institutionalized entertainment") and "an imagined *locus* of verisimilitude" of an enacted role, which privileges "the authority of what and who was represented."[9] Like the play it enacts, Shakespeare's *Hamlet,* Branagh's film suspends the links between actor and role, closing the gap between dramatic illusion and verisimilitude. But whereas in Shakespeare's play Hamlet narrows the frame by which he explores family guilt and murder through the encased events of the play within the play, Branagh opens the spectator's perspective to include the outer rim of the frame that is the actors' world. This outer circle of reference enables the characters within the film to exist both inside and outside the play, not unlike the way in which Bottom, also an aspiring actor and lover, explores the concentric layers of fictionality in *A Midsummer Night's Dream.* As in the Shakespearean comedy from which Branagh draws at least a portion of the title of his film, *A Midwinter's Tale* suggests that the relationship between levels of fictionality depends upon how the audience experiences the performance at its center, depending upon whether the audience percieves a "shift from spectacle to game—from encasing events to encased events."[10] For example, in Shakespeare's play Hamlet "plays" with the frame of the events in which he is immersed when he produces the "Mousetrap." When Hamlet introduces the play within a play, he introduces a change in framing, which "complicates the matter of brackets, leading to the possibility of sharply different perceptions, depending on whether the outer or inner realms are of chief concern."[11] Even as Hamlet introduces the fabricated theatrical frame to "catch the conscience of a king," to which Claudius violently responds, the staged audience who watches the performance is simply watching a play in progress. The staged audience need not know the outcome of the play, and, indeed, as Naomi Liebler observes, "the 'Mousetrap' seems to operate effectively only for Claudius and Hamlet; the rest of the courtly audience, arguably ignorant of Claudius's crime, see a performance they take to be entirely fictional."[12] Branagh confuses the bracketing of events even further when the character who plays Ophelia introduces out-of-frame behavior. During the opening night performance of *Hamlet,* when the entire cast believes that Joe Harper has been lured away from the production to be cast in a Hollywood science-fiction film, Harper suddenly reappears to assume his role as Hamlet. However, the woman who plays Ophelia falls back upon a self that is separate from the one relevantly projected in her Shakespearean role when she strikes Joe (as Hamlet) and hands the love letters back to him. Of course, the staged audience that watches their interaction is ignorant of any personal relationship outside the roles they play, and takes the performance to be entirely fictional, rather than a manifestation of out-of-frame behavior.

The film generates meaning through its framing practices that include an internal arrangement of space as well as that articulated by the boundaries between images. Yet these boundaries are challenged and confused when the film narrative requires that the viewer sustain simultaneously various levels of imaginative experience—the film, the play, the actors, and their personal stories. As partitions between frames collapse, the viewer experiences difficulty in prioritizing and isolating these multiple levels of experience. Branagh's film offers a spatialized model of knowledge in that the subject of the actor's jokes is "space" and the film viewer's experience of the play is of "actors in space" or "spacemen." It is part of the joke of the film that Branagh literalizes the staging or performance of consciousness as an explication of Joe's quest to enact *Hamlet* at Christmastime. The film asks whether representation might not always be distortion and dislocation, an interpretative process in which making one's dreams real involves a comically realized spatialization as disclosure and explication. The viewer discovers through the parodic employment of spatial metaphors and cinematic space that the play *Hamlet,* in its "original" condition, is also a product of distortion because it too is "'always already' in presentation."[13]

A Midwinter's Tale narratizes metaphorical space by revealing how meanings can be manipulated like things in space. As Joe's agent, Margaretta, tells the Hollywood producer who unexpectedly appears at their opening night performance, "You know Shakespeare. I mean, if you can get the spatial relationships right . . . it's . . . it's . . . often can be so much better."[14] Indeed, *A Midwinter's Tale* demonstrates an awareness of the varied rites of initiation, celebration, and exclusion through which a ceremonial order is defined, maintained, and manifested in time and space. The actors perform on the margins of the ordered town, and come to define their place as a space of cultural ambivalence and excess, where queens are gay fathers and where church ceremony has ceased, but faith is rekindled in the performative hopes of the actors and audience who congregate in the church of Hope — demonstrating how physical topography can merge with cultural topology.

In structuring a play within a film, Branagh also distinguishes between levels of fictionality inherent in the two acting media. The cinematic spectacle that constitutes the film's outer layer, and includes the story of the actors' lives and conflicts that animates the textual center, denies the viewer any direct access to its own mechanisms or to the film frame's frame. The viewer never witnesses Branagh directing the film, never is cued that the actor who plays Joe Harper is anything other than that character, although at various moments throughout the film Branagh introduces anti-illusionist techniques that recall the devices of film (as, for example, when Joe Harper's narrative is abruptly ended by the darkened screen that introduces the "Prologue"). However, these disruptions produce barely perceptible ruptures in the boundaries between viewer and performance when compared to the theatrical spectacle at the film's center, which continually alerts the audience to the circumstances of its own artifice and production. The performance of *Hamlet* that resides at the center of *A Midwinter's Tale* insists upon exposing its own theatricality, of "displaying its display," revealing what Barbara Freedman describes as "frames framed by their contexts."[15] Conflicted representations are thereby mutually sustained within the film, in that the film demands participation and identification while the theatrical center permits comic distancing and exposure. The spectator can be profoundly moved by Joe Harper's timely return for opening night, at great professional cost to himself, and yet at the same time laugh at the play itself when a flustered Gertrude bids Hamlet "cast off thy coloured nightie."[16]

The film challenges the play's discourse of similitude, decorum, and catharsis in adapting the poststructuralist concepts of the linguistic discontinuity between signs and meaning, played out in the space of the film and the stage it represents, a space that highlights the multiple cultural functions of performance. Gaps between the play text and its theatrical performance were a necessary condition of the Elizabethan stage, but, as Robert Weimann observes, "these gaps could more effectively be closed and these links more consequentially broken than in any other theatre culture before or since," because "social occasion and the uses of significations came together."[17] Branagh's film alerts its audience to the function of signs even as it parodies with laughable directness their lost relevance and function in contemporary culture. As the small car loaded with the actors drives past a signpost designating that they have entered the hamlet of "Hope," one actor chirps, "I think it's a sign." "Yes, love," responds another actor, "it's a road sign." "I think it's symbolical," murmurs another.[18] Yet, as this moment also (symbolically) reveals, the space of the theater holds the hope of a fluid traffic between the "signs" of dramatic representation and the social world the actor inhabits, in that the act of signification itself is "informed by the circumstances of the performance" and thereby invested with meaning.[19] Like Shakespeare's own theater, Branagh's film draws the viewer's attention to the interpenetration of "signs," in which the audience is continually aware of the relationship between the actor who represents a particular role and that actor's identity as understood in the context of the film's narrative, and extends that vision outward toward a larger circle of cultural, commercial, theatrical, and historical references the audience shares with the performer who plays the actor who plays a part in *Hamlet*.

Branagh's film self-consciously compares the theater in Shakespeare's time to the cinema of the modern age, for it is the cinematic medium that permits experimentation from a wide range of available perspectives and ponders the historical moment of its own possibility. *A Midwinter's Tale* is filled with references to other films, performances, and twentieth-century Shakespearean actors, and is as notably self-reflexive as *Hamlet*. As Barbara Everett observes, "There is an old joke about *Hamlet* being full of quotations. So it is; but perhaps so it always was, even for its audiences."[20] Branagh's *A Midwinter's Tale* is similarly intertextual in its agonistic relationship between theater and film, in its reliance on correspondences of similarity and difference between Olivier's *Hamlet* and this film, and in its critique of the commercialization of cultural and artistic legitimacy. And by using many of the same actors in this film and in his *Hamlet* (1996), Branagh rewrites or transforms one film by another in an intertextual relationship that is enormously powerful for film viewers. Branagh treats these processes themselves as subject matter for reframing. Casting and auditioning are essential components in the earliest scenes of *A Midwinter's Tale,* and illustrate an aspect of frame activity that establishes limits, in that the viewer quickly ascertains that casting is a critical moment in the production of a play, however comic the auditions may be, since they are viewed with a critical eye by Joe's agent, Margaretta (Joan Collins).

We see in Joe Harper, not unlike Hamlet himself, a troubled awareness of the simultaneous resemblance and discrepancy between the play and its older models. Joe, like Hamlet, selects an old play because he feels it mirrors his inner state ("I'm depressed"), but, like Hamlet's *Murder of Gonzago,* the staginess and stylistic archaisms of the drama separate it from

Hollywood and its values and the modern existence that frame and mock it. Much as Shakespeare's drama often contextualizes a character within the trappings of an archaic theatricality to demonstrate the character's identification with that past, Branagh dramatizes Joe Harper's struggle to make meaning from *Hamlet* within a theatrical space reminiscent of Olivier's *Hamlet*.[21] In using black-and-white cinematography and deep-focus camera shots, and in emphasizing the cavernous space of the church as Joe grows more and more despairing of ever producing *Hamlet,* Branagh visualizes Joe's (and the film's) own obsession with Olivier. However, the older models that Joe and Hamlet choose fail them because they discover a gap between role and character. Examples abound in *A Midwinter's Tale* in which Joe's repeated attempts to replicate Olivier's successes only lead to disappointment. When Joe sits, in profile, in the darkened space of his makeshift office (strategically situated in front of the church altar) and intones Hamlet's lines, "O God, O God, / How weary, stale, flat, and unprofitable / Seem to me all the uses of this world!" (I.ii.132–34), the moment parodies Hamlet's lines (in that Joe sits over a page of accounts and contemplates his pressing financial woes) as well as Olivier's cinematic treatment of the play (in the heightened lighting upon Joe's profile, his theatrical pose, and the camera's penetrating focus). At this moment Joe's sister's face suddenly intrudes into the darkened space of the cinematic screen opposite Joe and sarcastically remarks, "That's not bad, Sir Laurence," undercutting the heightened drama of the brother's portrayal.[22] Of course, as Joe repeatedly complains, his professional and personal life fail utterly to conform to that of Sir Laurence Olivier: "If everything had gone according to Laurence Olivier's book I would have known triumph, disappointment and married a beautiful woman. Instead I've known tedium, humiliation and got shacked up with the psycho from hell."[23]

However, out of the friction between life and older dramatic models — even the cinematic ones — can come the light of "meaning." When the actors first arrive at the church, a long shot down the main hallway of the building reveals its immensity and spatial vastness in an obvious parody of the spatial and aesthetic boundaries that define Olivier's *Hamlet*. Yet even as the film parodies the cinematic atmosphere of Olivier's film as "People in space, in smoke" (figure 7.1), it attests to the power of that image, as Fadge, the set designer, confirms when she first walks into the church: "You know this place is incredible. I feel something very powerful here. Very strange and powerful."[24] In these moments Branagh forces his audience to confront its own contradictory responses to an apparently subsumed but recognizably conventional model of Olivier's *Hamlet* which *A Midwinter's Tale* repudiates with the illusion that it uses no art at all. However, the film also promotes reflexivity by calling attention to the cinematic apparatus itself through abrupt cuts between scenes juxtaposed to the static frames that announce each sequence. The fleeting procession of images and rapid dialogue seem momentarily frozen in their progression—and mimetically derealized—when the spectator's view shifts from a conventional impression of reality to the darkened screen that compartmentalizes each sequence under subtitles such as "Prologue: 'I have to talk to my agent.'" The visual effect is a double movement, so to speak, from mimesis to deconstruction, in that the film gestures toward a conventional impression of reality that rejects Olivier's elaborate expressionistic sets while cinematically presenting a sort of visual semiotics that momentarily halts the viewers' identification with seamless characters and plots.

Yet by parodying the cinematic space in which Olivier dramatized *Hamlet* and the cultural space that appropriated Shakespeare's theater (including vaudeville, which, as Joe tells Terry, gave "Shakespeare a bad name"), the film works through representational strategies that authorize its concluding vision of dramatic practice. Branagh takes Hamlet's role, atrophied into predictable performances through critical commentary and theater history, and makes it unpredictable by exploring both the inner resources of the play—the ambiguity of textual signs in "play"— and the outer resources of actors determined to bring *Hamlet* to Hope during the Christmas season. Although the film confronts the problem that traditional genres may not be fully adequate to the imaginative needs of our time, the transformational context of the film brings the audience to a realization that, even within a multiple and decentered perspective, the play can still be meaningful. The film makes us aware of what Stephen Orgel has called the "poetics of incomprehensibility" in Shakespeare's drama. Orgel points to *The Winter's Tale,* a play whose elliptical and often

FIGURE 7.1. Joe Harper as Hamlet on stage in smoke. (Courtesy of
Castle Rock Entertainment. Photo credit: David Appleby)

obscure diction and syntax have resisted the elucidation of centuries of
editors and critics, and warns that although "plays may start as private
musings, they end as scripts performed by actors for spectators, and their
success depends on what they convey to those spectators."[25] Lynn Enterline also observes of *The Winter's Tale* that the play concentrates upon the
"misframing that happens in 'this place' of the theatre" when the stage
turns "into a space of unpredictable events" of self-reflexive "performative utterances" of the "here and now."[26] These observations have relevance to Branagh's film, not solely because of the film's derivative title,

but because it also begins with a "private musing" that ends as a playscript "misframed" in the space of unpredictable and self-reflexive theatrical performances, much as the sallies that bombard the actors' conversations necessitate that the audience reframe or transform language into the personalized speech of the performers themselves. As one of the characters asks, "Is this entire production going to be conducted through a stream of innuendo?"[27] When the actors read through the play for the first time together, around a large table and in an atmosphere that gets progressively smoke-filled and chaotic, the viewer also experiences how the play may be "read through" the dislocations of private musings and playful vulgarisms, criticism, and theater practice, thereby permitting a re-examination of the play from decentered and shifting perspectives (figure 7.2).

Although the film squarely counters theatrical aesthetics as idealized by the elderly Henry and his nostalgia for the legendary performances of Henry Irving and his resistence to gay casting, the film does so more to alert us to what has changed in the way we experience Shakespeare than to ridicule Henry as "old school" or because he is reluctant to embrace the obvious erosion of the humanistic certainties associated with the acting tradition. Similarly, although the film deromanticizes and exposes through burlesque and parody aspects of *Hamlet*—and its theatrical and cinematic past—the ultimate effect of Branagh's film is a nostalgic invocation of a great and distinctly English theatrical tradition, even as we sense how removed we are from that earlier time. *A Midwinter's Tale* actively encourages the cultivation of nostalgia: we see the play's Claudius and Gertrude in make-up that recalls the silent Shakespeare films of the early century, and we hear Joe romanticize about "Shakespeare's own theatre," when "a six-week season would have produced thirty-five performances of seventeen different plays including at times four world premieres."[28] As far from the plot of Shakespeare's *Hamlet* as this film seems to take the audience, it ultimately brings it deeper into the world of actor, script, and theater that is played out in the English countryside of Hope, in an abandoned church before the faithful few. The film immerses us in the nostalgic past of English theater even as it demythologizes the acting process and the supposed sanctity of the Shakespearean text, exploding

Figure 7.2. The actors read through *Hamlet*. (Courtesy of Castle Rock Entertainment. Photo credit: David Appleby)

the myths of the acting tradition even as it affirms the origins of English theater as a reflection of human aspirations and need.

"For O, for O, the hobbyhorse is forgot"

The film reimagines the connection between theater and the sacred, even as the speeches of Hamlet and Gertrude seem to recast the experience of *Hamlet* into a straightforward morality drama.[29] In fact, Hamlet's goal to "set it right" informs Joe Harper's impulses to redress what has become perverted, inverted, or aborted. Joe, like Hamlet, assumes a quest for clarification of the order and hierarchies and values of his world. When the actors first arrive in Hope, they comment that the church in which they will perform, like their own aspirations and intentions, has "fallen into disuse." But Joe enthusiastically announces: "We're not just doing a play. We're here on a mission. To save this place. To get the developer out and the people back in."[30] Harper's "moral journey," as an expression of his struggle with human issues of guilt and depression, is inseparable from his artistic one, which is not merely likened to Shakespeare's drama but demonstrates how Shakespeare's art can be a conduit of manifestation, even as his "layering" outside the dramatic frame has a distinctly ironic quality. For in giving up his worldly "stardom" (the coveted role as a "spaceman" in a three-picture Hollywood film deal) Harper takes an important step toward love and redemption, for himself and for his craft.

In both *Hamlet* and *A Midwinter's Tale* the function of tradition is almost identical with that of the theater itself, but in Shakespeare's play the signs and patterns of tradition and ritual suffer "the selective neglect of cultural structures," so that, as Naomi Liebler observes, "the commands of tradition and ritual processes run through *Hamlet* like the understage voice of the ghost."[31] Branagh's film takes the central issues of *Hamlet*—the changing times that problematize the value of the past and the evaporation of old customs—and highlights them through the actor's perception of living in changing times that value Hollywood spacemen over Shakespearean actors. The actors reveal how they, too, are "haunted" by the dead forms of tradition in their sepulchral theater. When two of the actors make their beds in the crypt, they joke about the relationship between the space in which they reside and their art. One actor asks, "Do they mean to suggest something about our acting?" to which the other actor puns, "That it's cryptic?" "No," the actor explains, "that it's *dead*."

In *Hamlet*, the play's rituals are either corrupted or truncated, as evidenced by the funeral-marriage-coronation that begins the play, Claudius's failed confessional, Ophelia's abbreviated funeral ceremony, and the funeral procession that crowns Fortinbras as king at the play's end. As Shakespeare's drama demonstrates, without the mediation of a shared set of references, however fractured, Hamlet experiences the collapse of traditional boundaries. Because, as Goffman observes, ritual illustrates the recursive character of framing, in that we perceive a particular scene or dramatic moment as having "some continuity, an existence before the scene occurs and an existence that continues on after the scene is over" so that it, too, becomes part of our reality, Joe Harper's recuperative gestures underscore that he is also radically detatched from these ritual patterns.[32] The film reveals the breakdown of the historical and cultural values of the past by exposing the contradictory possibilities of interpretation and the theater's absorption with its own artifacts, styles, and techniques. The actors repeatedly express nostalgia for a lost epoch of human faith in yearning for an earlier "romantic" time, when "the old Shakespeare Companies" traveled "from town to town on a Sunday" with hundreds of people waving them off from the platform, and for the great Shakespearean actors of an earlier day (in Henry Wakefield's tribute to Irving's Othello and Joe Harper's obsession with Olivier).[33] In their longing for the perennial wisdom of the theater, the actors self-consciously articulate their lack of continuity with a theatrical past that has been lost at the level of signs. Yet even as this production parodies theatrical tradition, for example, in casting the flamboyantly cross-dressed and homosexual Terry as Queen Gertrude, the actor underscores his relationship to the dramatic past he deconstructs: "Darling, just 'cos I'm in a frock at the end of a pier, doesn't mean I don't have a grasp of theatrical history."[34]

In that the actors' reminiscences at times verge on religious awe (as underscored by the circumstances of the actors' performance of Shakespearean tragedy in an abandoned church at Christmas time), the convergences of these rituals, both Shakespearean and religious, suggest the memory of our communal heritage, and the lost social function of that memory, a concern that Hamlet satirically articulates as "'For O, for O, the hobbyhorse is forgot'" (III.ii.133). Liebler observes that Hamlet's comment speaks to a paradoxical awareness of ritual both lost and recalled, its "continuity contested by suppression, while its remembrance signifies resistance to change."[35] In this respect, Branagh's comic references to tradition are as purposeful as Hamlet's, in that he claims legitimacy for an apparently abandoned theatrical tradition that, like the hobbyhorse, is forgotten. These lines are also meaningful in the context of the film's assertion that the public's rites of memory are inseparable from the cultural impact of Shakespeare's drama, in that the text remains essentially incomplete without them.

However, as Joe's agent, Margaretta, smugly suggests, the spiritual and psychological resources of theatrical ritual remain unabated, despite the public's loss of memory. When Joe admits that he's "feeling less suicidal now" with rehearsals for *Hamlet* actually in progress, Margaretta confidently asserts, "Then it's working. Marvellous. Good night sweet prince."[36] In likening Joe's resurrection to Hamlet's death, Margaretta connects Joe's psychological salvation with Hamlet's spiritual and secular salvation. For, as Howard Felperin argues, although Horatio's lines construct a morality play analogy for Hamlet's end, Hamlet's dying words articulate a concern for his "*secular* salvation" and his "wounded name" that survive him in history.[37] It seems that Branagh's film would have it both ways as well, in that Joe Harper seeks to preserve his "wounded" professional name before the all-too-worldly financial considerations of Hollywood producers and agents, while celebrating the miraculous transformative power of Shakespeare's drama as founded upon spiritual and theatrical ritual. The visual emphasis in the film shares this dual perspective, in that the cavernous Gothic church in which the actors rehearse inspires associations with the religious sanctifications of medieval art, while the actors' rehearsals within that space reveal that their craft is the product of hard work, not inspiration. So while the film pays homage to the actors' craft as a means of production by demystifying their art, the space of this theater quite literally resuscitates the memory of tradition and ritual processes.

In their comic rehearsals of *Hamlet,* the actors find some sense of continuity between the dramatic form and the spiritual resources it draws upon. Ironically, as unstable in dramatic form as *Hamlet* appears in Branagh's film, it supplies inspiration and feelings normally unavailable to ordinary people, revealing how Shakespeare's theater can function as an existential and nonfictional use of memory and emotion for ordinary mankind. Indeed, *A Midwinter's Tale* reveals how Shakespeare's *Hamlet* is the central catalyst for reviving an actor's faith in himself, recalling Wilson Knight's comment that "we need expect no Messiah, but we might, at this hour, turn to Shakespeare."[38]

Unlike Shakespeare's play, which tells its audience that this is *not* "that Season . . . / Wherein our Savior's Birth is celebrated," Branagh's film returns the viewer to the time of the Messiah. The ritual of putting on a play at Christmastime reveals the frame of a culture's collective values at the intersection of the traditional and the improvised, the sacred and the secular. The pivot of time in Branagh's *A Midwinter's Tale* is the authentic pivot of time, the Christ event, or Christmas, from which all meaning or typological representation flows. Yet in the film we immediately perceive a tension between what we might call theology and psychoanalysis, or the displacements of characters we associate with depression and hidden sexual thematics. It is significant that in this film there is a character who resolutely refuses to "see," but who is also associated with the typology of the Christ story through her story of sacrifice, loss, and restoration (Nina's husband, as Nina tells Joe Harper, died tragically at the age of thirty-three). In this respect *A Midwinter's Tale* is both nostalgia and parody—a comic union of desire and mystical insight—that enables this small community of actors to rekindle hope and redress its wrongs, motivated by an actor-Hamlet who discovers himself in the reciprocal relations of a community of actors and its individual members.

The film's emphasis upon the Christmas season alerts the viewer to an internal frame of reference even as it gestures outward toward a larger cultural frame, a concentration on what lies "inside" the play even as it expands to encompass what lies "outside." As Barbara Everett observes, *Hamlet* has a "Christmassy" quality for theater audiences, in that it is a drama frequently produced for the Christmas season, along with detective stories and thrillers, for reasons she believes have to do with the play's "profoundly reminiscential, nostalgic, obscurely looking back," qualities:

> The play would be different without this curiously stirring legend that "The Bird of Dawning singeth all night long"—it would lack some endorsement, some sense of otherwhere. Commentators don't seem to ask why Shakespeare failed to use the more conventional association of cockcrowing with Easter. But the New Arden editor is surely right to hint that the writer invented rather than found this myth of Christmas. And if Shakespeare did so, then his reason was that Christmas was needed in his play.[39]

The Christmas reference is intrinsic to Hamlet's story—perhaps as one more marker of "meaning" having been emptied out of the play's signs and rituals—even as Branagh's *A Midwinter's Tale* folds Christmastime back into *Hamlet* as holiday entertainment, comically illustrating the recursive character of framing. In an interview when he was starring in Adrian Noble's 1992–93 Royal Shakespeare Company production of *Hamlet*, Branagh was asked about "the reasoning behind setting the action against the Christmas season," and responded, "It was possibly that we were rehearsing near Christmas, that there was something in the air which just made it pungent."[40] Perhaps film audiences also unconsciously associate *Hamlet* with the Christmas season (in recent memory, both Zeffirelli's *Hamlet* and Branagh's *Hamlet* were released during the Christmas holidays), or, as Branagh suggests, the play savors of something that argues for connecting Hamlet's tragic drama—and Joe Harper's comic one—within this larger frame of cultural and literary history. Certainly Branagh's film is not the first narrative to comically place Hamlet's drama in conjunction with the Christmas season.[41] The film illustrates how dramaturgy invariably exceeds the boundaries of its representation, and suggests a continuity in the resources of representation, in which *A Midwinter's Tale* is a significant but partial link in the supplemental chain of cultural and literary references that work both inside and outside the play.

Not only does the film explore the margins of textuality, but it also explores theater at the margins, a place where negated actors, theaters, and performances come to the center, and where festive laughter urges a symbolic victory over the oppressive concerns of finances, personal loss, and Hollywood. Part of the film's interrogation of traditional boundaries and of any single, domineering interpretation is its subversion of the social hierarchies that preserve aesthetic unity, and, by implication, their political significance. Branagh illuminates how film occupies a space at the intersection of historical, theatrical, financial, and cultural dissonances, which are amplified in the cavernous interior of the play's church location rather than solved. Here the forces of Hollywood materialism and vulgarity finally intrude upon the church's theatrical space, luring away one of the actors to play a spaceman in latex and even carrying off some of Fadge's designs. But as Fadge's struggle to come up with a design for their production makes clear, the miniature model of the church and the cardboard people seated among the audience members simply reflect the actual space they inhabit, much as this film emphasizes that art unavoidably reveals the principles of construction (figure 7.3). And that includes financial aspects of art's creation. For although *A Midwinter's Tale* crystalizes and actualizes the utopian desires of the little community of actors, who pool their collective energies and resources to raise the funds for their production of *Hamlet,* it also exposes the enterprise's degraded expression. When Harper ruminates, "Well, we can't charge proper ticket prices, that's not what it's about anyway," in the same breath he obsesses about the financial arrangements by which he hopes to garner "an average donation of £2.50, that is £750 per night, which makes it £5,250 for the run, less £2,100 for the production budget and rent, less £100 per week per person profit-share (hopefully) for three weeks for eight people, less £150 for the first night drinks and Christmas dinner, less £600 for food and utilities."[42] In other words, market considerations and finances *are,* to a great extent, "what it's about." The film firmly rejects idealized conceptions of art and its romantic myths by dramatizing the economic forces that impinge upon the actor's craft.

FIGURE 7.3. The audience, both real and imaginary, on opening night. (Courtesy of Castle Rock Entertainment. Photo credit: David Appleby)

"Why must the show go on?" the film repeatedly asks. Joe's agent warns him, "at this time of year, everyone is doing Christmas shows or TV specials so all you are going to get is eccentrics, misfits and nutters."[43] The casting call that Joe advertises alerts the viewer to the peculiar enterprise that will unfold on Christmas eve with *Hamlet* as its vehicle: The agent reads "a co-operative experience," "profit-share, 'spirit share,'" "six fellow journeymen to enter the gloomy dane," "apply to the director and sweat prince."[44] The typographical errors alert the viewer to the flip side of Joe's dreamy visionary perspective, that the enterprise can be depressing and unrequited labor, work in a sweat shop and not the lofty enterprise he hopes.

Whereas *Hamlet* explores the constitutive liminalities of the protagonist and those of his community, Branagh's *A Midwinter's Tale* dramatizes the liminal status of Shakespeare's art in late-twentieth-century culture through the political and artistic vulnerability of the actor and his community. The film refracts the social realities of the theater practitioner through the prism of Shakespeare's drama, and exposes the ideology, false consciousness, and reification that render art nothing more than another economic category. The film exposes the devices of art while being itself a critical instrument of art, stripping the play of its mystical wrappings and seeming to devalue the play through parody (as may be seen in its parade of incompetent actors at the beginning of the film). But Branagh distances us from the play in order to allow us to come back into it, more involved, more fully believers in the illusions that foster hope. Harper's cynical comment to Nina — "Finally it's Shakespeare and nobody's interested" — is delivered just as he leaves the cast for a lucrative three-picture deal with a Hollywood producer.[45] But, like Hamlet, Joe returns to play out the final scene. His artistic integrity — and heart — win out over the temptations of Hollywood, commercialism, and material gain.

Out of the ashes of depression, alienation, and hopelessness, Joe develops a relationship with the "workers" of this "production." The film participates in the aims of Brechtian theater not only in defamiliarizing the audience with the play and in revealing the principles of construction upon which theatrical artifice is grounded, but also by introducing an actor who is alienated from his work and reduced by economic necessity to seriously competing for a role as a spaceman in a film. The scenario thematizes the issues of production and consumption, in which artists and intellectuals are the "producers." The film, in fact, performs a materialist variation on reflexivity by reminding the audience of the film's institutional infrastructure. The opening scenes unmask the alienated and depressed actor, speaking directly into the camera lens, modulating the circumstances of his alienation. The following black-and-white documentary-style film footage reveals a series of encounters that are anything but realistic. Not a single actor seems to be doing what is "natural" except for the film's "Ophelia," who falls on her face as soon as she starts to dance and sing about having "a heart of glass." With each successful audition, the viewer sees momentarily the publicity still that defines that actor, a crafted image for public consumption.

In Branagh's film the narrative of the two stories—Hamlet's and Joe's—follows parallel trajectories of the carnivalesque by implying an attitude of creative disrespect and a radical opposition to the illegitimately powerful. In the opening moments of the film Branagh distinguishes between a hierarchy of arts—with Hollywood film and television at its bottom, as hopelessly vulgar and tainted, and Shakespeare's drama at its apex, with its sacred space of ritual and ancient tragedy. The American producer, Nancy Crawford (Jennifer Saunders), who appears at the end of the film clearly represents the mundane and the average, the black hole into which the privileged space of theater has drifted. Hence her insistence upon rendering Fadge's name into a part of the female anatomy, taking all that is sublime or mysterious and rendering it carnal, banal, or absurd. Crawford degrades and vulgarizes the ritual of playing Shakespeare, even as she vulgarizes the play's spatial relationships, transforming Tom into a spaceman and Fadge into Vadge. Is this the "fairytale" that Joe envisions? Or, as another suggests, "Bloody nightmare more like it." Yet in the theatrical space of the Hope *Hamlet* even these opposing hierarchies of value become confused and conflated when high art meets low art. Here even a Hollywood producer can enjoy, however imperfectly, an imperfect Shakespearean production, and a Shakespearean actor obsessed with his craft discovers he has the requisite "character" to play a spaceman beneath layers of latex.

Joe begins the film questioning the meaning of things—whether life can be like an old movie— *The Wizard of Oz* with "family murders" and a fairytale ending—but it is Nina who intones the film's final message, "Listen, everyone, Merry Christmas!" in a long shot of the lit church, alive with love and hope on Christmas eve. Like Shakespeare's *The Winter's Tale,* Branagh's film reveals that, even as ritual is undone or questioned, it is remade again at the end. Perhaps not as Shakespeare envisioned it, but faithful, nonetheless, to the fragments perpetually in process that we call "Shakespeare." Although many of the jokes in this film derive from Branagh's cultural ransacking and his critique of the theater's advanced stages of consumerism, the film ultimately enshrines Shakespeare's art as a recourse to another plane of existence and means to begin a moral pilgrimage toward purification. The "blessing" that concludes *A Midwinter's Tale* resonates within the context of the parental blessings that affirm the bonds between parent and child in *The Winter's Tale* (in that Branagh conflates both theatrical and biological families in the comic resolution of the film) in a celebration of art as an expression of divine grace and good will, graciousness, and generosity. That blessing does not set itself apart from the experiences of the characters in the film, but exists at the convergence of the spaces of ritual, both sacred and theatrical. Nina's effusion affirms the sacredness of this world and the ordinary people in it, and, in particular, Joe Harper's decision to rejoin his theatrical community, which promises an enrichment of his personal identity.

Branagh's film embraces Shakespeare with a sophisticated awareness of generic expectations and constructs, not with creative exhaustion, but exhilarated by imaginative possibilities. *A Midwinter's Tale* is delirious with the prospect (one detects in certain scenes Branagh's anticipation of his own *Hamlet*) of breathing life into the language of the play, where speaking lines becomes again the language of living, breathing characters, and not the frozen forms of theatrical tradition. Ultimately, what "works" in this film is its ability to draw the audience from the textual center to a level beyond that of style, plot, character, or theme, where one may discover an immanence of meanings.

Notes

Introduction

1. Graham Holderness, *Shakespeare Recycled: The Making of Historical Drama* (New York: Barnes and Noble, 1992), pp. 178–210.

2. Virginia Mason Vaughan, *Othello: A Contextual History* (Cambridge: Cambridge University Press, 1994), p. 7.

3. For example, Herb Coursen's *Watching Shakespeare on Television* (Rutherford, N.J.: Fairleigh Dickinson University Press, 1993) argues that cinematic productions of *Hamlet* fail as adaptations, compared with television productions of the play, because they delete Fortinbras and thereby obscure the political implications that his invasion of the Danish court signals.

4. William Shakespeare, *A Midsummer Night's Dream*, in *The Complete Works of William Shakespeare*, 4th edition, ed. David Bevington (New York: Harper Collins, 1992). All references will be to this edition, unless otherwise noted.

5. Vivian Sobchack, *The Address of the Eye: A Phenomenology of Film Experience* (Princeton, N.J.: Princeton University Press, 1992), p. 134.

6. Voltaire, "Preface to Brutus" (1731), in *Shakespeare in Europe*, ed. Oswald LeWinter (London: Penguin, 1970), pp. 29–41; and Jan Kott, *Shakespeare Our Contemporary*, trans. Boleslaw Taborski (New York: Anchor, 1966), pp. 348–49.

7. Geoffrey H. Hartman, "Shakespeare and the Ethical Question: Leo Löwenthal *in Memoriam*," *ELH* 63 (1996): 7.

8. David Bordwell, *Narration in the Fiction Film* (Madison: University of Wisconsin Press, 1985), p. 7.

9. Noël Carroll, *Theorizing the Moving Image* (Cambridge: Cambridge University Press, 1996), pp. 86, 87.

10. Carroll, *Theorizing the Moving Image*, pp. 89, 91.

11. Samuel Crowl, *Shakespeare Observed: Studies in Performance on Stage and*

Screen (Athens: Ohio University Press, 1992); Barbara Hodgdon, *The End Crowns All: Closure and Contradiction in Shakespeare's History Plays* (Princeton, N.J.: Princeton University Press, 1991); Graham Holderness, *Shakespeare Recycled;* Peter Donaldson, *Shakespearean Films/Shakespearean Directors* (Boston: Unwin Hyman, 1990); John Collick, *Shakespeare, Cinema and Society* (Manchester: Manchester University Press, 1989).

12. Anthony Davies, *Filming Shakespeare's Plays: The Adaptations of Laurence Olivier, Orson Welles, Peter Brook, Akira Kurosawa* (Cambridge: Cambridge University Press, 1988), and Lorne M. Buchman, *Still in Movement: Shakespeare on Screen* (Oxford: Oxford University Press, 1991).

13. Graham Holderness, "Shakespeare Rewound," *Shakespeare Survey* 45 (1992): 64.

14. Holderness, "Shakespeare Rewound," pp. 64, 66.

15. Holderness, "Shakespeare Rewound," p. 66.

16. Holderness, "Shakespeare Rewound," p. 74.

17. Stephen Orgel, "What Is a Text?" in *Research Opportunities in Renaissance Drama* 26 (1981): 3–6. For editorial attempts to capture an imaginary ideal of the Shakespearean text, see Gabriel Egan, "Myths and Enabling Fictions of 'Origin' in the Editing of Shakespeare," *New Theatre Quarterly* 13.49 (February 1997): 41–47.

18. Leo Braudy, *The World in a Frame: What We See in Films* (Chicago: University of Chicago Press, 1976), p. 122. Braudy asserts that "the methods of the western, the musical, the detective film, or the science-fiction film are also reminiscent of the way Shakespeare infuses old stories with new characters to express the tension between past and present" (p. 108).

19. Inez Hedges, *Languages of Revolt: Dada and Surrealist Literature and Film* (Durham, N.C.: Duke University Press, 1983), p. 40.

20. Charles Altieri, *Canons and Consequences: Reflections on the Ethical Force of Imaginative Ideals* (Evanston, Ill.: Northwestern University Press, 1990), p. 41.

21. Altieri, *Canons and Consequences,* pp. 33, 37.

22. Susan Bennett, *Performing Nostalgia: Shifting Shakespeare and the Contemporary Past* (London and New York: Routledge, 1996), p. 16.

23. Leo Braudy, *Native Informant: Essays on Film, Fiction, and Popular Culture* (New York: Oxford University Press, 1991), p. 216.

24. Braudy, *Native Informant,* p. 223.

25. Erving Goffman, *Frame Analysis: An Essay on the Organization of Experience* (Cambridge, Mass.: Harvard University Press, 1974), p. 244.

26. Bertolt Brecht, *The Messingkauf Dialogues,* trans. John Willett (London: Eyre Methuen, 1965), p. 60.

27. Brecht, *The Messingkauf Dialogues,* pp. 57, 60.

28. Marvin Minsky, "A Framework for Representing Knowledge," in *The Psychology of Computer Vision,* ed. Patrick Henry Winston (New York: McGraw-Hill, 1975), p. 251.

29. Minsky, "A Framework for Representing Knowledge," p. 250.

30. Hedges, *Languages of Revolt,* p. 58.

31. Minsky, "A Framework for Representing Knowledge," p. 248.

32. Interestingly, Brecht perceived Shakespeare's drama in precisely these terms, as a problem-solving activity in which "the spectator does the constructing." Quoted in Margot Heinemann's essay "How Brecht Read Shakespeare," in *Political Shakespeare: New Essays in Cultural Materialism,* ed. Jonathan Dollimore and Alan Sinfield (Ithaca, N.Y.: Cornell University Press, 1985), p. 206.

33. Minsky, "A Framework for Representing Knowledge," p. 212.

34. Minsky, "A Framework for Representing Knowledge," p. 212.

35. Minsky, "A Framework for Representing Knowledge," p. 268.

36. Goffman, *Frame Analysis,* p. 238.

37. Bordwell, *Narration in the Fiction Film,* p. 31.

38. Goffman, *Frame Analysis,* p. 290.

39. Goffman, *Frame Analysis,* p. 80.

40. Goffman, *Frame Analysis,* p. 81.

41. Hedges, *Languages of Revolt,* p. 69.

42. Hedges, *Languages of Revolt,* p. 39.

43. Hedges, *Languages of Revolt,* p. 39.

44. For a discussion of this term see Joan Copjec's *"India Song/Son nom de Venise dans Calcutta desert:* The Compulsion to Repeat," *October* 17 (1981), and Raymond Bellous, "Cine-Repetitions," *Screen* 20.2 (1979).

45. Goffman, *Frame Analysis,* p. 39.

46. Hedges defines "breaking the frame" as the upsetting of audience expectations and understanding of how experience is organized, both psychologically and cognitively (the set of expectations that the viewer brings to the film). See *Languages of Revolt,* pp. 34–57, and *Breaking the Frame: Film Language and the Experience of Limits* (Bloomington: Indiana University Press, 1991). Also see Goffman, *Frame Analysis,* p. 364, for a discussion of frame breaking.

47. As Goffman observes, since "the longer in the past an event took place, the less can ready evidence about it be collected, and the more must reliance be placed on whatever can be dredged up" (*Frame Analysis,* p. 450).

48. Goffman, *Frame Analysis,* p. 388.

49. Goffman, *Frame Analysis,* pp. 413, 420.

50. Robert Stam, *Reflexivity in Film and Literature: From Don Quixote to Jean-Luc Godard* (Ann Arbor, Mich.: U.M.I. Research Press, 1985), p. 134.

51. Goffman, *Frame Analysis,* p. 82.

52. Barbara Freedman, *Staging the Gaze: Postmodernism, Psychoanalysis, and Shakespearean Comedy* (Ithaca, N.Y.: Cornell University Press, 1991), pp. 178–79.

53. Jean-Louis Baudry and Christian Metz, for example, argue that cinematic spectatorship is a dreamlike experience in which the viewer loses his awareness of the projected image as illusion.

54. Murray Smith, "Film Spectatorship and the Institution of Fiction," *The Journal of Aesthetics and Art Criticism* 53.2 (1995): 122.

Chapter 1

1. Richard Corliss, "Wanna Be . . . Or Wanna Not Be?" *Time,* January 7, 1991, p. 73.

2. Robert Hapgood observes in "Popularizing Shakespeare: The Artistry of Franco Zeffirelli," in *Shakespeare the Movie: Popularizing the Plays on Film, TV and Video,* ed. Lynda E. Boose and Richard Burt (London and New York: Routledge, 1997), that Zeffirelli's *Hamlet* seems more "durable" than Olivier's film, although he suspends judgment on Branagh's recent film version of the play (pp. 80–94).

3. Neil Taylor, "The Films of *Hamlet,*" in *Shakespeare and the Moving Image: The Plays on Film and Television,* ed. Anthony Davies and Stanley Welles (Cambridge: Cambridge University Press, 1994), p. 192.

4. Barbara Hodgdon, "The Critic, the Poor Player, Prince Hamlet, and the Lady in the Dark," in *Shakespeare Reread: The Texts in New Contexts,* ed. Russ McDonald (Ithaca and London: Cornell University Press, 1994), p. 292.

5. Hodgdon, "The Critic, the Poor Player, Prince Hamlet, and the Lady in the Dark," p. 292.

6. Kathleen Campbell, "Zeffirelli's *Hamlet*—Q1 in Performance," *Shakespeare on Film Newsletter* 16.1 (December 1991): 7.

7. Hodgdon, "The Critic, the Poor Player, Prince Hamlet, and the Lady in the Dark," p. 282.

8. Leo Braudy, *The World in a Frame,* p. 126.

9. Ruth M. Levitsky, "Rightly to Be Great," *Shakespeare Studies* 1 (1965): 142–67, for example, investigates *Hamlet* within the context of Renaissance notions of honorable behavior, and argues that Hamlet's dilemma is not whether he should act but how.

10. For example, in *Filming Shakespeare's Plays,* Anthony Davies discusses Olivier's *Henry V* as Western genre (pp. 35–37).

11. Braudy, *The World in a Frame,* pp. 108–9.

12. Lee Clark Mitchell, *Westerns: Making the Man in Fiction and Film* (Chicago: University of Chicago Press, 1996), p. 24.

13. Franco Zeffirelli, "Breaking the Classical Barrier," interview by John Tibbetts, *Literature/Film Quarterly* 22.2 (1994): 138.

14. Hodgdon, "The Critic, the Poor Player, Prince Hamlet, and the Lady in the Dark," p. 290.

15. Hodgdon, "The Critic, the Poor Player, Prince Hamlet, and the Lady in the Dark," pp. 276–77.

16. In "Shakespeare, Zeffirelli, and the Homosexual Gaze," *Literature/Film Quarterly* 20.4 (1992): 308–25, William Van Watson argues that Zeffirelli's film is an homage to patriarchy and to his mentor and predecessor, Laurence Olivier.

17. Franco Zeffirelli, *Zeffirelli: The Autobiography of Franco Zeffirelli* (New York: Weidenfeld and Nicolson, 1986), p. 201.

18. According to Lawrence Danson, "Gazing at Hamlet, or the Danish Cabaret," *Shakespeare Survey* 45 (1992), Olivier's performance of Hamlet comes out of "a long tradition of actresses playing Hamlet" of which Sarah Bernhardt is the most famous (43). Danson also detects elements of the female film star in Olivier's bleached blonde hair, "which in Hollywood films of the 1940s is the studio starlet's colour-of-choice," and his depiction of a "languidly passive" Hamlet as "object to be seen by the aggressive camera" (p. 50).

19. Hodgdon, "The Critic, the Poor Player, Prince Hamlet, and the Lady in the Dark," p. 278.

20. In fact, Robert Warshow's description of the Western hero as a reluctant player in a drama that has established formulations of plot and situation clearly alludes to—and echoes—*Hamlet:* "What 'redeems' him is that he no longer believes in this drama and nevertheless will continue to play the role perfectly: *the pattern is all"* (*The Immediate Experience: Movies, Comics, Theatre and Other Aspects of Popular Culture* [New York: Doubleday, 1962], p. 146). Nor is Warshow's allusion lost on Lee Clark Mitchell, who describes the Western as a "drama of self-restraint, where men *opposed by seas of troubles* refrained from arms until honorable means were exhausted" (*Westerns*, p. 223 [my emphasis]).

21. Mitchell, *Westerns,* pp. 161, 158.

22. Hodgdon, "The Critic, the Poor Player, Prince Hamlet, and the Lady in the Dark," p. 285.

23. Franco Zeffirelli, "Breaking the Classical Barrier," p. 137.

24. Mitchell, *Westerns,* p. 259.

25. Taylor, "The Films of *Hamlet*," p. 193.

26. Mitchell, *Westerns,* p. 159.

27. William Van Watson argues that Gibson's glamorous male movie-star characteristics are not the object of the camera's (homoerotic) gaze, and yet, according to Barbara Hodgdon, the viewer recognizes in Gibson a powerful and idealized representation of "excessive" masculinity.

28. Laura Mulvey, *Visual and Other Pleasures* (Bloomington: Indiana University Press, 1989), p. 20.

29. Bert O. States, *Hamlet and the Concept of Character* (Baltimore and London: Johns Hopkins University Press, 1992), p. 85.

30. States, *Hamlet and the Concept of Character*, p. 85.

31. States, *Hamlet and the Concept of Character*, p. 85.

32. John Andrew Gallagher and Sylvia Caminer, "Interview with Mel Gibson," *Films in Review* 47.5–6 (1996): 35.

33. Buchman, *Still in Movement*, p. 37.

34. Mitchell, *Westerns*, p. 167.

35. Mitchell, *Westerns*, p. 167.

36. Yvette Biró, *Profane Mythology: The Savage Mind of the Cinema,* trans. Imre Goldstein (Bloomington: Indiana University Press, 1982), p. 128.

37. According to Dale Silviria, *Laurence Olivier and the Art of Film Making* (Rutherford, N.J.: Fairleigh Dickinson University Press, 1985), Olivier's shooting script reveals that he originally intended to introduce a location scene of Hamlet on horseback. However, "Hamlet's horse had not cooperated; reportedly he wore a bored countenance capable of destroying the somber mood. Cost prohibited a reshooting of the location sequence" (p. 143).

38. Richard Slotkin, *Gunfighter Nation: The Myth of the Frontier in Twentieth-Century America* (New York: Atheneum, 1992), p. 387. Interestingly, this building is similar to a structure situated in the barren landscape of a postnuclear world in Gibson's early action film, *Road Warrior.*

39. Mitchell, *Westerns*, p. 168.

40. David Impastato, "Zeffirelli's *Hamlet:* Sunlight Makes Meaning," *Shakespeare on Film Newsletter* 16.1 (December 1991): 2.

41. Impastato, "Zeffirelli's *Hamlet,*" p. 2.

42. Zeffirelli, "Breaking the Classical Barrier," p. 140.

43. Annabel Patterson, *Shakespeare and the Popular Voice* (Cambridge: Basil Blackwell, 1989), p. 31.

44. The Western frequently incorporates Shakespeare in its film narrative, even as Zeffirelli's *Hamlet* incorporates elements from the Western. The acting troupe is a familiar component of the film Western, as in John Huston's *The Life and Times of Judge Roy Bean* (1972) when the actress Lily Langtry visits Texas, but Westerns also prominently feature moments from Shakespeare's drama, as when the Booth family

performs Shakespeare on a Western stage in Philip Dunne's *Prince of Players* (1955), or when an actor badly recites Hamlet's soliloquy in John Ford's *My Darling Clementine*. And, like the dumb show that informs *Hamlet*, these are moments in which the Western hero discovers his cue for action. For a discussion of *Hamlet*'s inclusion in Western film, see Scott Simmon's essay "Concerning the Weary Legs of Wyatt Earp: The Classic Western According to Shakespeare," *Literature/Film Quarterly* 24 (1996): 114–27.

45. Van Watson, "Shakespeare, Zeffirelli, and the Homosexual Gaze," p. 321.

46. Taylor, "The Films of *Hamlet*," p. 192.

47. Zeffirelli, *Zeffirelli*, p. 199.

48. Zeffirelli, *Zeffirelli*, p. 57.

49. Zeffirelli, *Zeffirelli*, pp. 57–58.

50. Donaldson, *Shakespearean Films/Shakespearean Directors*, p. 149.

51. Claire Gittings, *Death, Burial and the Individual in Early Modern England* (London and Sydney: Croom Helm, 1984), p. 122.

52. Gittings, *Death, Burial and the Individual in Early Modern England*, p. 121.

53. Whitgift quoted in Gittings, *Death, Burial and the Individual in Early Modern England*, p. 122.

54. Zeffirelli, *Zeffirelli*, p. 115.

55. Mitchell, *Westerns*, p. 174. Scholars of Western film discuss those moments in cemeteries in terms that invariably conjure comparisons with Shakespeare's *Hamlet*, as when Philip French observes that burial scenes in the Western function as a "grimly humorous *memento mori*," and often have "the mostly comic role assigned to the undertaker." French also warns that the burial scenes in Westerns are "not to be taken lightly," for death "is the great leveller" (*Westerns: Aspects of a Movie Genre* [New York: Oxford University Press, 1977], pp. 125, 123).

56. Mitchell, *Westerns*, p. 172.

57. Linda Charnes, "Dismember Me: Shakespeare, Paranoia, and the Logic of Mass Culture," *Shakespeare Quarterly* 48.1 (1997): 7.

58. Mitchell, *Westerns*, p. 207.

59. Mitchell, *Westerns*, p. 207.

60. Mulvey, *Visual and Other Pleasures*, pp. 33–34.

61. A brief review of recent critical interpretations illustrates my point: In "Shakespeare, Zeffirelli, and the Homosexual Gaze" Van Watson argues that the physical violence directed against the mother reveals Zeffirelli's "reactive focus from homophobia to its phallocentric corollary, misogyny" (p. 320), whereas Linda Charnes asserts that Zeffirelli literalizes Hamlet's oedipal "symptomology" by restoring the father "to his proper place through the 'classical' psychoanalytic logic of Oedipus" ("Dismember Me," pp. 10, 7). In "Freud's Footprints in Films of *Hamlet*," *Literature/Film Quarterly* 25.2 (1997), Philip Weller questions whether

Mel Gibson's Hamlet acts "to the modern understanding as a person with a neurotic Oedipus complex" at all because "unconscious problems are unconscious" (p. 124), whereas John P. McCombe argues in "Toward an Objective Correlative: The Problem of Desire in Franco Zeffirelli's *Hamlet*," *Literature/Film Quarterly* 25.2 (1997) that "Zeffirelli clearly displays, perhaps unconsciously, a debt to the *Hamlet* lecture of Jacques Lacan" (p. 128). "'In the Rank Sweat of an Enseamed Bed': Sexual Aberration and the Paradigmatic Screen *Hamlets*," *Literature/Film Quarterly* 25.2 (1997), James Simmons agrees that Zeffirelli "presented Hamlet's Oedipal confusion as fact" but concludes that the director contextualizes Hamlet's desires as the normal responses of a normal man, and not the "unprovoked sexual fantasies" of a "freak either unencouraged or only passively encouraged" (p. 116).

62. Lisa Jardine, *Reading Shakespeare Historically* (London and New York: Routledge, 1996), p. 153.

63. Biggs, "'He's Going to His Mother's Closet': Hamlet and Gertrude on Screen," *Shakespeare Survey* 45 (1992): 61.

64. Michael P. Jensen, "Mel Gibson on Hamlet," *Shakespeare on Film Newsletter* 15.2 (1991): 1–2.

65. French, *Westerns*, p. 67.

66. Mitchell, *Westerns*, p. 152.

67. Laura Mulvey, *Visual and Other Pleasures*, pp. 165–66.

68. Mitchell, *Westerns*, p. 218. As Noël Carroll explains regarding film metaphors, they "deploy homospatiality to suggest identity," in which disparate elements "are visually incorporated or amalgamated into one spatially bounded homogeneous entity" (*Theorizing the Moving Image*, pp. 213–14).

69. Braudy, *The World in a Frame*, p. 49.

70. Biró, *Profane Mythology*, p. 87.

71. Francis Barker, *The Culture of Violence: Essays on Tragedy and History* (Chicago: University of Chicago Press, 1993), p. 42.

72. Jack Jorgens, *Shakespeare on Film* (Bloomington: Indiana University Press, 1977), p. 217, and Davies, *Filming Shakespeare's Plays*, p. 45.

73. Braudy, *The World in a Frame*, p. 51.

74. Braudy, *The World in a Frame*, p. 71.

75. Biró, *Profane Mythology*, p. 125.

76. Michael Neill, *Issues of Death: Mortality and Identity in English Renaissance Tragedy* (Oxford: Clarendon Press, 1997), p. 239.

77. Mitchell, *Westerns*, p. 186.

78. Coursen interprets this "incompleteness" as "a need for the Fortinbras framing," in *Watching Shakespeare on Television*, p. 119.

79. Hodgdon, "The Critic, the Poor Player, Prince Hamlet, and the Lady in the Dark," p. 291.

Chapter 2

The first draft of this chapter was written as a paper for Barbara Freedman's seminar at the 1992 meeting of the Shakespeare Association of America in Kansas City, and expanded in 1993 for the Shakespearean Studies Seminar at Harvard University's Center for Literary and Cultural Studies, run by William Carroll and Virginia Vaughan.

1. Recent critical appraisals of *Othello* that underscore the voyeuristic impulse in the play are Barbara Everett's *Young Hamlet: Essays on Shakespeare's Tragedies* (Oxford: Clarendon Press, 1989), pp. 50–51, Patricia Parker's "*Othello* and *Hamlet*: Dilation, Spying, and the 'Secret Place' of Woman," in *Shakespeare Reread: The Texts in New Contexts,* ed. Russ McDonald (Ithaca and London: Cornell University Press, 1994), pp. 105–46, and Karen Newman's "'And wash the Ethiop white': Femininity and the Monstrous in *Othello,*" in *Shakespeare Reproduced: The Text in History and Ideology,* ed. Jean E. Howard and Marion F. O'Connor (New York and London: Methuen, 1987). Parker's essay emphasizes the contemporary apparatus of judicial power in *Othello* that panders to the horrified and fascinated gaze; Newman places the play within the context of "the male-dominated Venetian world of *Othello* . . . dominated by a scopic economy which privileges sight" in which Othello is "cast by Iago as eavesdropper and voyeur" (pp. 152–53).

2. Peter Donaldson, *Shakespearean Films/Shakespearean Directors,* p. 106.

3. James Naremore, *The Magic World of Orson Welles* (1978; rpt. Dallas: Southern Methodist University Press, 1989), p. 181.

4. *Filming Othello,* 16 mm color, directed and narrated by Orson Welles, photography by Klaus Hellwig and Juergen Hellwig, music by Gary Graver, edited by Marty Roth, documentary made for West German television, 1979, running time 84 minutes. My thanks to Peter Donaldson for alerting me to the existence of *Filming Othello* in Harvard University's Film Archives.

5. Barbara Leaming, *Orson Welles: A Biography* (New York: Penguin, 1983), p. 372.

6. Leaming, *Orson Welles,* p. 377.

7. Leaming, *Orson Welles,* p. 377.

8. Leaming, *Orson Welles,* p. 378.

9. Leaming, *Orson Welles,* p. 378.

10. Although David Pollard's essay "Iago's Wound," in *Othello: New Perspectives*, ed. Virginia Mason Vaughan and Kent Cartwright (Rutherford: Fairleigh Dickinson Press, 1991), pp. 89–96, is essentially a study of Iago, the essay has particular relevance for Orson Welles's development of the "voyeuristic pleasure of pain" in *Dr. Faustus* and later in the film *Othello*. Pollard's essay is instructive in making the connection between voyeurism and pain that we see operating in Eartha Kitt's account of Welles's behavior, and underscores the relationship between sadomasochism and scopophilia-exhibitionism as "parallel examples of how instincts may revert into their opposites," illustrating Freud's claim that the "passive aim (to be tortured, or looked at) has been substituted for the active aim (to torture and to look at)" (p. 91). Working from Freud's writing on sadomasochism in *Beyond the Pleasure Principle*, Pollard argues that "the sadistic and masochistic impulses are convertible, and when the one is transformed into the other, the process is always accompanied by a sense of guilt" (p. 90). In Kitt's narrative, Welles's behavior imitates this process, with the accompanying feelings of guilt.

11. Shakespeare, *Othello* (III.iv.67). All references to this play are from the Arden edition, ed. M. R. Ridley (1958; rpt. London and New York: Routledge, 1992).

12. Jorgens, *Shakespeare on Film*, p. 187.

13. Janet Bergstrom, "Enunciation and Sexual Difference," *Camera Obscura* 3–4 (1979): 33–59.

14. Jorgens, *Shakespeare on Film*, p. 185, has also noticed similarities between the scenes of these two films; however, his comments do not address the voyeuristic aspects of the Turkish bath scene.

15. Donaldson, *Shakespearean Films/Shakespearean Directors*, p. 107.

16. Leaming, *Orson Welles*, p. 41.

17. Leaming, *Orson Welles*, p. 47.

18. Leaming, *Orson Welles*, p. 47.

19. Leaming, *Orson Welles*, p. 367.

20. Leaming, *Orson Welles*, p. 370.

21. Leaming, *Orson Welles*, p. 43.

22. Kaja Silverman, *Male Subjectivity at the Margins* (New York: Routledge, 1992), p. 350.

23. Leaming, *Orson Welles*, pp. 370–371.

24. Leaming, *Orson Welles*, p. 371.

25. Laura Mulvey, *Visual and Other Pleasures*, p. 20.

26. Naremore, *The Magic World of Orson Welles*, p. 179.

27. Naremore, *The Magic World of Orson Welles*, p. 179.

28. Anthony Davies, *Filming Shakespeare's Plays*, p. 113.

29. Orson Welles, *Filming Othello*.

30. Davies, *Filming Shakespeare's Plays*, p. 118.

31. Davies, *Filming Shakespeare's Plays*, p. 118.

32. Barbara Hodgdon, "Kiss Me Deadly; or, The Des/Demonized Spectacle," in *Othello: New Perspectives*, ed. Virginia Mason Vaughan and Kent Cartwright (Rutherford, N.J.: Fairleigh Dickinson University Press, 1991), p. 226.

33. In *Put Money in Thy Purse: The Filming of Orson Welles' Othello* (London: Eyre Methuen, 1952) Micheal MacLiammoir quotes Welles: "All is to be Carpaccio, says Orson . . . . Carpaccio; which means hair falling wispishly to shoulders, small round hats of plummy red felt (though film not to be in colour), very short belted jackets, undershirt pulled in puffs through apertures in sleeves laced with ribbons and leather thongs, long hose, and laced boots" (p. 13).

34. Much in Welles's *Othello* is indebted to the sequence of paintings that constitutes the *Life of St. Ursula*. Carpaccio's "England" in "The Legend of St. Ursula" is very like the "Cyprus" in Welles's film. The social exoticism of Carpaccio's painted scene most likely was derived from geographical scenes depicted in the travel books of the age. In *Venetian Narrative Painting in the Age of Carpaccio* (New Haven: Yale University Press: 1989), p. 194, Patricia Fortini Brown reports that the "England" depicted in the *Leavetaking of the Betrothed Pair* has been identified as having been modeled on drawings of the Tower of the Cavaliers at Rhodes, from images portrayed in the engravings of Erhard Reeuwich in Breydenbach's *Opusculum Sanctarum Peregrinationum in Terram Sanctam,* published in Mainz in 1486. Brown points out that Carpaccio frames his *Return of the Ambassadors* as "two worlds separated by water, but connected in the front plane by the *déroulement* of the legend along a narrow wharf" (p. 185). The two worlds of Carpaccio's painting suggest the separation between the two worlds of Venice and Cyprus. The details that capture this moment in Carpaccio's painting—the arriving ships with full sails, the crashing waves, the trumpets raised, and the fortress walls peopled with spectators who view the meeting of the betrothed pair—are essential elements in Welles's depiction of the reunion of Shakespeare's betrothed pair, Desdemona and Othello. Even the inclined or bowing positions of two blonde figures in Carpaccio's "Leavetaking" suggest the canted shot of Desdemona and Cassio's greeting in Cyprus.

35. Norbert Huse and Wolfgang Wolters, *The Art of Renaissance Venice: Architecture, Sculpture, and Painting, 1460-1590,* trans. Edmund Jephcott (Chicago: University of Chicago Press, 1990), p. 203.

36. Huse and Wolters, *The Art of Renaissance Venice*, p. 203. For more on the significance of the dog, see Patrik Reutersward, "The Dog in the Humanist's Study," *Konsthistorisk tidskrift: revy for konst och konstforskning* 50.2 (1981): 53–69.

37. Ironically, the artistic achievements of Carpaccio, like those of Welles himself, evolved from circumstances that supposedly limited or hampered his performance. Much as film critics frequently attribute the visual fragmentation in Welles's *Othello* to the circumstances (financial, emotional, and artistic) in which he created his film, Peter Humfrey claims that Carpaccio's "looser, more broken and suggestive handling" of his paint was due to his working in the relatively new medium of canvas, which, unlike fresco, had a rougher and textured surface that would not accommodate the meticulously smooth brushwork of fresco painting (*Painting in Renaissance Venice* [New Haven, Conn.: Yale University Press, 1995], p. 82). Huse suggests that the emphasis upon objects within Carpaccio's paintings derives from the spatial restrictions Carpaccio encountered when forced to work in a low, horizontal and rectangular format; the proliferation of objects within Carpaccio's painting was the result of the artist's difficulty in filling the unusually large spaces designated for the narrative of the saints' lives. Consequently, "the artist's imagination was spurred far more by the accessories than by [the saints]" (Huse and Wolters, *The Art of Renaissance Venice*, p. 201). However, Patricia Fortini Brown cautions that Carpaccio deliberately sought a documentary accuracy in detail which intended that the central narrative of the painting should not be the central focus in the frame (Brown, *Venetian Narrative Painting in the Age of Carpaccio*, p. 125).

38. Terisio Pignatti, *Carpaccio* (New York: Editions d'Art Albert Skira, 1958), p. 59.

39. Brown, *Venetian Narrative Painting in the Age of Carpaccio*, p. 161.

40. In "Kiss Me Deadly," Barbara Hodgdon employs this term to describe the death of Desdemona, which she describes as reduced to the "metonymical representation" of "the bed; the lighted, and then extinguished, candle; the handkerchief" (p. 226).

41. Michael Neill, "Unproper Beds: Race, Adultery, and the Hideous in *Othello*," *Shakespeare Quarterly* 40 (1989): 406.

42. That Welles detected in Carpaccio "the stage designer" something of great affinity with the theatrical vision of Shakespeare should not be surprising. More recently, Philip Brockbank has also noted "analogous principles of perspective and order . . . at work on our ethical imaginations in certain paintings of Carpaccio and plays of Shakespeare," reflecting that "painting performed for fifteenth-century Venice some of the functions that theatre performed in sixteenth-century London" (Brockbank, "Urban Mysteries of the Renaissance: Shakespeare and Carpaccio" in his *The Creativity of Perception: Essays in the Genesis of Literature and Art* [Oxford: Basil Blackwell, 1991], p. 146). Brockbank intuits a sympathetic vision between these two great Renaissance artists, explaining that "While Shakespearean

perspectives are a theatrical complex of word and spectacle, Carpaccio offers us a painter's theatre," though he denies any "direct and literal" connections between the paintings of Carpaccio and Shakespeare's plays (p. 152). It is only through the filmic imagination of Orson Welles that the theatrical vision of Shakespeare and the visual theatricality of Carpaccio are finally literally and directly united.

43. In fact, the deceptive movements of the Turkish forces, contradictory to the various messengers, was much as Richard Knolles in *The Generall Historie of the Turkes* (London 1603) reported them at the famous battle of Lepanto: "For *Mustapha,* author of that expedition . . . had before appointed *Piall Bassa* at a time prefixed, to meet him at the Rhodes, and that he that came first should tarrie for the other, that so they might together saile unto Cyprus" (quoted in Geoffrey Bullough, ed., *Narrative and Dramatic Sources of Shakespeare* [London: Routledge and Kegan Paul, 1973], 7:263. Knolles's contemporary account states that the Turkish fleet comprised two hundred galleys, a number reported by the last of the Venetian messengers to the Senate in *Othello.* In writing his *Othello* Shakespeare may have had in mind the real battle strategies of the Turks at this famous battle. Though it had occurred nearly thirty years prior to the writing of *Othello,* interest in the battle was revived with the reprinting of James I's heroic poem "Lepanto" in 1603, the same year as the king's coronation (earliest known edition is 1591).

44. Brown, *Venetian Narrative Painting in the Age of Carpaccio,* p. 186. Certainly the relationship between the cinematic screen and Renaissance painting was a natural one. Jean-Louis Baudry has also found that Italian Renaissance painting and the camera's mode of inscription are based upon similar conceptions of space and constructions of perspective, so that the frame of the cinematic screen "permits the construction of an image analogous to the perspective projections developed during the Italian Renaissance" ("Ideological Effects of the Basic Cinematographic Apparatus," *Film Quarterly* 28 [winter 1974-75]: 39-47).

45. Brown, *Venetian Narrative Painting in the Age of Carpaccio,* p. 280.

46. In "Kiss Me Deadly," Hodgdon argues that the structure of Welles's film exploits "two classical forms, tragedy and Hollywood cinema" and points to the opening funeral procession as "an extended (and enclosed) flashback to explain the enigma posed by the opening (and framing) funeral procession" in which Welles reconstructs "Shakespeare's narrative to conform to an investigative model not unlike that of his earlier *Citizen Kane* (1941) or the later *Touch of Evil* (1958)" (p. 223).

47. Brown, *Venetian Narrative Painting in the Age of Carpaccio,* p. 184.

48. Brown, *Venetian Narrative Painting in the Age of Carpaccio,* p. 186.

49. Brown, *Venetian Narrative Painting in the Age of Carpaccio,* p. 95.

50. Brown, *Venetian Narrative Painting in the Age of Carpaccio*, p. 186.

51. Donaldson, *Shakespearean Films / Shakespearean Directors*, p. 116.

52. Lorne M. Buchman, "Orson Welles's 'Othello': A Study of Time in Shakespeare's Tragedy," *Shakespeare Survey* 39 (1986), p. 54.

53. Buchman, "Orson Welles's 'Othello,'" p. 55.

54. Jorgens, *Shakespeare on Film*, p. 178; Davies, *Filming Shakespeare's Plays*, p. 116.

55. Buchman, "Orson Welles's 'Othello,'" p. 54.

56. Davies, *Filming Shakespeare's Plays*, p. 108.

57. MacLiammoir, *Put Money in Thy Purse*, p. 27. Welles also states in *Filming Othello* that "Carpaccio was the source of the costumes and the general aesthetic of the movie."

58. Brown, *Venetian Narrative Painting in the Age of Carpaccio*, p. 132.

59. Brown, *Venetian Narrative Painting in the Age of Carpaccio*, p. 132. Coincidentally, Venetian patrons required that art provide demonstrable and tangible evidence of their honor and reputation, and the paintings they commissioned in the "eyewitness style" in Quattrocentro Venice reflect their need to register their proof of "worth" and honor in the abundance of often isolated details that appear in these paintings.

60. Brown, *Venetian Narrative Painting in the Age of Carpaccio*, p. 125. Brown notes the popularity of the chronicle histories of the period, which reflected the trend within the visual arts in attempting to create meaning from the cumulative weight of detailed observations. Narratives of expeditions to foreign and exotic lands emphasized description and detail, so that the "truth" of the narrative was judged by the plentitude of details and weight of exotic description. A particularly relevant example of the "eyewitness style" in the chronicle narratives of the period is Josafa Barbaro's description of his journey to Tana and Persia. Merchant, diplomat, and patrician of the Scuola di San Marco, Barbaro describes his travels in language that evokes Othello's, replete with an emphasis upon the fantastic in an account of "wonders" which only copious detail might affirm:

> . . . seeing that I have spent all of my yowthe and a great parte of myne age in ferre cuntries, amongst barbarouse people and men without civilitie, much different in all things from our customes, wheare I have proved and seene many things that, bicause they be not vsed in our parties, shulde seem fables to them (as who wolde saie) that were never out of Venice. (Josafa Barbaro and Ambrogio Contrarini, *Travels to Tana and Persia*, trans. William Thomas, ed. Lord Stanley of Alderley [London: Hakluyt Society, 1873], pp. 3–4).

Shakespeare may have known of William Thomas's English translation of Barbaro's travel narrative, *History of Italy* (1549); at least Geoffrey Bullough thinks so: see Bullough, *Narrative and Dramatic Sources of Shakespeare*, 7:212.

61. J. H. Plumb, *The Italian Renaissance* (1961; rpt. Boston: Houghton Mifflin, 1987), p. 102.

62. Plumb, *The Italian Renaissance*, p. 103.

63. Shakespeare's source for the play *Othello*, Giraldi Cinthio's *Gli Hecatommithi*, first published in 1565, according to Geoffrey Bullough, "is marked by a verisimilitude of detail which has made some scholars suspect that it was based on some police-court case of the sixteenth century" (*Narrative and Dramatic Sources of Shakespeare*, 7:195). Bullough cites several notorious cases that might have served to give the tale of Cinthio's "Disdemona" the requisite realistic detail that appealed to Venetians. Recounting a case from the records of the Avogadori, Guido Ruggiero quotes from the records the case of Maria Bono, wife of Roberto Bono, whose handkerchief was carried off by Tomaso Querini: "As a result of this deed the said Tomaso entered the home of Roberto many times during the day and night and committed many dishonesties with this lady with the highest dishonor for ser Robert" (*The Boundaries of Eros: Sex Crime and Sexuality in Renaissance Venice* [Oxford: Oxford University Press, 1985], p. 62).

64. Ruggiero, *The Boundaries of Eros*, p. 5. As one might expect, records of the Council of Ten were much less detailed that those of the Forty, since cases were heard internally by the Council of Ten and secrecy was paramount.

65. Guido Ruggiero, *Violence in Early Renaissance Venice* (New Brunswick, N.J.: Rutgers University Press, 1980), p. 43.

66. Ruggiero, *Violence in Early Renaissance Venice*, p. 43.

67. Brockbank, *The Creativity of Perception*, p. 157.

68. C. L. Barber and Richard P. Wheeler. *The Whole Journey: Shakespeare's Power of Development* (Berkeley: University of California Press, 1986), p. 22.

69. Gaylyn Studlar, *In the Realm of Pleasure: Von Sternberg, Dietrich, and the Masochistic Aesthetic* (New York: Columbia University Press, 1988), p. 124.

70. Gilles Deleuze and Felix Guattari, *Anti-Oedipus: Capitalism and Schizophrenia*, trans. Robert Hurley, Mark Seem, and Helen R. Lane (New York: Viking Press, 1977), p. 31, quoted in Studlar's *In the Realm of Pleasure*, p. 125.

71. Studlar, *In the Realm of Pleasure*, p. 124.

72. Jonathan Dollimore, *Sexual Dissidence: Augustine to Wilde, Freud to Foucault* (Oxford: Oxford University Press, 1991), p. 164.

73. Welles's filmic representation of Carpaccio's painterly world challenges Donaldson's assertion that "there is no indication . . . that the repression the film

evokes is the expression of a particular society at a particular historical moment" (*Shakespearean Films/Shakespearean Directors*, p. 116).

Chapter 3

1. Kenneth Branagh, *Beginning* (New York: St. Martin's Press, 1989), p. 144.

2. Stephen Greenblatt, *Shakespearean Negotiations: The Circulation of Social Energy in Renaissance England* (Berkeley: University of California Press, 1988), p. 63.

3. William P. Shaw, "Textual Ambiguities and Cinematic Certainties in *Henry V*," *Literature/Film Quarterly* 22.2 (1994): 121.

4. Sara Munson Deats, "Rabbits and Ducks: Olivier, Branagh, and *Henry V*," *Literature/Film Quarterly* 20.4 (1992): 285; and Donald Hedrick, "War Is Mud: Branagh's Dirty Harry V and the Types of Political Ambiguity," in *Shakespeare the Movie: Popularizing the Plays on Film, TV, and Video*, ed. Lynda E. Boose and Richard Burt (London and New York: Routledge, 1997), p. 47.

5. Hedrick, "War Is Mud," p. 47.

6. Hedrick, "War Is Mud," p. 59.

7. Noël Carroll, *Theorizing the Moving Image*, p. 279.

8. Erving Goffman, *Frame Analysis*, p. 310.

9. Linda Woodbridge, *The Scythe of Saturn: Shakespeare and Magical Thinking* (Urbana: University of Illinois Press, 1994), pp. 109–10.

10. Norman Rabkin, "Rabbits, Ducks, and *Henry V*," *Shakespeare Quarterly* 28 (1977): 279–96.

11. Peter Donaldson, "Taking on Shakespeare: Kenneth Branagh's *Henry V*," *Shakespeare Quarterly* 42.1 (1991): 63. However, in "Shakespeare's Kingly Mirror: Figuring the Chorus in Olivier's and Branagh's *Henry V*," *Literature/Film Quarterly* 25.1 (1997), Derek Royal argues that in the play "the Chorus undermines the heroic by way of example" but is cinematically muted in Branagh's film to "significantly temper any possible radical critique" (pp. 104, 105).

12. Murray Smith, "Film Spectatorship and the Institution of Fiction," *The Journal of Aesthetics and Art Criticism* 53.1 (1995): 116.

13. Smith, "Film Spectatorship and the Institution of Fiction," p. 117.

14. Branagh, *Beginning*, p. 233.

15. This is Goffman's term in *Frame Analysis*, p. 341.

16. Carroll, *Theorizing the Moving Image*, p. 285.

17. Leonard Tennenhouse, "Strategies of State and Political Plays: *A Midsummer Night's Dream, Henry IV, Henry V, Henry VIII*," in *Political Shakespeare: New Essays in Cultural Materialism*, ed. Jonathan Dollimore and Alan Sinfield (Ithaca: Cornell University Press, 1985), p. 120.

18. Woodbridge, *The Scythe of Saturn,* p. 12.

19. Woodbridge, *The Scythe of Saturn,* p. 96.

20. Branagh, *Beginning,* p. 223.

21. Brownell Salomon argues in "The Myth Structure and Rituality of *Henry V,*" *Yearbook of English Studies* 23 (1993), that the play correlates "in its entirety, point for point, with that selfsame ageless pattern of folktale and myth" (p. 257).

22. Yvette Biró, *Profane Mythology,* p. 75.

23. Joel B. Altman, "'Vile Participation': The Amplification of Violence in the Theatre of *Henry V,*" *Shakespeare Quarterly* 42 (1991): 16.

24. Altman, "'Vile Participation,'" p. 16.

25. Altman, "'Vile Participation,'" p. 17.

26. Altman, "'Vile Participation,'" p. 18.

27. Robert Lane, "'When Blood Is Their Argument': Class, Character, and Historymaking in Shakespeare's and Branagh's *Henry V,*" *ELH* 61.1 (1994): 37.

28. Branagh, *Beginning,* pp. 224–25.

29. Branagh, *Beginning,* p. 149.

30. Branagh, *Beginning,* pp. 143, 15, 16.

31. Branagh, *Beginning,* p. 15.

32. Branagh, *Beginning,* p. 224.

33. Graham Holderness, *Shakespeare Recycled,* p. 197.

34. Branagh, *Beginning,* p. 225.

35. Carroll, *Theorizing the Moving Image,* p. 111.

36. Carroll, *Theorizing the Moving Image,* p. 113.

37. Samuel Crowl, *Shakespeare Observed,* p. 170.

38. Michael Manheim, "The English History Play on Screen," in *Shakespeare and the Moving Image: The Plays on Film and Television,* ed. Anthony Davies and Stanley Welles (Cambridge: Cambridge University Press, 1994), p. 129. Lane also argues that Branagh's expressions of personal temperament historically disembody the king ("'When Blood Is Their Argument,'" p. 37).

39. Hedrick, "War Is Mud," p. 53.

40. Branagh, *Beginning,* p. 234.

41. Biró, *Profane Mythology,* p. 36.

42. Branagh, *Beginning,* p. 236.

43. Manheim, "The English History Play on Screen," p. 130.

44. Royal, "Shakespeare's Kingly Mirror," p. 109; Lane, "'When Blood Is Their Argument,'" p. 44; and Michael Neill, "Broken English and Broken Irish: Nation, Language, and the Optic of Power in Shakespeare's Histories," *Shakespeare Quarterly* 45 (1994): 22.

45. Royal, "Shakespeare's Kingly Mirror," p. 109.

46. Alan Sinfield (written with Jonathan Dollimore), "History and Ideology, Masculinity and Miscegenation: The Instance of *Henry V,*" in *Faultlines: Cultural Materialism and the Politics of Dissident Reading* (Berkeley: University of California Press, 1992), p. 139.

47. Carroll, *Theorizing the Moving Image,* p. 285.

48. Salomon, "The Myth Structure and Rituality of *Henry V,*" p. 266.

49. Woodbridge, *The Scythe of Saturn,* p. 197.

Chapter 4

1. Stephen Prince, *The Warrior's Camera: The Cinema of Akira Kurosawa* (Princeton, N.J.: Princeton University Press, 1991), p. 288.

2. Akira Kurosawa, *Something Like an Autobiography,* trans. Audie Block (New York: Alfred A. Knopf, 1982), p. 35.

3. Inez Hedges, *Breaking the Frame: Film Language and the Experience of Limits* (Bloomington: Indiana University Press, 1991), p. 98.

4. Kurosawa, *Something Like an Autobiography,* p. 35.

5. Kurosawa, *Something Like an Autobiography,* p. 35.

6. Kurosawa quoted in Donald Richie, *The Films of Akira Kurosawa* (Berkeley: University of California Press, 1984), p. 218.

7. David Desser, *The Samurai Films of Akira Kurosawa* (Ann Arbor, Mich.: U.M.I. Research Press, 1981), p. 14.

8. Jennifer Robertson, "Gender-Bending in Paradise: Doing 'Female' and 'Male' in Japan," *Genders* 5 (1989): 51.

9. Robertson, "Gender-Bending in Paradise," p. 51.

10. Robertson, "Gender-Bending in Paradise," p. 59.

11. John Collick, *Shakespeare, Cinema and Society* (Manchester and New York: Manchester University Press, 1989), p. 184.

12. Collick, *Shakespeare, Cinema and Society,* p. 184.

13. Prince, *The Warrior's Camera,* p. 289.

14. Claudine Hermann, quoted in Hedges, *Breaking the Frame,* p. 88.

15. Gregory Barrett, *Archetypes in Japanese Film: The Sociopolitical and Religious Significance of the Principal Heroes and Heroines* (Selinsgrove, Pa.: Susquehanna University Press, 1989), p. 98.

16. Hedges, *Breaking the Frame,* p. 102.

17. Hedges, *Breaking the Frame,* p. 102.

18. Hedges, *Breaking the Frame,* p. 103.

19. Prince, *The Warrior's Camera,* p. 290.

Chapter 5

1. Terrence Rafferty, "Time Out of Joint: The Hyperkinetic '12 Monkeys' and a Fascist-Era 'Richard III,'" *The New Yorker,* January 22, 1996, p. 86. Olivier, however, was a similarly ruthless expunger of the text and incorporated many of Colley Cibber's eighteenth-century emendations in his film adaptation of *Richard III.*

2. James Bowman, "Bard to Death," *The American Spectator* 29 (March 1996): 58.

3. Thomas Elsaesser, "The New German Cinema's Historical Imaginary," in *Framing the Past: The Historiography of German Cinema and Television,* ed. Bruce A. Murray and Christopher J. Wickam (Carbondale and Edwardsville: Southern Illinois University Press, 1992), p. 305.

4. Loncraine quoted in Porter's "Bringing Shakespeare to a '90s Audience: Loncraine, McKellen Join Forces for *Richard III,"* Interview with Richard Loncraine, *The Film Journal* 99.1 (1996): 34.

5. Marjorie Garber, "Descanting on Deformity: Richard III and the Shape of History," in *The Historical Renaissance: New Essays on Tudor and Stuart Literature and Culture,* ed. Heather Dubrow and Richard Strier (Chicago: University of Chicago Press, 1988), p. 96.

6. Loncraine quoted in Porter, "Bringing Shakespeare to a '90s Audience," p. 42.

7. Loncraine quoted in Porter, "Bringing Shakespeare to a '90s Audience," p. 42.

8. Ian McKellen, *William Shakespeare's Richard III* (Woodstock, N.Y.: Overlook Press, 1996), p. 65.

9. Laurence Olivier, quoted in Scott Colley, *Richard's Himself Again: A Stage History of Richard III* (New York: Greenwood Press, 1992), p. 172. Colley observes that by the late 1950s directors of theatrical productions "could not take delight in the merry pranks of Richard III in an era of Nazis and in the aftermath of millions of deaths in concentration camps. Olivier's histrionics must have seemed out of touch with grim post-war reality" (p. 184).

10. Colley, *Richard's Himself Again,* p. 169.

11. Benedict Nightingale, "A Very Modern Nightmare," *Times* (26 July 1990), quoted in Colley, *Richard's Himself Again,* p. 258.

12. Ben Brantley, Review of *Richard III, New York Times,* Sunday, January 21, 1996, p. 25.

13. Goebbels, quoted in Ian Kershaw, *The "Hitler Myth": Image and Reality in the Third Reich* (Oxford: Clarendon Press, 1987), p. 59.

14. Linda Charnes, *Notorious Identity: Materializing the Subject in Shakespeare* (Cambridge, Mass.: Harvard University Press, 1993), p. 65.

15. Morton J. Frisch, "Shakespeare's *Richard III* and the Soul of the Tyrant," *Interpretation* 20.3 (1993), p. 283. Frisch echoes Sigmund Freud in "Some Character-Types Met with in Psycho-Analytic Work," in *The Freud Reader,* ed. Peter Gay (New York: W. W. Norton, 1989), who observes of Richard's opening soliloquy that when the "bitterness and minuteness with which Richard has depicted his deformity make their full effect . . . we clearly perceive the fellow-feeling which compels our sympathy even with a villain like him." Freud concludes that "we feel that we ourselves might become like Richard, that on a small scale, indeed, we are already like him" (p. 593).

16. Anton Kaes, *From Hitler to Heimat: The Return of History as Film* (Cambridge, Mass.: Harvard University Press, 1989), p. 221.

17. Elsaesser, "The New German Cinema's Historical Imaginary," p. 286.

18. Davies, *Filming Shakespeare's Plays,* p. 71.

19. Goffman, *Frame Analysis,* p. 450.

20. Ernst Nolte, "Between Historical Legend and Revisionism? The Third Reich in the Perspective of 1980," in *Forever in the Shadow of Hitler?: Original Documents of the Historikerstreit, The Controversy Concerning the Singularity of the Holocaust,* trans. James Knowlton and Truett Cates (Atlantic Highlands, N.J.: Humanities Press, 1993), pp. 3–4.

21. Nolte, "Between Historical Legend and Revisionism?," p. 15.

22. Sachvertändigenkommission, *Konzeption für ein "Deutsches Historisches Museum,"* p. 17, quoted in Charles S. Maier, *The Unmasterable Past: History, Holocaust, and German National Identity* (Cambridge, Mass.: Harvard University Press, 1988), p. 132.

23. Holocaust denial has been one response to German history's "vivid negativity." In 1976 Arthur R. Butz, a tenured engineering professor at Northwestern University in Evanston, Illinois, published *The Hoax of the Twentieth Century* in an attempt to win historical and scholarly legitimacy for Holocaust denial. It is particularly ironic (when one considers that Hitler effectively used the film media in his own propaganda campaign) that Butz blames historical revisionism on the mass media in Western democracies, which he calls "a lie machine of vaster extent than even many of the more independent minded have perceived" (quoted in Deborah Lipstadt, *Denying the Holocaust: The Growing Assault on Truth and Memory* [New York: Plume, 1994], p. 132).

24. Eric L. Santner, "On the Difficulty of Saying 'We': The Historians' Debate and Edgar Reitz's *Heimat,*" in *Framing the Past: The Historiography of German Cinema and Television,* ed. Bruce A. Murray and Christopher J. Wickam (Carbondale and Edwardsville: Southern Illinois University Press, 1992), p. 269.

25. Susan Sontag, Preface to Hans-Jürgen Syberberg's *Hitler: A Film from Germany,* trans. Joachim Neugroschel (New York: Farrar, Straus, Giroux, 1982), pp. x–xi.

26. Kaes, *From Hitler to Heimat,* p. 57.

27. John Calhoun, *"Richard III"* (film review), *TCI: Business of Entertainment Technology and Design* 30 (April 1996): 34.

28. McKellen, *William Shakespeare's Richard III,* p. 249.

29. Richard Corliss, "Pulp Elizabethan Fiction," *Time,* January 15, 1996, p. 67.

30. Leo Braudy, *Native Informant,* p. 231.

31. Bertolt Brecht, *Journals, 1934–1955,* trans. Hugh Rorrison, ed. John Willett (New York: Routledge, 1993), p. 137.

32. Eugene Roscow, *Born to Lose: The Gangster Film in America* (New York: Oxford University Press, 1978), p. 310.

33. Susan Bennett, *Performing Nostalgia,* p. 33.

34. Ian McKellen, *William Shakespeare's Richard III,* p. 13.

35. Erwin Leiser, *Nazi Cinema,* trans. Gertrud Mander and David Wilson (New York: Macmillan, 1975), p. 124.

36. Michael E. Geisler, "The Disposal of Memory: Fascism and the Holocaust on West German Television," in *Framing the Past: The Historiography of German Cinema and Television,* ed. Bruce A. Murray and Christopher J. Wickam (Cardondale and Edwardsville: Southern Illinois University Press, 1992), p. 233.

37. Loncraine quoted in Porter, "Bringing Shakespeare to a '90s Audience," p. 34.

38. Loncraine quoted in Porter, "Bringing Shakespeare to a '90s Audience," p. 34.

39. Loncraine quoted in Porter, "Bringing Shakespeare to a '90s Audience," p. 34.

40. Charnes, *Notorious Identity,* p. 6.

41. Rafferty, "Time Out of Joint," p. 86.

42. Kershaw, *The "Hitler Myth,"* p. 72. Between 1933 and 1942, Goebbels consolidated the crisis-prone German film industry as a vehicle for propaganda, so that during the 1930s Hitler's Propaganda Ministry had the best technical facilities in Europe. According to Marc Silberman, "Shooting Wars: German Cinema and the Two World Wars," in *1914/1939: German Reflections of the Two World Wars,* ed. Reinhold Grimm and Jost Hermand (Madison: University of Wisconsin, 1992), "the Nazi cinema remained one of the strongest European producers through the onset of war in 1939, with an average of 80 feature-length films per year, as well as documents, shorts, and newsreels" (p. 121).

43. This fabricated scene also recalls Michel de Montaigne's translation of a Greek proverb, "The lame man doth it best," in *The Complete Essays of Montaigne,* ed. Donald M. Frame (Stanford, Calif.: Stanford University Press, 1943), p. 791.

44. Although Hitler did not "scapegoat" women in the way he did Jews, gypsies, and homosexuals, he did blame women in the workforce for many social problems, including the unemployment of men. However, Hitler also recognized the significance of women in his drive to power, as Richard does. He insisted that Goebbels advertise his celibacy "as the sacrifice of personal happiness for the welfare of the nation," which Hitler regarded as a "functional necessity directed at avoiding any loss of popularity among German women, whose support he saw as vital to his electoral success." As Kershaw points out, "All this was closely related to Hitler's known views on the 'psychology of the masses,' already expounded in *Mein Kampf*" (*The "Hitler Myth,"* p. 3).

45. Phyllis Rackin, "History into Tragedy: The Case of *Richard III,*" in *Shakespeare: Tragedy and Gender,* ed. Shirley Nelson Garner and Madelon Sprengnether (Bloomington: Indiana University Press, 1996), p. 40.

46. Michael E. Mooney, *Shakespeare's Dramatic Transactions* (Durham, N.C.: Duke University Press, 1990), p. 42.

47. Mulvey, *Visual and Other Pleasures,* p. 159.

48. Ian Frederick Moulton, "'A Monster Great Deformed': The Unruly Masculinity of Richard III," *Shakespeare Quarterly* 47.3 (1996): 267.

49. The production designer for Loncraine's film, Tony Burroughs, confirms in an interview in *TCI* 30 (April 1996) that "When Richmond arrives at the set (which happens to be a power station) and the two of them have their confrontation atop the girders, the end recalls the climax of Jimmy Cagney's *White Heat*" (p. 37).

50. McKellen says of Richard's death, "I relished the double irony of the Al Jolson song which he [Loncraine] had overlaid on the final frames of his film. Richmond and Richard simultaneously feel, in the moment when their fates collide, that they are sitting on top of the world" (*William Shakespeare's Richard III,* p. 286).

51. Moulton, "'A Monster Great Deformed,'" p. 260.

52. Robert Sklar, *Movie Made America* (New York: Random House, 1975), p. 181.

53. John McCarty, *Hollywood Gangland: The Movie's Love Affair with the Mob* (New York: St. Martin's Press, 1993), p. 98. McKellen similarly observes of Loncraine's *Richard III* that "if the action of the play often looks back, the film is centred on the living moment and then looks forward" (*William Shakespeare's Richard III,* p. 17).

54. Mulvey, *Visual and Other Pleasures*, p. 162.

55. Goffman, *Frame Analysis*, p. 420.

56. Goffman, *Frame Analysis*, p. 439.

57. Leah Marcus, *Puzzling Shakespeare: Local Reading and Its Discontents* (Berkeley: University of California, 1988), p. 217.

58. Robert Leicht, "Only By Facing the Past Can We be Free. We Are Our Own Past," in *Forever in the Shadow of Hitler?: Original Documents of the Historikerstreit, The Controversy Concerning the Singularity of the Holocaust*, trans. James Knowlton and Truett Cates (Atlantic Highlands, N.J.: Humanities Press, 1993), p. 244.

59. Ron Burnett, *Cultures of Vision: Images, Media and the Imaginary* (Bloomington: Indiana University Press, 1995), p. 136.

Chapter 6

1. Anthony Davies, *Filming Shakespeare's Plays*, p. 134.

2. Gus Van Sant, *Even Cowgirls Get the Blues and My Own Private Idaho* (London and Boston: Faber and Faber, 1993), p. xxxviii.

3. Michael Anderegg, "'Every Third Word a Lie': Rhetoric and History in Orson Welles's *Chimes at Midnight*," *Film Quarterly* 40 (1987): 18-24.

4. Barbara Leaming, *Orson Welles*, p. 462.

5. Fredric Jameson, *Signatures of the Visible* (New York and London: Routledge, 1992), p. 16.

6. Jean Renoir quoted in Orson Welles and Peter Bogdanovich, *This Is Orson Welles*, ed. Jonathan Rosenbaum (New York: Harper Collins, 1992), p. 212.

7. Welles, *This Is Orson Welles*, p. 108.

8. Jameson, *Signatures of the Visible*, p. 14.

9. Jameson, *Signatures of the Visible*, p. 14.

10. Jameson, *Signatures of the Visible*, p. 14.

11. Jack Jorgens, *Shakespeare on Film*, p. 115.

12. Roberta E. Pearson and William Uricchio convincingly argue for the popular appropriation of Shakespeare's plays during the first decade of the twentieth century. In their essay "How Many Times Shall Caesar Bleed in Sport: Shakespeare and the Cultural Debate about Moving Pictures," *Screen* 31 (1990): 243-61, Pearson and Uricchio conclude that examples such as Vitagraph's *A Midsummer Night's Dream* (1910), *Richard III* (1908), *Antony and Cleopatra* (1908), and *Taming of the Shrew* (1908) captured the popular audience of their day, although these films, unlike Van Sant's *My Own Private Idaho*, "specifically referenced the films' high cultural associations and benefits, echoing the sentiments

of civic reformers and uplifters" (p. 249). However, these early films did spawn parodic forms of the Shakespearean plays, so that "while cultural arbiters and educators may have played up the Bard's uplifting and even Americanizing potential, lard and corned beef manufacturers circulated 'vernacular' Shakespeares which counted on an easy familiarity with the 'great' works" (p. 259).

13. Davies, *Filming Shakespeare's Plays,* p. 123.

14. Welles, *This Is Orson Welles,* p. 100.

15. Welles, *This Is Orson Welles,* p. 100.

16. Welles, *This Is Orson Welles,* p. 101.

17. Jorgens, *Shakespeare on Film,* p. 111; Davies, *Filming Shakespeare's Plays,* p. 141.

18. Leaming, *Orson Welles,* p. 16.

19. Welles, *This Is Orson Welles,* p. 67.

20. Leaming, *Orson Welles,* p. 18.

21. Welles, *This Is Orson Welles,* p. 100.

22. Welles quoted from Juan Cobos and Miguel Rubio, "Welles and Falstaff: An Interview," *Sight and Sound* 35 (Autumn 1966): 159.

23. Welles, quoted in Juan Cobos and Michael Rubio, "Welles and Falstaff," p. 160.

24. Jameson, *Signatures of the Visible,* p. 34.

25. As my colleague Marina Leslie points out in *Renaissance Utopias and the Problem of History* (Ithaca, N.Y.: Cornell University Press, 1998), the differences between utopian reform and dystopian satire are not clear, if they exist at all. Both utopia and dystopia share the same critical attitude toward the old world and employ the same themes, formal patterns, and framing devices. Robert Stam also observes, "the utopian propensity can look backward or forward in its negation of the present, just as it can function positively or negatively, positing an ideal commonwealth or an inverted utopia" (*Reflexivity in Film and Literature,* p. 210).

26. Fredric Jameson, *The Political Unconscious: Narrative as Socially Symbolic Act* (Ithaca, N.Y.: Cornell University Press, 1981), p. 289.

27. Phyllis Rackin, *Stages of History: Shakespeare's English Chronicles* (Ithaca, N.Y.: Cornell University Press, 1990), p. 22.

28. Rackin, *Stages of History,* p. 28.

29. Van Sant, *Even Cowgirls Get the Blues and My Own Private Idaho,* p. xxxvii.

30. Graham Holderness, *Shakespeare Recycled,* p. 173.

31. Welles, *This Is Orson Welles,* pp. 99–100.

32. Caryl Flinn emphasizes that "the escapist, excessive, and utopian properties of film music must be considered in light of the cultural, institutional, and

ideological functions it serves at a particular time" (*Strains of Utopia: Gender, Nostalgia, and Hollywood Film Music* [Princeton, N.J.: Princeton University Press, 1992), p. 93).

33. Robert C. Elliot, *The Shape of Utopia: Studies in a Literary Genre* (Chicago: University of Chicago Press, 1970).

34. Phyllis Rackin observes in "Foreign Country: The Place of Women and Sexuality in Shakespeare's Historical World," in *Enclosure Acts: Sexuality, Property, and Culture in Early Modern England,* ed. Richard Burt and John Michael Archer (Ithaca and London: Cornell University Press, 1994), that not only is the Boar's Head "the name of at least six real taverns in Shakespeare's London, one of them used for a theatre," but also that the tavern itself was anachronistic to the historical world the play claims to represent: "The Boar's Head Tavern in Eastcheap is a plebeian, comic, theatrical, anachronistically modern world that mirrors the disorderly push and shove of the playhouse itself" (pp. 80-81).

35. See Peter Clark, "The Alehouse and the Alternative Society," in *Puritans and Revolutionaries: Essays in Seventeenth-Century History Presented to Christopher Hill,* ed. Donald Pennington and Keith Thomas (Oxford: Clarendon, 1978), pp. 47-72. According to Clark, circumstances began to change in the early decades of the sixteenth century, and by "1577 there were at least 14,000 houses in 27 counties" (p. 50).

36. Susan Dwyer Amussen, *An Ordered Society: Gender and Class in Early Modern England* (New York: Columbia University Press, 1988), p. 166. However, historians point out that contemporaries' anxieties about the alehouse and tavern belie the social realities that provoked their outrage. For although circumstances often drove poor men or those of questionable status and reputation to the tavern's doors, the frequenters of the alehouses were a heterogeneous group.

37. Peter Clark, "The Alehouse and the Alternative Society," p. 48.

38. Robert B. Manning notes that "the proliferation of illegal alehouses and lodging houses is a measure of the problem of masterless men in both rural and urban areas. In some towns as many as one in ten houses functioned as alehouses; perhaps 20 per cent of the urban households contained lodgers. People who brewed ale and kept alehouses and lodging houses were themselves poor and needed to supplement meagre incomes. Alehouses were regulated by justices of the peace after the passing of the Licensing Act of 1552 (5 and 6 Edw. VI, c. 25); taking in lodgers was prohibited by a variety of late-Elizabethan enactments (31 Eliz., c. 7 and 35 Eliz., c.6) and municipal ordinances" *(Village Revolts: Social Protest and Popular Disturbances in England, 1509-1640* [Oxford: Clarendon Press, 1988], p. 164).

39. Manning, *Village Revolts,* p. 163. However, contrary to contemporary anxieties about the tavern and depictions in the plays of Thomas Dekker and Ben

Jonson of underworld crimes conceived within the alehouse environs, "there is little evidence to support allegations that the alehouse was the nexus of a tightly knit popular subculture" (Clark, "The Alehouse and the Alternative Society," p. 67). Nevertheless, Shakespeare's Boar's Head Tavern illustrates many contemporaries' fears concerning these inns and eating establishments, particularly that they were "the command post of men who sought to turn the traditional world upside down and create their own alternative society" (Clark, "The Alehouse and the Alternative Society," p. 48).

40. According to Paul Slack's *Poverty and Policy in Tudor and Stuart England* (London and New York: Longman, 1988), "between 1576 and 1610 there were 35 bills on drunkenness, inns, and alehouses" (p. 130), yet laws that regulated the sumptuousness of the rich (on covetousness, usury, or regulating fashions) were mostly repealed by 1604.

41. Peter Stallybrass and Allon White, *The Politics and Poetics of Transgression* (Ithaca, N.Y.: Cornell University Press, 1986), p. 37.

42. Bennett, *Performing Nostalgia,* p. 10.

43. Much has recently been written on this subject; in particular, see Alan Bray's essay "Homosexuality and the Signs of Male Friendship in Elizabethan England," in *Queering the Renaissance,* ed. Jonathan Goldberg (Durham and London: Duke University Press, 1994), pp. 40-61, and Jonathan Goldberg's *Sodometries: Renaissance Texts/Modern Sexualities* (Stanford, Calif.: Stanford University Press, 1992). Goldberg (seconding Bray) distinguishes between homosexual sexual practices and the homosocial world of the English Renaissance: "While it is certainly fair enough to invoke the term *homosocial* to describe male/male relations in the plays, relations between homosociality and the modern regimes of hetero-and homosexualities cannot be presumed. The importation of the term *homosexuality* would seriously misconstrue the place of sexuality, if only because it obscures what Alan Bray has shown, that much in the ordinary transactions between men in the period, in their negotiations of the social hierarchies, took place sexually" (p. 162).

44. Naremore, *The Magic World of Orson Welles,* p. 222, and Davies, *Filming Shakespeare's Plays,* 131.

45. Ronald Hutton explains in *The Rise and Fall of Merry England: The Ritual Year, 1400-1700* (Oxford: Oxford University Press, 1994) that "the Marians of the Elizabethan May games were there principally to provide rough humour, being men in female dress, often deliberately selected for their beards, brawny muscles, and general inability to make convincing transvestites" (p. 118). He cites growing contemporary intolerance for traditional festivities as indicated in Christopher Fetherston's *Dialogue against Light, Lewd and Lascivious Dauncing* (1582), which specifically targets the transvestite Maid Marians as offensive: "'men in woman's

apparell, whom you do most commonly call maymarions, whereby you infringe Deut. 22.5' (the Mosaic law against transvestism)" (p. 131). Peter Stallybrass, in "'Drunk with the Cup of Liberty': Robin Hood, the Carnivalesque, and the Rhetoric of Violence in Early Modern England," in *The Violence of Representation: Literature and the History of Violence,* ed. Nancy Armstrong and Leonard Tennenhouse (London and New York: Routledge, 1989), pp. 45–76, asserts that the long history of Maid Marian's participation in May games suggests that her role (played by an actual woman or a transvestite man) "was used to legitimate political action by the powerless" (p. 55).

46. William Hale, *A Series of Precedents and Proceedings in Criminal Causes Extending from the Year 1475 to 1640* (London: Francis and John Rivington, 1847), p. 180.

47. Quoted from Bruce Smith's *Homosexual Desire in Shakespeare's England: A Cultural Poetics* (Chicago: University of Chicago Press, 1991), p. 186.

48. Van Sant, *Even Cowgirls Get the Blues and My Own Private Idaho,* p. 134.

49. Jonathan Goldberg, *Sodometries,* p. 174.

50. Stallybrass, "'Drunk with the Cup of Liberty,'" p. 46.

51. Richard Lanham, *The Motives of Eloquence: Literary Rhetoric in the Renaissance* (New Haven and London: Yale University Press, 1976), p. 195.

52. Steven Mullaney, *The Place of the Stage: License, Play, and Power in Renaissance England* (Chicago and London: University of Chicago Press, 1988), p. 82.

53. Mullaney, *The Place of the Stage,* p. 80.

54. Van Sant, *Even Cowgirls Get the Blues and My Own Private Idaho,* pp. xlii–xliii.

55. Van Sant, *Even Cowgirls Get the Blues and My Own Private Idaho,* p. xliii.

56. Davies, *Filming Shakespeare's Plays,* p. 124.

57. François Laroque, *Shakespeare's Festive World: Elizabethan Seasonal Entertainment and the Professional Stage,* trans. Janet Lloyd (Cambridge: Cambridge University Press, 1991), p. 202.

58. Laroque, *Shakespeare's Festive World,* p. 202.

59. Paul M. Cubeta, "Falstaff and the Art of Dying," *Studies in English Literature, 1500–1900* 27.2 (1987): 209.

60. Laroque, *Shakespeare's Festive World,* p. 201.

61. Laroque, *Shakespeare's Festive World,* p. 230.

62. Van Sant, *Even Cowgirls Get the Blues and My Own Private Idaho,* p. xxviii.

63. Mulvey, *Visual and Other Pleasures,* p. 167.

64. Robert Stam, *Subversive Pleasures: Bakhtin, Cultural Criticism, and Film* (Baltimore and London: Johns Hopkins University Press, 1989), p. 96.

65. Stam, *Subversive Pleasures,* p. 114.

66. For this point I am indebted to my colleague Marina Leslie and her essay "Mapping out Ideology: The Case of Utopia," *Recherches semiotiques/Semiotic Inquiry* 12 (1992): 73–94, which discusses the protean boundaries of utopian discourse in early modern literature and the problem of "reading" utopia; she argues that utopias are essentially a problem of figuration.

67. Jameson, *Signatures of the Visible,* p. 26.

Chapter 7

1. Paul Meier, "Kenneth Branagh with Utter Clarity: An Interview," *The Drama Review: The Journal of Performance Studies* 41.2 (1997): 88.

2. Meier, "Kenneth Branagh with Utter Clarity," p. 84.

3. In fact, Branagh's film comically recalls Robert Lepage's directoral strategies in a Royal National Theatre production of *A Midsummer Night's Dream,* which, according to Susan Bennett, attempted "to disavow the fetish of Shakespeare's text" by introducing "the text 'at the end' of the rehearsal period" (*Performing Nostalgia,* pp. 19–20).

4. Leo Braudy, *Native Informant,* p. 201.

5. Kenneth Branagh, *A Midwinter's Tale: The Shooting Script* (New York: Newmarket Press, 1996), p. 30.

6. Braudy, *Native Informant,* p. 211.

7. As Erving Goffman points out, Hamlet's "quiet change of some dozen or sixteen lines in the script" is "a fabricated theatrical framing," that is ultimately all part of "the play that Shakespeare wrote, a play that persons who are actors stage before persons who are really members of an audience" (*Frame Analysis,* p. 183).

8. Branagh, *A Midwinter's Tale,* p. 74.

9. Robert Weimann, "Representation and Performance: The Uses of Authority in Shakespeare's Theatre," *PMLA* 107.3 (1992): 503.

10. Goffman, *Frame Analysis,* p. 262.

11. Goffman, *Frame Analysis,* p. 263.

12. Naomi Conn Liebler, *Shakespeare's Festive Tragedy: The Ritual Foundations of Genre* (London: Routledge, 1995), p. 27.

13. Barbara Freedman, *Staging the Gaze,* p. 177.

14. Branagh, *A Midwinter's Tale,* p. 112.

15. Freedman, *Staging the Gaze,* p. 70.

16. Branagh, *A Midwinter's Tale,* p. 104

17. Weimann, "Representation and Performance," p. 499.

18. Branagh, *A Midwinter's Tale,* p. 17.

19. Weimann, "Representation and Performance," p. 498.

20. Everett, *Young Hamlet*, p. 14.

21. See Stephen M. Buhler's article "Double Takes: Branagh Gets to *Hamlet*," *Post Script* 17.1 (fall 1997): 43–52, for a discussion of the relationship between Branagh's *A Midwinter's Tale* and Olivier's *Hamlet*.

22. Branagh, *A Midwinter's Tale*, p. 64.

23. Branagh, *A Midwinter's Tale*, p. 2.

24. Branagh, *A Midwinter's Tale*, p. 22.

25. Stephen Orgel, "The Poetics of Incomprehensibility," *Shakespeare Quarterly* 42 (1991): 436.

26. Lynn Enterline, "'You speak a language that I understand not': The Rhetoric of Animation in *The Winter's Tale*," *Shakespeare Quarterly* 48.1 (1997): 37.

27. Branagh, *A Midwinter's Tale*, p. 22.

28. Branagh, *A Midwinter's Tale*, p. 62.

29. Howard Felperin, *Shakespearean Representations: Mimesis and Modernity in Elizabethan Tragedy* (Princeton, N.J.: Princeton University Press, 1977), observes that in his speech in the closet scene Hamlet assumes the role of Virtue and Gertrude is cast as the misguided sinner seduced by Vice (p. 52).

30. Branagh, *A Midwinter's Tale*, p. 19.

31. Liebler, *Shakespeare's Festive Tragedies*, 192.

32. Goffman, *Frame Analysis*, p. 299.

33. Branagh, *A Midwinter's Tale*, p. 63.

35. Branagh, *A Midwinter's Tale*, p. 64.

35. Liebler, *Shakespeare's Festive Tragedies*, p. 194.

36. Branagh, *A Midwinter's Tale*, p. 53.

37. Felperin, *Shakespearean Representations*, p. 65.

38. Wilson Knight, *The Olive and the Sword* (Oxford: Oxford University Press, 1944), p. 3.

39. Barbara Everett, *Young Hamlet*, p. 14.

40. Samuel Crowl, "Hamlet 'Most Royal': An Interview with Kenneth Branagh," *Shakespeare Bulletin* 12.4 (1994): 7.

41. Henry Fielding's *Tom Jones* (1749) is notable among the film's literary predecessors in its depiction of the critical intervals and asides that punctuate Garrick's performance of *Hamlet* at a time close to the winter solstice in 1745, in which Patridge's emotional response to Garrick's performance and the appearance of the ghost expose an unsettling indeterminacy of boundaries between fictional levels. See John Allen Stevenson, "Fielding's Mousetrap: Hamlet, Patridge, and the '45," *Studies in English Literature* 37 (1997): 559–60.

42. Branagh, *A Midwinter's Tale*, p. 65.
43. Branagh, *A Midwinter's Tale*, p. 3.
44. Branagh, *A Midwinter's Tale*, pp. 4-5.
45. Branagh, *A Midwinter's Tale*, p. 95.

Bibliography

Altieri, Charles. *Canons and Consequences: Reflections on the Ethical Force of Imaginative Ideals.* Evanston, Ill.: Northwestern University Press, 1990.

Altman, Joel B. "'Vile Participation': The Amplification of Violence in the Theatre of *Henry V.*" *Shakespeare Quarterly* 42 (1991): 1–32.

Amussen, Susan Dwyer. *An Ordered Society: Gender and Class in Early Modern England.* New York: Columbia University Press, 1988.

Anderegg, Michael. "'Every Third Word a Lie': Rhetoric and History in Orson Welles's *Chimes at Midnight.*" *Film Quarterly* 40 (spring 1987): 18–24.

Barber, C. L., and Richard Wheeler. *The Whole Journey: Shakespeare's Power of Development.* Berkeley: University of California Press, 1986.

Barker, Francis. *The Culture of Violence: Essays on Tragedy and History.* Chicago: University of Chicago Press, 1993.

Barrett, Gregory. *Archetypes in Japanese Film: The Sociopolitical and Religious Significance of the Principal Heroes and Heroines.* Selinsgrove, Pa.: Susquehanna University Press, 1989.

Baudry, Jean-Louis. "Ideological Effects of the Basic Cinemographic Apparatus." *Film Quarterly* 28 (winter 1974–75): 39–47.

Bazin, Andre. *What Is Cinema?,* trans. Hugh Gray. Berkeley: University of California Press, 1967.

Bellous, Raymond. "Cine-Repetitions." *Screen* 20.2 (1979).

Bennett, Susan. *Performing Nostalgia: Shifting Shakespeare and the Contemporary Past.* London and New York: Routledge, 1996.

Bergstrom, Janet. "Enunciation and Sexual Difference." In *Camera Obscura* 3–4 (summer 1979): 33–59.

Biggs, Murray. "'He's Going to His Mother's Closet': Hamlet and Gertrude on Screen." *Shakespeare Survey* 45 (1992), pp. 53–62.

Biró, Yvette. *Profane Mythology: The Savage Mind of the Cinema.* Trans. Imre Goldstein. Bloomington: Indiana University Press, 1982.

Bordwell, David. *Narration in the Fiction Film.* Madison: University of Wisconsin Press, 1985.

Bowman, James. "Bard to Death." *The American Spectator* 29 (March 1996): 58.

Branagh, Kenneth. *Beginning.* New York: St. Martin's Press, 1989.

————. *A Midwinter's Tale: The Shooting Script.* New York: Newmarket Press, 1996.

Brantley, Ben. Review of *Richard III. New York Times,* January 21, 1996, p. 14.

Braudy, Leo. *Native Informant: Essays on Film, Fiction, and Popular Culture.* New York: Oxford University Press, 1991.

————. *The World in a Frame: What We See in Films.* Chicago: University of Chicago Press, 1976.

Bray, Alan. "Homosexuality and the Signs of Male Friendship in Elizabethan England." In *Queering the Renaissance,* ed. Jonathan Goldberg. Durham and London: Duke University Press, 1994, pp. 40–61.

Brecht, Bertolt. *Journals, 1934–1955.* Trans. Hugh Rorrison. Ed. John Willett. New York: Routledge, 1993.

————. *The Messingkauf Dialogues.* Trans. John Willett. London: Eyre Methuen, 1965.

Bredbeck, Gregory. *Sodomy and Interpretation: Marlowe to Milton.* Ithaca, N.Y.: Cornell University Press, 1991.

Brockbank, Philip. *The Creativity of Perception: Essays in the Genesis of Literature and Art.* Oxford: Basil Blackwell, 1991.

Brown, Patricia Fortini. *Venetian Narrative Painting in the Age of Carpaccio.* New Haven, Conn.: Yale University Press, 1989.

Buchman, Lorne M. "Orson Welles's 'Othello': A Study of Time in Shakespeare's Tragedy." *Shakespeare Survey* 39 (1986): 53–65.

————. *Still in Movement: Shakespeare on Screen.* Oxford: Oxford University Press, 1991.

Buhler, Stephen M. "Double Takes: Branagh Gets to *Hamlet.*" *Post Script* 17.1 (1997): 43–52.

Bullough, Geoffrey, ed. *Narrative and Dramatic Sources of Shakespeare.* Vol. 7. London: Routledge and Kegan Paul, 1973.

Burnett, Ron. *Cultures of Vision: Images, Media and the Imaginary.* Bloomington: Indiana University Press, 1995.

Calhoun, John. *"Richard III"* (motion picture review*). TCI: Business of Entertainment Technology and Design* 30 (April 1996): 34–37.

Campbell, Kathleen. "Zeffirelli's *Hamlet*—Q1 in Performance." *Shakespeare on Film Newsletter* 16.1 (December 1991): 7.

Carroll, Noël. *Theorizing the Moving Image.* Cambridge: Cambridge University Press, 1996.

Charnes, Linda. "Dismember Me: Shakespeare, Paranoia, and the Logic of Mass Culture." *Shakespeare Quarterly* 48.1 (1997): 1–16.

———. *Notorious Identity: Materializing the Subject in Shakespeare.* Cambridge, Mass.: Harvard University Press, 1993.

Clark, Peter. "The Alehouse and the Alternative Society." In *Puritans and Revolutionaries: Essays in Seventeenth-Century History Presented to Christopher Hill,* ed. Donald Pennington and Keith Thomas. Oxford: Clarendon, 1978, pp. 47–72.

Cobos, Juan, and Michael Rubio. "Welles and Falstaff." *Sight and Sound* 35 (autumn 1966): 158–63.

Colley, Scott. *Richard's Himself Again: A Stage History of Richard III.* New York: Greenwood Press, 1992.

Collick, John. *Shakespeare, Cinema and Society.* Manchester and New York: Manchester University Press, 1989.

Copjec, Joan. "*India Song/Son nom de Venise dans Calcutta desert:* The Compulsion to Repeat." *October* 17 (1981).

Corliss, Richard. "Pulp Elizabethan Fiction." *Time,* January 15, 1996, 67.

———. "Wanna Be . . . Or Wanna Not Be?" *Time,* January 7, 1991, 73.

Coursen, H. R. *Watching Shakespeare on Television.* Rutherford: Fairleigh Dickinson University Press, 1993.

Crowl, Samuel. "Hamlet 'Most Royal': An Interview with Kenneth Branaugh." *Shakespeare Bulletin* 12.4 (1994).

———. *Shakespeare Observed: Studies in Performance on Stage and Screen.* Athens: Ohio University Press, 1992.

Cubeta, Paul M. "Falstaff and the Art of Dying." *Studies in English Literature, 1500–1900* 27.2 (1987): 197–211.

Danson, Lawrence. "Gazing at Hamlet, or the Danish Cabaret." *Shakespeare Survey* 45 (1992): 37–51.

Davies, Anthony. *Filming Shakespeare's Plays: The Adaptations of Laurence Olivier, Orson Welles, Peter Brook, Akira Kurosawa.* Cambridge: Cambridge University Press, 1988.

Deats, Sara Munson. "Rabbits and Ducks: Olivier, Branagh, and *Henry V.*" *Literature/Film Quarterly* 20.4 (1992): 284–93.

Desser, David. *The Samurai Films of Akira Kurosawa.* Ann Arbor, Mich.: U.M.I. Research Press, 1981.

Dollimore, Jonathan. *Sexual Dissidence: Augustine to Wilde, Freud to Foucault.* Oxford: Oxford University Press, 1991.

Donaldson, Peter. "Taking on Shakespeare: Kenneth Branagh's *Henry V.*" *Shakespeare Quarterly* 42.1 (1991): 60-70.

————. *Shakespearean Films/Shakespearean Directors.* Boston: Unwin Hyman, 1990.

Egan, Gabriel. "Myths and Enabling Fictions of 'Origin' in the Editing of Shakespeare." *New Theatre Quarterly* 13.49 (February 1997): 41-47.

Eggert, Katherine. "Nostalgia and the Not Yet Late Queen: Refusing Female Rule in *Henry V.*" *ELH* 61.2 (1994): 523-50.

Elliot, Robert C. *The Shape of Utopia: Studies in a Literary Genre.* Chicago: University of Chicago Press, 1970.

Enterline, Lynn. "'You speak a language that I understand not': The Rhetoric of Animation in *The Winter's Tale*," *Shakespeare Quarterly* 48.1 (1997): 17-44.

Everett, Barbara. *Young Hamlet: Essays on Shakespeare's Tragedies.* Oxford: Clarendon Press, 1989.

Felperin, Howard. *Shakespearean Representations: Mimesis and Modernity in Elizabethan Tragedy.* Princeton, N.J.: Princeton University Press, 1977.

Flinn, Caryl. *Strains of Utopia: Gender, Nostalgia, and Hollywood Film Music.* Princeton, N.J.: Princeton University Press, 1992.

Framing the Past: The Historiography of German Cinema and Television. Ed. Bruce A. Murray and Christopher J. Wickam. Carbondale and Edwardsville: Southern Illinois University Press, 1992.

Freedman, Barbara. *Staging the Gaze: Postmodernism, Psychoanalysis, and Shakespearean Comedy.* Ithaca, N.Y.: Cornell University Press, 1991.

French, Philip. *Westerns: Aspects of a Movie Genre.* New York: Oxford University Press, 1977.

Frisch, Morton J. "Shakespeare's *Richard III* and the Soul of the Tyrant." *Interpretation* 20.3 (1993): 275-84.

Gallagher, John Andrew, and Sylvia Caminer. "Interview with Mel Gibson." *Films in Review* 47.5-6 (1996): 31-39.

Garber, Marjorie. "Descanting on Deformity: Richard III and the Shape of History." In *The Historical Renaissance: New Essays on Tudor and Stuart Literature and Culture.* Ed. Heather Dubrow and Richard Strier. Chicago: University of Chicago Press, 1988, pp. 79-103.

Girard, Rene. *Violence and the Sacred.* Trans. Patrick Gregory. Baltimore: Johns Hopkins University Press, 1972.

Gittings, Claire. *Death, Burial and the Individual in Early Modern England.* London and Sydney: Croom Helm, 1984.

Goffman, Erving. *Frame Analysis: An Essay on the Organization of Experience.* Cambridge, Mass.: Harvard University Press, 1974.

Goldberg, Jonathan. *Sodometries: Renaissance Texts, Modern Sexualities.* Stanford, Calif.: Stanford University Press, 1992.

Greenblatt, Stephen. *Shakespearean Negotiations: The Circulation of Social Energy in Renaissance England.* Berkeley and Los Angeles: University of California Press, 1988.

Hale, William. *A Series of Precedents and Proceedings in Criminal Causes Extending from the Year 1475 to 1640.* London: Francis and John Rivington, 1847.

Hapgood, Robert. "Popularizing Shakespeare: The Artistry of Franco Zeffirelli." In *Shakespeare the Movie: Popularizing the Plays on Film, TV and Video,* ed. Lynda E. Boose and Richard Burt. London and New York: Routledge, 1997, pp. 80–94.

Hartman, Geoffrey H. "Shakespeare and the Ethical Question: Leo Löwenthal in Memoriam." *ELH* 63 (1996): 1–23.

Hedges, Inez. *Breaking the Frame: Film Language and the Experience of Limits.* Bloomington: Indiana University Press, 1991.

———. *Languages of Revolt: Dada and Surrealist Literature and Film.* Durham, N.C.: Duke University Press, 1983.

Hedrick, Donald K. "War Is Mud: Branagh's Dirty Harry V and the Types of Political Ambiguity." In *Shakespeare the Movie: Popularizing the Plays on Film, TV, and Video,* ed. Lynda E. Boose and Richard Burt. London and New York: Routledge, 1997, pp. 45–66.

Heinemann, Margot. "How Brecht Read Shakespeare." In *Political Shakespeare: New Essays in Cultural Materialism,* ed. Jonathan Dollimore and Alan Sinfield. Ithaca, N.Y.: Cornell University Press, 1985.

Hodgdon, Barbara. "The Critic, the Poor Player, Prince Hamlet, and the Lady in the Dark." In *Shakespeare Reread: The Texts in New Contexts,* ed. Russ McDonald. Ithaca and London: Cornell University Press, 1994, pp. 259–93.

———. *The End Crowns All: Closure and Contradiction in Shakespeare's History Plays.* Princeton, N.J.: Princeton University Press, 1991.

———. "Kiss Me Deadly; or, The Des/Demonized Spectacle." In *Othello: New Perspectives,* ed. Virginia Mason Vaughan and Kent Cartwright. Rutherford, N.J.: Fairleigh Dickinson Press, 1991, pp. 214–55.

Holden, Stephen. "An Arch-Evil Monarch, Updated to the 1930's." *New York Times,* December 29, 1995, C3.

Holderness, Graham. *Shakespeare Recycled: The Making of Historical Drama.* New York: Barnes and Noble, 1992.

———. "Shakespeare Rewound." *Shakespeare Survey* 45 (1992): 63–74.

Humfrey, Peter. *Painting in Renaissance Venice.* New Haven, Conn.: Yale University Press, 1995.

Huse, Norbert, and Wolfgang Wolters. *The Art of Renaissance Venice: Architecture, Sculpture, and Painting, 1460–1590.* Trans. Edmund Jephcott. Chicago: University of Chicago Press, 1990.

Hutton, Ronald. *The Rise and Fall of Merry England: The Ritual Year, 1400–1700.* Oxford: Oxford University Press, 1994.

Impastato, David. "Zeffirelli's *Hamlet:* Sunlight Makes Meaning." *Shakespeare on Film Newsletter* 16.1 (1991): 1–2.

Jameson, Fredric. *The Political Unconscious: Narrative as Socially Symbolic Art.* Ithaca, N.Y.: Cornell University Press, 1981.

———. *Signatures of the Visible.* New York and London: Routledge, 1992.

Jardine, Lisa. *Reading Shakespeare Historically.* London and New York: Routledge, 1996.

Jensen, Michael P. "Mel Gibson on Hamlet." *Shakespeare on Film Newsletter* 15.2 (1991): 1–2, 6.

Jorgens, Jack. *Shakespeare on Film.* Bloomington: Indiana University Press, 1977.

Kaes, Anton. *From Hitler to Heimat: The Return of History as Film.* Cambridge, Mass.: Harvard University Press, 1989.

Kershaw, Ian. *The "Hitler Myth": Image and Reality in the Third Reich.* Oxford: Clarendon Press, 1987.

Kliman, Bernice W. *Hamlet: Film, Television, and Audio Performance.* London and Toronto: Associated University Presses, 1988.

Knight, Wilson. *The Olive and the Sword.* Oxford: Oxfrod University Press, 1944.

Kott, Jan. *Shakespeare Our Contemporary.* Trans. Boleslaw Taborski. New York: Anchor, 1966.

Kurosawa, Akira. *Something Like an Autobiography.* Trans. Audie Block. New York: Alfred A. Knopf, 1982.

Lane, Robert. "'When Blood Is Their Argument': Class, Character, and Historymaking in Shakespeare's and Branagh's *Henry V.*" *ELH* 61.1 (1994): 27–52.

Lanham, Richard. *The Motives of Eloquence: Literary Rhetoric in the Renaissance.* New Haven and London: Yale University Press, 1976.

Laroque, François. *Shakespeare's Festive World: Elizabethan Seasonal Entertainment and the Professional Stage.* Trans. Janet Lloyd. Cambridge: Cambridge University Press, 1991.

Leaming, Barbara. *Orson Welles: A Biography.* New York: Penguin, 1983.

Leiser, Erwin. *Nazi Cinema.* Trans. Gertrud Mander and David Wilson. New York: Macmillan, 1975.

Leslie, Marina. "Mapping Out Ideology: The Case of Utopia." *Recherches semiotiques/Semiotic Inquiry* 12 (1992): 73–94.

———. *Renaissance Utopias and the Problem of History.* Ithaca, N.Y. Cornell University Pree, 1998.

Levitsky, Ruth M. "Rightly to Be Great." *Shakespeare Studies* 1 (1965): 142–67.

Liebler, Naomi Conn. *Shakespeare's Festive Tragedy: The Ritual Foundations of Genre.* London: Routledge, 1995.

Lipstadt, Deborah. *Denying the Holocaust: The Growing Assault on Truth and Memory.* 1993; rpt. New York: Plume, 1994.

MacLiammoir, Micheal. *Put Money in Thy Purse: The Filming of Orson Welles' Othello.* London: Eyre Methuen, 1952.

Maier, Charles S. *The Unmasterable Past: History, Holocaust, and German National Identity.* Cambridge, Mass.: Harvard University Press, 1988.

Manheim, Michael. "The English History Play on Screen." In *Shakespeare and the Moving Image: The Plays on Film and Television,* ed. Anthony Davies and Stanley Wells. Cambridge: Cambridge University Press, 1994, pp. 121–45.

Manning, Roger B. *Village Revolts: Social Protest and Popular Disturbances in England, 1509–1640.* Oxford: Clarendon Press, 1988.

Marcus, Leah. *Puzzling Shakespeare: Local Reading and Its Discontents.* Berkeley: University of California Press, 1988.

McCarty, John. *Hollywood Gangland: The Movies' Love Affair with the Mob.* New York: St. Martin's Press, 1993.

McCombe, John P. "Toward an Objective Correlative: The Problem of Desire in Franco Zeffirelli's *Hamlet.*" *Literature/Film Quarterly* 25.2 (1997): 125–31.

McKellen, Ian. *William Shakespeare's Richard III.* Woodstock, N.Y.: The Overlook Press, 1996.

Meier, Paul. "Kenneth Branagh with Utter Clarity: An Interview." *The Drama Review* 41.2 (1997): 82–89.

Mindle, Grant B. "Shakespeare's Demonic Prince." *Interpretation* 20.3 (1993): 259–74.

Minsky, Marvin. "A Framework for Representing Knowledge." In *The Psychology of Computer Vision,* ed. Patrick Henry Winston. New York: McGraw-Hill Book Company, 1975, 211–78.

Mitchell, Lee Clark. *Westerns: Making the Man in Fiction and Film.* Chicago: University of Chicago Press, 1996.

Mooney, Michael E. *Shakespeare's Dramatic Transactions.* Durham, N.C.: Duke University Press, 1990.

Moulton, Ian Frederick. "'A Monster Great Deformed': The Unruly Masculinity of Richard III." *Shakespeare Quarterly* 47.3 (1996): 251–68.

Mullaney, Steven. *The Place of the Stage: License, Play, and Power in Renaissance England.* Chicago and London: University of Chicago Press, 1988.

Mulvey, Laura. *Visual and Other Pleasures.* Bloomington: Indiana University Press, 1989.

Murray, Bruce A., and Christopher J. Wickam, eds. *Framing the Past: The Historiography of German Cinema and Television.* Carbondale and Edwardsville: Southern Illinois University Press, 1992.

Naremore, James. *The Magic World of Orson Welles.* 1978; rpt. Dallas: Southern Methodist University Press, 1989.

Neill, Michael. "Broken English and Broken Irish: Nation, Language, and the Optic of Power in Shakespeare's Histories." *Shakespeare Quarterly* 45 (1994): 1–33.

———. *Issues of Death: Mortality and Identity in English Renaissance Tragedy.* Oxford: Clarendon Press, 1997.

———. "Unproper Beds: Race, Adultery, and the Hideous in *Othello.*" *Shakespeare Quarterly* 40 (1989): 383–412.

Newman, Karen. "'And Wash the Ethiop White': Femininity and the Monstrous in *Othello.*" In *Shakespeare Reproduced: The Text in History and Ideology.* Ed. Jean E. Howard and Marion F. O'Connor. New York and London: Methuen, 1987, pp. 143–162.

Nolte, Ernst. "Between Historical Legend and Revisionism? The Third Reich in the Perspective of 1980." In *Forever in the Shadow of Hitler?: Original Documents of the Historikerstreit, The Controversy Concerning the Singularity of the Holocaust.* Trans. James Knowlton and Truett Cates. Atlantic Highlands, N.J.: Humanities Press, 1993.

Orgel, Stephen. "The Poetics of Incomprehensibility." *Shakespeare Quarterly* 42 (1991): 431–37.

———. "What Is a Text?" In *Research Opportunities in Renaissance Drama* 26 (1981): 3–6.

Parker, Patricia. "*Othello* and *Hamlet:* Dilation, Spying, and the 'Secret Place' of Woman." In *Shakespeare Reread: The Texts in New Contexts.* Ed. Russ McDonald. Ithaca and London: Cornell University Press, 1994, pp. 105–46.

Patterson, Annabel. *Shakespeare and the Popular Voice.* Cambridge: Basil Blackwell, 1989.

Pearson, Roberta E., and William Uricchio. "How Many Times Shall Caesar Bleed in Sport: Shakespeare and the Cultural Debate about Moving Pictures." *Screen* 31 (1990): 243-61.

Pignatti, Terisio. *Carpaccio.* New York: Editions d'Art Albert Skira, 1958.

Plumb, J. H. *The Italian Renaissance.* 1961; rpt. Boston: Houghton Mifflin, 1987.

Pollard, David. "Iago's Wound." In *Othello: New Perspectives.* Ed. Virginia Mason Vaughan and Kent Cartwright. Rutherford, N.J.: Fairleigh Dickinson University Press, 1991, pp. 89-96.

Porter, Beth. "Bringing Shakespeare to a '90s Audience: Loncraine, McKellen Join Forces for *Richard III.*" Interview with Richard Loncraine. *The Film Journal* 99.1 (1996): 34, 42.

Prince, Stephen. *The Warrior's Camera: The Cinema of Akira Kurosawa.* Princeton, N.J.: Princeton University Press, 1991.

Rabkin, Norman. "Rabbits, Ducks, and *Henry V.*" *Shakespeare Quarterly* 28 (1977): 279-96.

Rackin, Phyllis. "Foreign Country: The Place of Women and Sexuality in Shakespeare's Historical World." In *Enclosure Acts: Sexuality, Property, and Culture in Early Modern England,* ed. Richard Burt and John Michael Archer. Ithaca and London: Cornell University Press, 1994, pp. 68-95.

———. "History into Tragedy: The Case of *Richard III.*" In *Shakespeare: Tragedy and Gender,* ed. Shirley Nelson Garner and Madelon Sprengnether. Bloomington: Indiana University Press, 1996, pp. 31-53.

———. *Stages of History: Shakespeare's English Chronicles.* Ithaca, N.Y.: Cornell University Press, 1990.

Rafferty, Terrence. "Time Out of Joint: The Hyperkinetic '12 Monkeys' and a Fascist-Era 'Richard III.'" *The New Yorker,* January 22, 1996, pp. 84-86.

Rappaport, Steve. *Worlds within Worlds: Structures of Life in Sixteenth-Century London.* 1989; rpt. Cambridge: Cambridge University Press, 1991.

Reutersward, Patrik. "The Dog in the Humanist's Study." *Konsthistorisk tidskrift: revy for konst och konstforskning* 50.2 (1981): 53-69.

Richie, Donald. *The Films of Akira Kurosawa.* Berkeley: University of California Press, 1984.

Robertson, Jennifer. "Gender-Bending in Paradise: Doing 'Female' and 'Male' in Japan." *Genders* 5 (1989): 50-69.

Roscow, Eugene. *Born to Lose: The Gangster Film in America.* New York: Oxford University Press, 1978.

Royal, Derek. "Shakespeare's Kingly Mirror: Figuring the Chorus in Olivier's and Branagh's *Henry V.*" *Literature/Film Quarterly* 25.1 (1997): 104-10.

Ruggiero, Guido. *The Boundaries of Eros: Sex Crime and Sexuality in Renaissance Venice.* Oxford: Oxford University Press, 1985.

———. "Marriage, Love, Sex, and Renaissance Civic Morality." In *Sexuality and Gender in Early Modern Europe: Institutions, Texts, Images.* Ed. James Grantham Turner. Cambridge: Cambridge University Press, 1993, pp. 10–30.

———. *Violence in Early Renaissance Venice.* New Brunswick, N.J.: Rutgers University Press, 1980.

Salomon, Brownell. "The Myth Structure and Rituality of *Henry V.*" *Yearbook of English Studies* 23 (1993): 254–69.

Santner, Eric L. "On the Difficulty of Saying 'We': The Historians' Debate and Edgar Reitz's *Heimat.*" In *Framing the Past: The Historiography of German Cinema and Television.* Ed. Bruce A. Murray and Christopher J. Wickam. Carbondale and Edwardsville: Southern Illinois University Press, 1992.

Seduction and Theory: Readings of Gender, Representation, and Rhetoric. Ed. Dianne Hunter. Urbana: University of Illinois Press, 1989.

Shakespeare, William. *The Complete Works of William Shakespeare,* 4th edition. Ed. David Bevington. New York: Harper Collins, 1992.

———. *Othello.* Ed. M.R. Ridley (1958; rpt. London and New York: Routledge, 1992).

Shaw, William P. "Textual Ambiguities and Cinematic Certainties in *Henry V.*" *Literature/Film Quarterly* 22.2 (1994): 117–28.

Silberman, Marc. "Shooting Wars: German Cinema and the Two World Wars." In *1914/1939: German Reflections of the Two World Wars,* ed. Reinhold Grimm and Jost Hermand. Madison: University of Wisconsin Press, 1992, pp. 116–36.

Silverman, Kaja. *Male Subjectivity at the Margins.* New York: Routledge, 1992.

Silviria, Dale. *Laurence Olivier and the Art of Film Making.* Rutherford, N.J.: Fairleigh Dickinson University Press, 1985.

Simmon, Scott. "Concerning the Weary Legs of Wyatt Earp: The Classic Western According to Shakespeare." *Literature/Film Quarterly* 24 (1996): 114–27.

Simmons, James R., Jr. "'In the Rank Sweat of an Enseamed Bed': Sexual Aberration and the Paradigmatic Screen *Hamlets.*" *Literature/Film Quarterly* 25.2 (1997): 111–18.

Sinfield, Alan. *Faultlines: Cultural Materialism and the Politics of Dissident Reading.* Berkeley: University of California Press, 1992.

Sklar, Robert. *Movie Made America.* New York: Random House, 1975.

Slack, Paul. *Poverty and Policy in Tudor and Stuart England.* London and New York: Longman, 1988.

Slotkin, Richard. *Gunfighter Nation: The Myth of the Frontier in Twentieth-Century America*. New York: Atheneum, 1992.

Smith, Bruce. *Homosexual Desire in Shakespeare's England: A Cultural Poetics*. Chicago: University of Chicago Press, 1991.

Smith, Murray. "Film Spectatorship and the Institution of Fiction." *The Journal of Aesthetics and Art Criticism* 53.2 (1995): 113–27.

Sobchack, Vivian. *The Address of the Eye: A Phenomenology of Film Experience*. Princeton, N.J.: Princeton University Press, 1992.

Sontag, Susan. Preface to Hans-Jurgen Syberberg's *Hitler: A Film from Germany*. Trans. Joachim Neugroschel. New York: Farrar, Straus, Giroux, 1982, pp. x–xi.

Stallybrass, Peter. "'Drunk with the Cup of Liberty': Robin Hood, the Carnivalesque, and the Rhetoric of Violence in Early Modern England." In *The Violence of Representation: Literature and the History of Violence*, ed. Nancy Armstrong and Leonard Tennenhouse. London and New York: Routledge, 1989, pp. 45–76.

Stallybrass, Peter, and Allon White. *The Politics and Poetics of Transgression*. Ithaca, N.Y.: Cornell University Press, 1986.

Stam, Robert. *Reflexivity in Film and Literature: From Don Quixote to Jean-Luc Godard*. Ann Arbor, Mich.: U.M.I. Research Press, 1985.

———. *Subversive Pleasures: Bakhtin, Cultural Criticism, and Film*. Baltimore and London: Johns Hopkins University Press, 1989.

States, Bert O. *Hamlet and the Concept of Character*. Baltimore and London: Johns Hopkins University Press, 1992.

Stevenson, John Allen. "Fielding's Mousetrap: Hamlet, Partridge, and the '45." *Studies in English Literature* 37 (1997): 553–71.

Studlar, Gaylyn. *In the Realm of Pleasure: Von Sternberg, Dietrich, and the Masochistic Aesthetic*. New York: Columbia University Press, 1988.

Syberberg, Hans-Jürgen. *Hitler: A Film From Germany*. Trans. Joachim Neugroschel. New York: Farrar, Straus, and Giroux, Inc., 1982.

Taylor, Neil. "The Films of *Hamlet*." In *Shakespeare and the Moving Image: The Plays on Film and Television*, ed. Anthony Davies and Stanley Welles. Cambridge: Cambridge University Press, 1994, pp. 180–95.

Tennenhouse, Leonard. "Strategies of State and Political Plays: *A Midsummer Night's Dream, Henry IV, Henry V, Henry VIII*." In *Political Shakespeare: New Essays in Cultural Materialism*. Ed. Jonathan Dollimore and Alan Sinfield. Ithaca: Cornell University Press, 1985, pp. 109–28.

Underdown, David. *Revel, Riot, and Rebellion: Popular Politics and Culture in England, 1603–1660*. Oxford: Oxford University Press, 1987.

Van Sant, Gus. *Even Cowgirls Get the Blues and My Own Private Idaho.* London and Boston: Faber and Faber, 1993.

Van Watson, William. "Shakespeare, Zeffirelli, and the Homosexual Gaze." *Literature/Film Quarterly* 20.4 (1992): 308–25.

Vaughan, Virginia Mason. *Othello: A Contextual History.* Cambridge: Cambridge University Press, 1994.

Voltaire, François Marie Arouet. "Preface to Brutus" (1731). In *Shakespeare in Europe,* ed. Oswald LeWinter. London: Penguin, 1970, pp. 29–41.

Warshow, Robert. *The Immediate Experience: Movies, Comics, Theatre and Other Aspects of Popular Culture.* New York: Doubleday, 1962.

Weimann, Robert. "Representation and Performance: The Uses of Authority in Shakespeare's Theatre." *PMLA* 107.3 (1992): 497–510.

Weller, Philip. "Freud's Footprints in Films of *Hamlet.*" *Literature/Film Quarterly* 25.2 (1997): 119–24.

Welles, Orson. *Filming Othello* (documentary film). Photography: Gary Graver. Editing: Marty Roth. Produced by: Klaus Hellwig and Juergen Hellwig. 1978.

Welles, Orson, and Peter Bogdanovich. *This Is Orson Welles,* ed. Jonathan Rosenbaum. New York: Harper Collins, 1992.

Woodbridge, Linda. *The Scythe of Saturn: Shakespeare and Magical Thinking.* Urbana and Chicago: University of Illinois Press, 1994.

Zeffirelli, Franco. "Breaking the Classical Barrier." Interviewed by John Tibbetts. *Literature/Film Quarterly* 22.2 (1994): 136–40.

————. *Zeffirelli: The Autobiography of Franco Zeffirelli.* New York: Weidenfeld and Nicolson, 1986.

Filmography

CHIMES AT MIDNIGHT: Spain, 1966. 119 minutes. Internacional Films Escolano [Madrid]/Alpine [Basel]. Black and white. 35 mm. *Production, direction, and adaptation:* Orson Welles. *Camera:* Edmund Richard. *Music:* Alberto Lavignino. *Cast:* Orson Welles (Falstaff); John Gielgud (Henry IV); Keith Baxter (Hal); Margaret Rutherford (Mistress Quickly); Jeanne Moreau (Doll Tearsheet); Norman Rodway (Henry Percy); Marina Vlady (Kate Percy); Fernando Rey (Worcester); Andrew Faulds (Westmoreland); Jose Nieto (Northumberland); Alan Webb (Justice Shallow); Wlater Chiari (Silence); Michael Aldridge (Pistol); Tony Beckley (Poins); Beatrice Welles (Page); and others.

HAMLET: U.K., 1948. 152 minutes. Two Cities Films, released by J. Arthur Rank. Black and White. 35mm. *Producer, Director:* Laurence Olivier. *Cinematography:* Desmond Dickerson. *Sets:* Roger Furse. *Music:* William Walton. *Cast:* Laurence Olivier (Hamlet); Eileen Herlie (Gertrude); Basil Sydney (Claudius); Jean Simmons (Ophelia); Felic Aylmer (Polonius); Norman Wooland (Horatio); Terence Morgan (Laertes); Harcourt Williams (First Player); Patrick Troughton (Player King); Toney Tarver (Player Queen); Peter Cushing (Osric); Stanley Holloway (Gravedigger); Russell Thorndike (Priest); John Laurie (Francisco); Esmond Knight (Bernardo): Anthony Quale (Marcellus); Niall MacGinnis (Sea Captain).

HAMLET: U.K., 1990. 135 minutes. Warner Brothers Prod. Color. Producer: Dyson Lovell. *Director:* Franco Zeffirelli. *Music:* Ennio Morricone. *Designer:* Dante Ferreti. *Costumes:* Maurizio Millenotti. *Cast:* Mel Gibson

(Hamlet); Glenn Close (Gertrude); Alan Bates (Claudius); Paul Scofield (Ghost); Ian Holm (Polonius); Helena Bonham-Carter (Ophelia); Stephen Dillane (Horatio); Nathaniel Parker (Laertes); Sean Murray (Guildernstern); Michael Maloney (Rosencrantz); Trevor Peacock (Gravedigger); John McEnery (Osric); Richard Warwick (Bernardo); Christien Anholt (Marcellus); Dave Dufy (Francisco); Vernon Dobtcheff (Reynaldo); Pete Postlethwaite (Player King); Christopher Fairbank (Player Queen); and Sarah Phillips, Ned Mendez, Roy York, Marjorie Bell, Justin Case, Roger Low, Pamela Sinclair, Baby Simon Sinclair, Roy Evans (players).

HENRY V: U.K., 1944. 137 minutes. A Two Cities Film, released by United Artists. Technicolor. 35 mm. *Producer/Director:* Sir Laurence Olivier. *Screenplay:* Sir Laurence Olivier, Alan Dent. *Cinematography:* Robert Krasker. *Music:* Sir William Walton. *Art Direction:* Paul Sheriff and Carmen Dillon. *Costumes:* Roger Furse. *Editing:* Reginald Beck. *Sound:* John Dennis and Desmond Dew. *Cast:* Sir Laurence Olivier (Henry V); George Robey (Falstaff); Renée Asherson (Princess Katharine); Freda Jackson (Mistress Quickly); Michael Warre (Gloucester); Robert Newton (Pistol); Nicholas Hannen (Exeter); Esmond Knight (Fluellen); Griffith Jones (Salisbury); Roy Emerton (Bardolph); Gerald Case (Westmoreland); Frederick Cooper (Nym); Felix Aylmer (Canterbruy); Jimmy Hanley (Williams); Robert Helpman (Ely); Niall MacGinnis (MacMorris); Harcourt Williams (Charles VI); John Laurie (Jamy); Janet Burnell (Queen Isabel); Brian Nissen (Court); Max Adrian (Dauphin); Arthur Hambling (Bates); Valentine Dyall (Burgundy); Michael Shepley (Gower); Francis Lister (Orleans); Leo Genn (Constable); Russell Thorndike (Bourbon); George Cole (Boy); Ivy St. Helier (Alice); Leslie Banks (Chorus); Jonathan Field (Montjoy); Morland Graham (Erpingham).

HENRY V: U.K., 1989. 138 minutes. Renaissance Film Company, Ltd. Color. 35 mm. *Executive Producer:* Stephen Evans *Producer:* Bruce Sharman *Director:* Kenneth Branagh. *Producer:* Bruce Sharman. *Director and screenplay:* Kenneth Branagh. *Cinematography:* Kenneth MacMillan. *Script:* Kenneth Branagh. *Music:* Patrick Doyle. *Costumes:* Phyllis Dalton. *Editing:* Michael Bradsell. *Cast:* Kenneth Branagh (Henry V); Robbie Coltrane (Falstaff); Emma Thompson (Katharine); Judi Dench (Dame Quickly); Simon Shepherd (Gloucester); Robert Stephens (Pistol); Brian Blessed (Exeter); Ian Holm (Fluellen); James Larkin (Bedford); Richard Briers

(Bardolph); Paul Gregory (Westmoreland); Geoffrey Hutchings (Nym); Charles Kay (Canterbury); Michael Williams (Williams); Alec McCowen (Ely); John Sessions (MacMorris); Paul Scofield (Charles VI); Jimmy Yuill (Jamy); James Simmons (York); Pat Doyle (Court); Michael Maloney (Dauphin); Shaun Prendergast (Bates); Harold Innocent (Burgundy); Daniel Webb (Gower); Richard Clifford (Orleans); Richard Easton (Constable); Edward Jewesbury (Erpingham); Christian Bale (Boy); Geraldine McEwan (Alice); Derek Jacobi (Chorus); Christopher Ravenscroft (Mountjoy).

A MIDWINTER'S TALE: U.K., 1995. 97 minutes. Sony Picture Classics. Black and white. 35 mm. *Producer:* David Barron. *Director:* Kenneth Branagh. *Music:* Jimmy Yuill. *Production Design:* Caroline Harris. *Cinematography:* Roger Lanser. *Cast:* Richard Briers (Henry Wakefield, Claudius, the Ghost, and the Player King); Hetta Charnley (Molly); Joan Collins (Margaretta D'Arcy); Nicholas Farrell (Tom Newman, Laertes, Fortinbras, and messengers); Mark Hadfield (Vernon Spatch, Polonius, Marcellus, and First Gravedigger); Gerard Horan (Carnforth Greville, Rosencrantz, Guildenstern, Horatio); Celia Imrie (Fadge); Michael Maloney (Joe Harper, Hamlet); Jennifer Saunders (Nancy Crawford); Julia Sawalha (Nina Raymond, Ophelia); John Sessions (Terry Du Bois, Gertrude); Ann Davies (Mrs. Branch); James D. White (Tim); Robert Hines (Mortimer); Allie Byrne (Tap Dancer); Adrian Scarborough (Young Actor); Brian Petifer (Ventriloquist); Patrick Doyle (Scotsman); Shaun Prendergast (Mule Train Man); Carol Starks (Audience Member); Edward Jewesbury (Nina's Father); Katy Carmichael (Mad Puppet Woman).

MY OWN PRIVATE IDAHO: U.S.A., 1991. 104 minutes. New Line Cinema. Color. 35 mm. *Producer:* Laurie Parker. *Executive Producer:* Gus Van Sant. *Co-Executive Producer:s:* Gus Van Sant and Allan Mindel. *Director:* Gus Van Sant *Directors of. Photography:* Eric Alan Edwards, John Campbell. *Editor:* Curtiss Clayton. *Screenplay:* Gus Van Sant, additional dialogue by Shakespeare. *Costume Designer:* Beatrix Aruna Pasztor. *Music:* Bill Stafford. *Cast:* River Phoenix (Mike Waters); Keanu Reeves (Scott Favor); James Russo (Richard Waters); William Reichert (Bob Pigeon); Rodney Harvey (Gary); Chiara Caselli (Carmella); Michael Parker (Digger); Jessie Thomas (Denise); Flea (Budd); Grace Zabriskie (Alena); Tom Troupe (Jack Favor); Udo Kier (Hans); Sally Curtice (Jane Lightwork); Robert

Lee Pitchlynn (Walt); Mickey Cottrell (Daddy Carroll); Wade Evans (Wade).

OTHELLO: U.S.A., 1952. 91 minutes. Mercury Productions, released by United Artists. Black and white. 35 mm. *Producer/Director:* Orson Welles. *Cinematography:* Anchise Brizzi, G. Araldo, George Fanto. *Music:* Francesco Lavahnino, Alberto Narberis. *Cast:* Orson Welles (Othello); Micheal MacLiammoir (Iago); Suzanne Cloutier (Desdemona); Robert Coote (Roderigo); Hilton Edwards (Brabantio); Michael Lawrence (Cassio); Fay Compton (Emilia); Nicholas Bruce (Lodovico); Jean David (Montano); Doris Dowling (Bianca).

RAN [CHAOS]: Japan, 1985. 160 minutes. A Serge Silberman Production for Greenwich Film Production/Herald Ace Inc./Nippon Herald Films, Inc. Color. 35 mm. *Producers:* Serge Silberman and Masato Hara. *Director:* Akira Kurosawa. *Screenplay:* Akira Kurosawa, Hideo Oguni, and Masato Ide. *Photographers:* Takao Saito and Masaharu Ueda. *Art Director, Editor, Music:* Toru Takemitsu. *Cast:* Tatsuya Nakadai (Lord Hidetora Ichimonji); Akira Terao (Taro); Jinpachi Nezu (Jiro); Daisuke Ryu (Saburo); Mieko Harada (Lady Kaede); Yoshiko Miyazaki (Lady Sué); Masayuki Yui (Tango); Kazuo Kato (Ikoma); Peter (Kyoami); Hitoshi Ueki (Fujimaki); Jun Tazaki (Ayebe); Norio Matsui (Ogura); Hisashi Ikawa (Kurogane); Kenji Kodama (Shirane); Toshiya Ito (Naganuma); Takeshi Kato (Hatakeyama); Takeshi Normura (Tsurumaru).

RICHARD III: U.K., 1995. 104 minutes. First Look Pictures. Color. 35 mm. *Producer:* Lisa Katdelas Pare and Stephen Bayly. *Executive Producers:* Ellen Dinenman Little, Ian McKellen, Joe Simon, Maria Apodiagos *Director:* Richard Loncraine *Director of Photography:* Peter Biziou *Editor:* Paul Green *Screenplay:* Ian McKellen and Richard Loncraine. *Costume Design:* Shuna Harwood. *Music:* Trevor Jones. *Cast:* Ian McKellen (Richard III); John Wood (King Edward); Christopher Bowen (Prince Edward); Edward Jewesbury (King Henry); Bill Paterson (Ratcliffe); Annette Bening (Queen Elizabeth); Matthew Groom (Young Prince); Nigel Hawthorne (Clarence); Maggie Smith (Duchess of York); Katie Steavenson-Payne (Princess Elizabeth); Robert Downey, Jr. (Rivers); Tim McInnery (Catesby); Jim Carter (Hastings); Jim Broadbent (Buckingham); Edward Hardwicke (Stanley); Ryan Gilmore (George Stanley); Dominic West (Richmond): Kristin Scott Thomas (Lady Anne); Adrian Dunbar (Tyrell); Marco Williamson (Prince of Wales).

RICHARD III: U.K., 1956. 155 minutes. Presented by Laurence Olivier in association with London Films, released by Lopert Films Distribution Corporation. Technicolor. 35mm VistaVision. *Producer and Director:* Laurence Olivier. *Photographer:* Otto Heller. *Art Director:* Carmen Dillon. *Editor:* Helga Cranston. *Music:* William Walton. *Cast:* Laurence Olivier (Richard III); Ralph Richardson (Buckingham); John Gielgud (Clarence); Claire Bloom (Lady Anne); Cedric Hardwicke (King Edward IV); Alex Clunes (Hastings); Pamela Brown (Jane Shore); Mary Kerridge (Queen Elizabeth); Norman Wooland (Catesby); Helen Hayes (Duchess of York—Queen Mother); George Woodbridge (Lord Mayor of London); John Phillips (Norfolk).

Index